Red All Over t'...World
Liverpool FC C

Steven Horton

Vertical Editions
www.verticaleditions.com

First published in the United Kingdom in 2013 by Vertical Editions, Unit 4a, Snaygill Industrial Estate, Skipton, North Yorkshire BD23 2QR

www.verticaleditions.com

ISBN 978-1-904091-77-6

A CIP catalogue record for this book is available from the British Library

Cover design by HBA, York

Printed and bound by CMP (uk) Limited

Contents

Introduction and Acknowledgements   5

1   Gaelic Beginnings   8

2   Early Viking Adventures   12

3   Italy and Gay Paree   27

4   Entertaining the Troops   39

5   Czech-Ing Out the East   43

6   Across the Ocean Waves   53

7   Costa Capers   76

8   Mainland Europe – Tests of Physical and Mental Strength   84

9   The Irish Kop   104

10   Mini-Tournaments   119

11   Great Sheikhs   135

12   Building Bridges and Confidence   140

13   Holidays in the Holy Land   157

14   Into Africa   163

15   Going Global   172

16   Alpine Retreats   191

17   Soccer Tours   201

18   Down Under   214

19   The Future   217

Endnotes   219

Introduction and Acknowledgements

As a keen football historian, traveller and Liverpool fan of 35 years that has seen them in both competitive and friendly action all over Europe it is perhaps inevitable that I would look to put all of these elements together.

The idea for this book came during the research into my previous effort concerning the Reds, Ending the Seven Year Itch, which told the story of the 1972-73 title and UEFA Cup winning season. Some of the seeds of that success were sown in West Germany and Holland, as Bill Shankly took his players away to tackle two top quality sides in warm up games that would have them in prime condition for the season ahead. Add to this the tales told to me by Chris Wood, one of less than 100 fans who went to those games and who has been to countless others on foreign tours and I believed there were plenty of stories to tell.

Liverpool's title success of 1946-47 is commonly accredited to the decision to take the squad on a month-long tour of North America where they were fattened up on steaks in a ration-free country. On the opposite end of the scale, the dismal start to the 1964-65 season that prevented them retaining the title could be attributed to the North American tour of that summer, which cut the summer break to a minimum. It still paid dividends in a way though, as the Reds then concentrated exclusively on the cups in the second half of the season, earning a first-ever FA Cup and only going out of the European Cup at the semi-final stage due to dubious refereeing decisions.

There are various aims to this book. One has been to tell the stories of the tours and one-off friendlies that laid the foundations for success. There is an almost perfect correlation for example between the type of tours that the Reds undertook under Bob Paisley's managerial reign and the subsequent season's league position. The club's fourth European Cup success in 1984 was widely put down to the decision to take the team to Israel for a week in the run up to the final, allowing them to relax, bond and get away from the pressures of home.

Another aim has been to show how the purpose of the pre/post-season tour has changed over time. For many years they were very much a way of rewarding players with a holiday for their services over the season, in the days when maximum wage meant cash bonuses couldn't be paid. They then emerged into careful pre-season training exercises and have now evolved further into money making jaunts which are hard to believe do the players' fitness much good, given the number of time zones that are crossed and hours spent on planes.

The reporting of the tours has also taken great strides over time. The first tours saw letters posted back that were printed a week after they were written, but now players are tweeting what they are up to and the information is around the world within seconds. No journalists would accompany the early tours and even after correspondents did regularly accompany the team from the 1970s onwards, fans would be waiting until 24 hours after the match for the result. Since the development of satellite and cable television in the 1990s live television coverage has also become the norm. What Bill Shankly or Bob Paisley would have thought of every move being scrutinised as they tried to lay the foundations for the coming season out of the media glare is anybody's guess.

In writing this book I have tried to avoid a simple chronology of each year, but instead have divided up the tours (and occasional one-off friendlies in unusual places) into locations and themes. Generally speaking tours were post-season until the mid 1960s, with the 1967 trip to West Germany being the first time that one was part of a specific pre-season training plan. As such post-season tours to specific regions are covered in individual chapters, before direction change to pre-season tours takes shape, where once again I group things regionally or by theme. Interspersed, to try and break the monotony a little, I have covered various one-off friendlies, or trips where a holiday was the main name of the game, putting them together on a regional scale such as Ireland and the Spanish Costas. Because of the way the chapters are done it is inevitable that some backtracking occurs, an example being of Rafa Benitez's first summer in charge, which saw the Reds visit North America, being covered later than his visits to the Far East. Essentially though, each specific tour is a ringfenced story in itself and as such I hope this doesn't detract from the flow of the book for the reader.

This book does not cover every friendly Liverpool have ever played as it would move away from the aims of it. In fact I am certain there are plenty which the club's historians still don't know about – I uncovered two in Denmark for the 1932 tour for example that were previously 'lost.' However I am confident that club historians do have details of every tour that they have carried out. The vast majority of, but not all, tours are featured in this book. The reason some are missing is to avoid too much repetition and tedium. The 1948 tour of North America is not covered for example, as it was made using more or less the same players as two years earlier and included many of the same venues. Given the Reds toured Scandinavia every year from 1986 to 1993, I did not see any benefit in detailing all of those visits.

There are many who have helped me to research and write this book and in no particular order I thank the following:

- Arnie Baldursson and Gudmundur Magnusson for their website www. lfchistory.net, by far the most comprehensive collection of statistics not just regarding Liverpool FC, but arguably any football club in the world. Additional thanks to Arnie for the photos he has provided to me and also sharing his copies of George Kay's letters.

- Chris Wood for sharing his memories of following the Reds on so many of the tours covered in this book and also for his studious checks on the content of the book.

- Stephen Done for the foreword.

- Torbjørn Flatin for sharing his memories of watching Liverpool FC in his native Norway.

- All the staff from Liverpool Central Library for their assistance in working the machinery and careful work collating the newspaper archives.

- Lynne and Luke for their support and patience.

- Karl Waddicor at Vertical Editions.

- Phil Rimmer for his memories of games attended and scans of ticket stubs.

- Jan Schnell for uploading his Swaziland video to Youtube and recollections of it.

- Erik Delacy for his take on being an Irish fan of Liverpool FC.

1

Gaelic Beginnings

During the 1890s, with league seasons consisting of less than 30 games, it was common for clubs to play a number of friendly games to increase income and also keep the players fit. In 1892-93, Liverpool FC's first season for example, they played 22 Lancashire League games and 30 friendlies. These included glamour matches at Anfield against the much more illustrious opposition of Aston Villa and Preston North End, as well as Irish side Cliftonville. They also ventured to Scotland in October 1892 to play Rangers at Ibrox.

All of the friendlies during the first four years were one-off matches, although the side did play away friendlies on successive days against Bolton Wanderers and then Blackburn Rovers on Christmas and Boxing Day in 1895, which almost certainly involved an overnight stop so it was a mini-tour in some ways.

The arrival of Tom Watson from Sunderland as manager in 1896 led to many changes at Anfield, with the blue and white halved shirts being replaced by red ones and a new training regime introduced. It is probably more than a coincidence too that after Watson's arrival the club started taking proper tours with players being away for several days at a time, the first of which saw them go north of Hadrian's Wall.

SCOTLAND 1897

Liverpool's first extended visit to Scotland came in April 1897 when the Reds went there to play five games, with the *Liverpool Echo* reporting that Tom Watson had charge of the arrangements.

The tour was made on the back of two glamour friendlies against new Scottish Champions Heart of Midlothian. The first of these was played at Anfield on 6th March, with Liverpool winning 2-1. The return fixture was arranged to be played at Tynecastle on Saturday 24th April, a fortnight after the league campaign had ended. The travelling party took a train to Preston from Exchange Station on the Friday night at 5.15pm, connecting there with a London and North Western service where they dined in the saloon car during the journey, arriving in Edinburgh at 10.30pm.

After spending the night at the now long gone Douglas Hotel in Princes Street the players were given a sightseeing tour on the morning of the match. The *Liverpool Courier* reported that the game kicked off at 4.05pm in beautiful weather and that 5,000 fans had attended. The Reds were unable to repeat their Anfield victory and went down 3-0, their cause not having been helped when Robert Neill, who had played against Hearts for Hibernian in the previous season's Scottish Cup final, was forced off with injury after 15 minutes after being badly kicked. It meant Liverpool had to play the rest of the game with ten men with one of the forwards dropping back into Neill's half back position, although the *Liverpool Mercury* believed this was no excuse for what it called an 'utterly feeble display by the front rank.'

The Hearts game had been by far the most important match of the tour, with the *Courier, Echo* and *Mercury* making no mention of the other matches played and only the *Mercury* publishing any itinerary. That paper stated in its report of the Hearts game on the following Monday that the Reds would be playing further games in Falkirk and Aberdeen on the Monday and Wednesday before returning to Liverpool on the Thursday. The Reds drew 2-2 with East Stirlingshire then beat Victoria United (one of three clubs that would form Aberdeen FC in 1903) 1-0. However rather than return home as planned on the Thursday another game was arranged with Dundee at their Carolina Port ground, which was situated in the harbour and overlooked by a shale mountain. Despite the short notice at which the game was arranged a large crowd attended and Dundee, who had finished fifth in the Scottish league that season comfortably beat the Reds 4-0. That still wasn't quite it, as they were in action again on the Friday night, beating Lanarkshire side Wishaw Thistle 4-3 in front of 2,000 fans.

SCOTLAND 1898

Having established relations with Hearts, Liverpool would be back in Edinburgh in January 1898 as they went on a brief two-match tour of Scotland, playing a game at Tynecastle and then travelling to Paisley to face St Mirren. Although this was a mid-season jaunt for the Reds, Hearts had already completed their 18 league fixtures and lay third in the table, with St Mirren having a chance to overhaul them if they won their last two games. It meant the Reds knew they faced two games likely to be equally as tough as each other.

The Hearts match was arranged for Monday 3rd January and the party headed by Tom Watson, secretary John McKenna and William Houlding (club founder John Houlding's son), took a sleeper train from Liverpool to Edinburgh the night before, arriving at 7am. They rested at the Douglas Hotel before the game but went down 3-1 after being 1-0 up at half-time. The *Liverpool Mercury* reported that early in the second half: 'Liverpool fairly bombarded the home goal, shot after shot being sent in.' However

Hearts got a breakaway goal and after taking the lead the home side added a third late on through another counter attack after the Reds had been chasing an equaliser. The crowd for this game was just 2,000 and considerably lower than had attended the previous season's fixture, partly down to the fact another friendly was also taking place in the city between St Bernard's and Corinthians.

Immediately after the Hearts game, the players and officials travelled to Glasgow where they spent the night. Neighbours Everton were in Glasgow as well, preparing for a friendly with Rangers although there is no record as to whether the two sets of players fraternised with each other. The Reds set off for Paisley at noon the following day where their match with St Mirren kicked off at 2.15pm. The *Liverpool Courier* described the playing conditions as 'abominable', with puddles all over the pitch and this no doubt kept the attendance down to 1,000. St Mirren were 2-0 up within 15 minutes and although the Reds rallied and pulled one back through Andrew McCowie, they tired in the second half and it was no surprise when the home side scored a third.

The Liverpool party then returned home to resume their league campaign, the next match being against Blackburn Rovers on the Saturday. Later in the season though there would be a return match with Hearts, who came to Anfield and won 2-0, while the Reds would be back in Edinburgh in April 1899, losing 3-2.

IRELAND 1903

Liverpool first crossed the seas to play friendly matches in 1903 with a brief two-game tour of Ireland in April, playing matches in Dublin and Belfast.

The season wasn't quite over, the Reds still having three games to play when they sailed to Dublin for the game with Bohemians at Dalymount Park on Monday 13th April. Now one of the Republic of Ireland's leading clubs, Bohemians had been formed in 1890 and in 1902 became the first Dublin side to join the Irish League, which was dominated by teams from the Belfast area. They had finished seventh out of eight clubs in the league and were no match for the Reds, who in unseasonably snowy conditions ran out 5-2 winners. The crowd was a disappointing 4,000 due to a race meeting in the locality.

From Dublin the Liverpool side travelled to Belfast, where they faced a much harder game against Irish League champions Distillery. The club is now known as Lisburn Distillery, having moved there in 1980 after their Grosvenor Park ground had been destroyed by an arson attack during the Troubles. Founded in 1880, they had won four league titles and seven Irish Cups and they provided a much sterner test for the Reds on a wet and windy afternoon which kept the crowd down to 3,000, half what had seen them take on Sheffield United the day before. The hosts had an early goal disallowed in a game that Liverpool ran out 3-2 winners and the *Liverpool Courier* reported: 'play was generally interesting and slightly in favour of Liverpool.'

Liverpool would be back in Ireland the following April, this time playing just the one game against Bohemians, who they beat 4-1 at Dalymount Park, where the now League of Ireland side still play. They didn't return until after the Second World War, when the island of Ireland was two countries.

2

Early Viking Adventures

Liverpool may have been regular visitors to Denmark, Norway and Sweden in the 1980s and 1990s, with further visits to the Norwegian capital of Oslo having taken place in recent years, but the very first away matches against Continental opposition took place in Scandinavia as well. Although the players had gone on a trip to Paris as a reward for winning the league championship in 1906 no matches were played. However before the outbreak of the First World War, they twice went on combined tours of Denmark and Sweden and in later years went to Denmark in 1932, then Sweden in 1939 and 1951.

SCANDINAVIA 1910

Liverpool's first trip to the Continent where they would play matches came in 1910, with a four-game tour to Denmark and Sweden. It took place against the backdrop of the death of King Edward VII, who died of bronchitis late in the evening of 6th May and would not be buried for two weeks afterwards.

The *Evening Express* predicted that the tour would be 'a most enjoyable one', with The Critic observing that: 'The Danes have made rapid strides in the association code, and the fact that they were able to beat an English representative team is proof of their advance.'[1] The Reds would be hoping they were going out to better weather than that faced by the FA XI, who saw a planned game against a Danish XI rained off on 9th May.

The party set off from Liverpool Central station at noon on Wednesday 11th May, taking a train to Hull. The most notable absentee amongst the 15 players was goalkeeper Sam Hardy who had injured his arm and his place was taken by Augustus Beeby, whilst the team were accompanied by secretary-manager Tom Watson and trainer Bill McConnell, as well as directors J. Astbury and W.C. Briggs. There were unsurprisingly no journalists on the tour and the local papers relied on telegraphs to get the results. The *Evening Express* was also able to provide additional information a few days in arrears thanks to Watson sending letters to them. His first letter published described the terrible sea crossing they had endured that had led to them arriving 10 hours late:

'We left Hull at 7.30pm on Wednesday by one of the Finland Steamship

Company's steamships the Polaris, Mr Langley the manager of Hull City FC seeing us off. The party of 19 were all in high spirits. The dinner was quite a novelty as many of the party had not yet tasted a dinner in the Finnish style. I may say it was the last meal many of the party had for 36 hours, for after dropping the pilot at the mouth of the Humber we experienced a north-east gale and during the time it lasted it was pretty severe. The majority of the party was not seen for at least 24 hours and with the exception of three or four the dining room was empty. But nearing the shores of Jutland the weather improved greatly and in a very short time all the inconveniences had been forgotten and the party resumed its cheerful mood and the dining room its bustle and stir.[2]'

After two nights in Copenhagen, the party moved on to Gothenburg on Sunday 15th May, a train and ferry journey that took seven-and-a-half hours. The following day they played a Stockholm XI at the ground of the Örgryte club, who Watson described as having a fine stand. Liverpool showed no signs of any travel weariness or being affected by the heat with temperatures registering 80 in the shade, as they cruised to a 2-0 win, James Stewart and Samual Gilligan getting the goals. The first fans got to know about this match, though, was on 19th May when the *Evening Express* published a letter from Tom Watson, the other local papers not having reported the game.

After the game, both sides were the guests of Örgryte at the Royal Swedish Yacht Club in Långedrag, with Watson describing the evening as 'an enjoyable one and very much appreciated by us.' The next day the players went on a visit to the waterfall at Trolhättan, 40 miles to the north of Gothenburg, a sight that Watson believed would be 'long remembered by those privileged to see it.'

Just two days after beating the Stockholm side, the Reds were back at Örgryte's ground for a match against the home club, which Watson predicted would be far tougher although given the heat he would have been glad that the game was to be played in the evening kicking off at 7.15pm. Liverpool had no problems against their hosts, winning 3-0 with Gilligan again on the scoresheet and the other two goals coming from Sam Bowyer. Unlike the first match, this did actually make the papers the next day, with the *Daily Post and Mercury* reporting: 'The Liverpool football team who are touring on the Continent yesterday met the Gothenburg team at Gothenburg, whom they defeated by three goals to nil.' The length of coverage given in the papers immediately after the matches was the same as given to some other clubs, for example readers could also learn that Southend United were beaten by Hertha Berlin.

The Reds party had been due to leave Gothenburg the day after the Örgryte match as they had two games scheduled in Copenhagen on Friday

20th and Sunday 22nd May. However as a mark of respect due to the King's funeral, with Denmark also being in mourning as Queen Alexandra was Danish, the games were put back to the 22nd and 24th. It meant the players stayed in Sweden for an extra day, visiting some islands around Gothenburg harbour and then socialising with the players of Manchester City, who arrived that evening from Copenhagen for the start of the Swedish leg of their tour. When the party did leave on the day of the funeral, the send off was low key and when they arrived in Copenhagen they found that the heat was even higher than in Gothenburg, with temperatures touching the 90s.

After touring the harbour on the Saturday, the Reds faced a Danish FA XI in searing heat on the Sunday afternoon, with Watson describing the crowd as containing a number of women whose 'summer dresses gave the occasion quite a holiday appearance'. The amateur Danes, who had previously lost 5-2 to Manchester City, shocked Liverpool by winning 3-0 and Watson described it as a fully deserved win for them. He said: 'I can fully see them beating any amateur team sent over from England, their knowledge of the game was an eye opener to all.' The circumstances of the defeat were only known to fans the following Thursday when Watson's letter was published in the *Evening Express*, with the Monday's *Daily Post and Mercury* having published a Reuters telegraph that said: 'Copenhagen Sunday – A team representing the Danish Football Union today defeated the Liverpool Football Club by three goals to nil.'

After the game the Reds' players dined at a dinner hosted by Danish veteran player Johannes Gandil, who had the unusual distinction of having represented his country at the Olympics in both athletics (100m) and football. Watson described in a letter how 'our healths were drunk with the usual "rar, rar, rar"'. The final game of the tour was on Tuesday 24th May when the Reds faced the Danish Football Union XI again. This time, in far cooler conditions given it was played of an evening, Liverpool won 1-0 in a game where the scorer remains unknown due to no more letters being posted by Watson. The following day's *Daily Post and Mercury* simply said in the results section: 'Liverpool 1 Denmark 0'.

Despite the last match being on the Tuesday, the players were given a few more days in Denmark before beginning their journey home on Friday 27th May, finally arriving back at Liverpool Central station at 7pm on the Sunday evening. The *Evening Express* reported that the players were in excellent condition and had 'evidently thoroughly enjoyed themselves'. Scandinavia had obviously made a mark on the party, as they would be back there the next time they were abroad four years later.

SCANDINAVIA 1914

After reaching the FA Cup final for the first time in their history Liverpool's players were rewarded with another trip to Scandinavia, where they would play a total of seven games, four in Sweden and three in Denmark.

The party of 16 players, two directors, secretary-manager Tom Watson and trainer Bill Connell set off at 2.30pm on Thursday 7th May from Liverpool Central station for Harwich, from where they took an overnight ferry to Hook of Holland. This meant it was a much shorter sea crossing than the one they undertook four years earlier that resulted in so much seasickness. A ten-hour train journey to Hamburg followed and after a few hours to stretch their legs in the German city, they took a sleeper train to Gothenburg. They finally arrived there shortly before 2pm on the Saturday and checked into the Hotel Eggers, situated next to the railway station.

With no journalists present on the tour, Liverpool's four daily newspapers had different methods of obtaining information about the games. As in 1910 the two morning papers, the *Daily Post & Mercury* and *Liverpool Courier* both relied on extremely brief telegraphs sent by Tom Watson, allowing them to publish the result with a brief comment the following day. The *Evening Express* received the same information but due to their later publication were able to receive additional newswires from Scandinavia as to what had been published in the morning papers there. However the *Liverpool Echo,* which sometimes didn't even publish the results, did have a trump card up its sleeve in the form of a contract with half back Tom Fairfoul to send letters to football columnist Bee Edwards. They would arrive a few days later but contain much more details of the games and in time they have also proved invaluable in gleaning information regarding this tour, as they contained the team line-ups and also news on what the players got up to in their free time.

Despite the gruelling journey, the Reds first game was on Sunday 10th May, the day after they arrived, against Örgryte. They were by far the best team in Sweden, having won 11 of the 18 Swedish championships that had been contested to date but were no match for the Reds, who ran out 4-1 winners courtesy of a hat-trick from Tom Miller and a goal by Robert Terris. The win was reported very briefly in the *Courier* and *Post* but by 14th May Fairfoul's letter had arrived at the offices of the *Echo* and gave a much greater insight into the game:

> 'The prevalent opinion of those who profess to know something about Continental football was that we would have to play our very best to win. We had a fine reception on appearing, better even than the home team. Lacey and Terris gave the spectators a sample of their ability right off. A nice combined run by the whole front rank ended in Terris scoring after about five minutes play. Our boys began giving an exhibition and as is generally the case in these games everything they tried came off. Sheldon beat four players in succession then placed to Miller who scored

the second goal. A neat header by Banks placed the ball at Miller's foot and shooting first time our centre forward scored one of the finest goals I have ever seen. Shortly after the Swedish centre ran through on his own and shooting from 18 yards left Campbell helpless. This effort was enthusiastically cheered by the spectators and our defenders were not displeased, as the centre was worthy of his goal. The second half calls for very little comment, our boys doing a lot of trickery which pleased the crowd immensely. Miller got the fourth goal and so performed the hat-trick. The Swedish players gave our boys three cheers before leaving the field.'

The win had been achieved on a pitch that left a lot to be desired and forced Terris off 10 minutes from time when he twisted his ankle after he stepped in a hole whilst running. Fairfoul wrote of the players' concerns:

'We had an inspection of the ground previous to turning out. It is really a skating pond but they run the water off in the summer. The surface is covered with gravel and rolled as hard as our toll roads. I must say the look of the pitch caused serious misgivings among our boys, especially the wing players, as a cement cycle track runs right along the touchline and it is much closer than Aston Villa's used to be.'

A gathering of both sets of players was arranged for the night following the game, which Fairfoul described as 'a great success' and included unexpected displays of singing from Tom Watson and Bill Connell. Initially the Reds had intended to play two games in Gothenburg, but the itinerary changed and the morning after the fraternisation the party left for Stockholm a few days earlier than anticipated for a nine-hour train journey. The Swedish press had described Liverpool as the finest team seen in Gothenburg for years, something that caused quite a stir in Stockholm. Up to 5,000 were present at the railway station to greet the Reds off the train and follow them on the one kilometre journey to the luxurious Strand Hotel, built for the 1912 Olympics.

They would now be playing three games in the Swedish capital, the first of them the following night against Djurgårdens, whose one title to date had come two years earlier. The game was attended by a record crowd which included the heir to the Swedish throne, the Crown Prince Gustaf Adolf. The *Liverpool Courier* reported briefly on 14th May that the Reds had received a great reception and won 6-2, but the *Evening Express*, which had been able to gather a bit more detail by receiving news of what had been published in that morning's Swedish papers wrote:

'The Reds did not put themselves out of their way as in the former match; that is they confined themselves to the exhibition style rather than the keen "all out" league play and some fancy work was interspersed between the goals . The spectator had quite a lot to enthuse over. The home forwards had the satisfaction it will be noticed of scoring a couple of goals so that the attacking line evidently included marksmen of no mean ability. The Stockholm papers in hand speak in glowing terms of the Liverpool club and almost a page is devoted to pictures and details about the cup finalists.'

On how the tour had gone to date, the *Express* commented that there was some surprise at the quality of some of the strikers the Reds had come up against and that 'there are one or two forwards who would not be considered second raters in English football.'

Tom Fairfoul's letter was not published in the *Liverpool Echo* until six days after the game, but it went along the lines of what the *Express* had said, that Liverpool had played an exhibition style and the crowd had been appreciative, saying: 'The game was keenly contested, our boys giving a brilliant exposition which was greatly admired by the crowd who never failed to applaud the finer points shown. These people seem to have a thorough knowledge of the game and are a fine sporting race'. The players were also much more appreciative of the pitch, which he described as being 'much better than at Gothenburg, there being a fine old yielding turf and our boys appreciated the change in playing conditions.'

After two goals from Bill Lacey and one from William Banks gave the Reds a 3-0 half-time lead Fairfoul got on the scoresheet himself in the second half, finding the net for the first time since his move to Liverpool from Third Lanark a year earlier. He wrote of the goal:

'When play was resumed we began pressing right off. After 10 minutes play the ball came right out to me and taking a happy-go-lucky shot I had the satisfaction of scoring my first goal for Liverpool FC. There was quite a demonstration and my fellow players came from their respective positions to shake my hand and offer congratulations. The crowd entered into the humour of the situation by cheering all over the field.'

Such was the appreciation of the locals that Fairfoul wrote how the streets were lined all the way from the ground to the hotel, a distance of about a mile, by crowds who cheered throughout. The following day the players took a steamer onto the Baltic Sea before being given a motor car tour of Stockholm and attending a banquet laid on by the Swedish FA.

On Friday 15th May the Reds faced Djurgårdens' biggest rivals Allmänna Idrottsklubben Stockholm – AIK for short. Meaning 'General Sports Club', AIK had been formed in 1891, with the football division being created five years later. They had been crowned Swedish champions three times and would go on to win the championship in 1914. Watson wired to the *Liverpool Courier* to say that the Reds won 3-0 and that the large crowd had appreciated the tourists' efforts. Tom Fairfoul wrote that this was

Liverpool's toughest game of the tour so far and the scores were level at the break, but admitted that the amount of Swedish punch consumed at the banquet the night before may have had something to do with their lacklustre performance. Early in the second half the AIK left back put through his own goal and buoyed by this, the Reds improved and added another couple through Bill Lacey and Robert MacDougall. One of the more surprising elements of this match was Watson's decision to play reserve keeper Elisha Scott at outside half, a position in which he did not look out of place.

The Reds then played their third game in five days, facing a Swedish Select XI on 17th May and running out 8-0 winners, Bill Lacey scoring twice. Tom Watson wired the *Liverpool Courier* to say that the Reds were superior in all departments and that their play was widely applauded. The following day they made the 13-hour journey to Copenhagen, checking into the Phoenix Hotel and spending the next day being shown around the city in chartered taxis.

The Reds first game in Denmark was on 20th May against KB Copenhagen, who had in the past month played exhibition matches against Clapton Orient, Crystal Palace and a Holland XI, avoiding defeat in all three games. But they were no match for the Reds who ran out 5-2 winners. The *Evening Express* didn't underestimate the importance of the win, describing the Danes as the 'most progressive of Continental footballers' and that Liverpool's 'exposition must be seen as one of the finest seen on the Continent'.

On 24th May the Reds faced a Copenhagen Select XI and were stretched for the first time on the tour, drawing 3-3 in a fast and keenly contested game. The Reds were 2-1 down at half-time and Tom Fairfoul noted that unlike in previous games the crowd hadn't applauded the Liverpool goal, writing: 'Our success didn't meet with much appreciation, it was evident this crowd was not a sporting one.' In the second half it was an improved Liverpool display and in the end the players were disappointed not to win, Fairfoul saying they only had themselves to blame due to weak finishing.

Back home though, the Reds, along with Bradford City, were being criticised at the Annual General Meeting of the Football League which took place on 25th May. A resolution agreed that both clubs should be asked on their return why they hadn't furnished accounts of their tours, while Everton's representative Mr Clayton was annoyed at being unable to finalise fixtures as Liverpool had no responsible official present.

The Reds must have been grateful for the way they were being treated in Scandinavia, compared to the difficulties Tottenham Hotspur were facing in Germany. The *Liverpool Echo* reported on 26th May that in a game with Pforzheim the Spurs captain complained to the referee over some of their players being kicked and his German counterpart, on hearing this said in

English: 'You are in Germany now, we are going to win.' At the end of the game, which Spurs won 4-0 the German keeper kicked their winger Wally Tattersall three times before a pitch invasion ensued, which resulted in John Joyce being hit over the head with an umbrella and having to be treated for bleeding. Chairman Mr C. D. Roberts was robbed of £15 and he told the press that the team had to leave the ground by a roundabout way whilst having stones and flints thrown at them.

It was far easier going for the Reds, whose tour ended on 26th May with a 7-1 win over a Danish Select XI, no details of which were furnished to the morning papers due to the party having to prepare to leave that night on the midnight sleeper bound for Hamburg. After a gruelling train journey through Germany and Holland, followed by an overnight sea crossing to Harwich, the party arrived back at Liverpool Central station just after 3pm on Thursday 28th May and were described by the *Liverpool Courier* as being in 'the pink of condition'. A large crowd turned out to greet them, including two directors who hadn't gone on the tour, Mr Martindale and Mr Williams. Manager Tom Watson was carrying a silver shield presented to the team from the Swedes, while his coat was adorned with a number of club badges. Described as looking 'particularly well' by the *Evening Express*, he immediately took a cab to Anfield leaving others to speak to the press. The paper reported of one unnamed player:

'He had enjoyed the trip immensely, everywhere the team had been well received and the spectators appeared to appreciate the finer points of the game in full. The grounds he said were much better than here and the players knew the finer points of the game all right, but were less experienced.'

Full backs Ephraim Longworth and Donald McKinlay agreed that the grounds were of a high standard, while winger Bill Lacey spoke briefly to the paper, saying they had had a good time and he had scored nine or 10 goals. Lacey, who hailed from Wexford in Ireland, then made his apologies before rushing home to prepare for a trip across the Irish Sea to visit relatives. Director Mr E.A. Bainbridge believed the Danes had been very hospitable but that they had no intention of treating the games as friendlies, being determined to try and win. To sum up, the *Evening Express* said of only the club's second Continental sojourn: 'Altogether the trip was one of the most enjoyable any club has had and the success of the Anfield team made them famous and, as indicated, big crowds were the order wherever they appeared.'

DENMARK 1932

After the resumption of football in 1919-20 following the end of the First

World War Liverpool took a different direction with their end of season tours, being rewarded for the title successes of 1922 and 1923 with trips to Italy and France respectively. There were no more foreign adventures that decade though as funds were used to make ground improvements, including the new roof on the Kop. At the end of 1931-32 the Reds set off for Denmark again, 18 years after their last visit.

Everton had been making all the headlines on Merseyside that season as they secured the title just a year after being promoted. The Reds finished 10th as poor home form prevented them challenging at the top and the season came to an extremely disappointing end as they were thrashed 8-1 at Bolton on the final day, at the time the club's record defeat.

This was Liverpool's first foreign tour since 1923 and they would be without leading scorer Gordon Hodgson, who had hit 26 league goals during the season, due to his cricket commitments to Lancashire. A large crowd, including local featherweight boxer Dom Volante who would be fighting at Anfield while the Reds were away, gathered at Lime Street station on the afternoon of 19th May to see them off. The party of 15 players, manager George Patterson, trainer Charlie Wilson and director Mr W. Harvey Webb went first to London, from where they took another train to Harwich, sailing at 10pm on the 23-hour crossing to Esbjerg. This was completed three hours ahead of schedule due to the calm conditions, the sea being described by Gordon Gunson as 'like a mirror.[3]'

After spending the night in Esbjerg they took a train to Aarhus, a five-hour journey and checked into the Regina Hotel, in readiness for the first game of the tour against Aarhus Workers' Sports Club on Sunday 22nd May. A pre-match shower followed by sunshine left the pitch in a perfect state for the players and the Reds won 8-0 in front of 2,000 fans with Edmund Hancock, Archie McPherson and Dave Wright each getting two goals.

The following day the party took the train to Odense, where they spent the night in the Park Hotel. Hancock got a double again as the Reds ran out 3-0 winners against an Odense Select XI, with Gordon Gunson getting the other. The Reds strikers may well have been keen to prove their worth considering back at home the Board were making reinforcements for the next season, with the *Liverpool Echo* reporting on 15th May that they had signed Edmund Crawford from Halifax. Afterwards the party remained in Odense for the night then the following day took the train to Copenhagen, where they would be staying for four nights at the Hotel Cosmopolite. Two games were arranged in the Danish capital, one against a Danish League XI and another against a select side from teams in the Copenhagen area.

The Danish teams were managed by ex Scottish international David Steele, who had played for the Huddersfield side that won a hat-trick of league championships in the 1920s. They were expected to provide the Reds with a far sterner test than the ones against the provincial sides, with the Danish league XI having secured a 2-2 draw with Steele's old club a few days before the Reds arrived. They went on to give Liverpool a shock by taking an early lead, but the Reds came back to win 3-1 with the goals coming from Hancock, Gunson and Harold Barton. That game was played in a downpour which restricted the crowd to 6,000 but for the game against the Copenhagen XI played two days later on 29th May the weather was extremely hot. The Reds again went behind early on after a penalty was conceded for handball, but they came back to win 4-1 in front of 10,000 fans. Amongst the spectators were the Birmingham City team, who had arrived in Copenhagen that morning as they began their own tour of Denmark. The victory completed a 100% tour record for the Reds, who had enjoyed themselves with the *Evening Express* printing a letter from Gordon Gunson on 31st May:

'The first night we stayed at Esbjerg, a quite little place but really very nice. We then went on to Aarhus, a place with more life and bigger in every way. Our lads have played brilliant football and we were given a great welcome everywhere we went. The great drawback of our tour was that none of us could understand the language and after a lot of trouble we could only make them understand as a result of our actions.'

The morning after the last match the party departed by train for Esbjerg for the crossing to Harwich. The party arrived in London on the evening of 31st May and spent the night in the Grafton Hotel in Tottenham Court Road. They then took the train back to Liverpool the next day, although six players stayed behind to go and watch The Derby horse race at Epsom, which was won by *April the Fifth*. The *Evening Express* reported their arrival at Lime Street on 1st June, stating that all the players looked well and that in the views of George Patterson and Mr Harvey Webb the tour had been a success from both a playing and financial point of view.

SWEDEN 1939

What turned out to be Liverpool's last foreign adventure before the outbreak of the Second World War came in May and June 1939, when they undertook a five-match tour of Sweden. In the seven years since their last trip across the North Sea they had been to the Canary Islands, Czechoslovakia, Yugoslavia and Romania, so this was set to be quite a different adventure altogether for the players.

Preliminary arrangements for the tour had been made the previous November when it was intended to play games in Denmark too, but those fell through and it was instead limited to just Sweden. A squad of 16 players along with manager George Kay, trainer Charlie Wilson and six directors set off from Lime Street station for Harwich on the morning of Monday 22nd May. Kay told Ranger from the *Liverpool Echo* before boarding the train:

'We hope to maintain the high standard that has been set in past years on the Continent by English touring teams. The players are looking forward to the trip with enthusiasm and are determined to show our Scandinavian friends good football and good sportsmanship.'

On arrival in Harwich the party took a 24 hour ferry crossing to Esbjerg in Denmark, followed by a train to Copenhagen, the *Echo* reporting that the players would not need to leave their train despite a one-hour ferry crossing being required between Funen and Zealand, as the boat had rails on it. They finally arrived in Malmö on 24th May, where they played their first game that night, losing a nine goal thriller 5-4 against a Swedish Combination side. The following day they headed to Stockholm, where they were beaten 2-0 by AIK on 26th May.

Both Kay and vice captain Matt Busby had agreed to send letters to Pilot at the *Evening Express*, with Kay also writing to the *Liverpool Echo* during the tour. The first letters arrived at the *Express* offices on 29th May, Kay putting the first defeat down to tiredness. This letter appeared to have been posted in Malmö as he described how the directors and some players were ready for a bridge school on the nine hour journey to Stockholm. He also described how he was impressed by the manners and quality of the food in Sweden:

'The bowing here wherever we are met is almost as good as physical jerks. Fortunately for us there is no demand for a curtsey. No wonder they have big fellows over there, they feed so well. The Swedish hors-d'oeuvre consisted of 24 varieties, just like a quick lunch counter, but that was only the start of the meal.'

Busby sent his letter after the Stockholm game in which he described how Berry Nieuwenhuys had kept them entertained on the 350 mile journey from Malmö by playing his ukulele. Busby felt Liverpool had been unfortunate to lose the game against AIK. He wrote:

'I'm afraid the breaks are going against us, for after 20 minutes when it seemed a question of only how many we would score, Phil Taylor was carried off with concussion. With 10 men we could not hold them, for they play attractive football. One of their goals however was doubtful but the 2-0 result against us stands. These two defeats have been disappointing for us all but if we can steer clear of injuries in the remaining matches I'm sure we can atone. Phil Taylor and Jim Harley now look as if they had been sparring with Joe Louis.'

Given his injury in this game Taylor must have wondered if he had made the right decision to go on this tour, having turned down the opportunity to spend the summer playing cricket for Gloucestershire. After spending four days sightseeing in Stockholm, which included a trip to the races, the party took an overnight sleeper train back to the west coast on 30th May, where the Reds claimed their first win of the tour the following evening, beating a Gothenburg combined team 2-0 thanks to goals from Taylor and Nieuwenhuys. After the game they were criss-crossing the country again, returning to Stockholm on another sleeper train.

In their next game they recorded an emphatic 6-0 win against a Södermanland XI at the Tunavallen Stadium in Eskilstuna on 2nd June, with Taylor netting a hat-trick. Before this game Liverpool were given a commemorative plate from the local Fotbollforbund, which is now displayed in the Liverpool FC museum at Anfield. The Gothenburg and Södermanland games took up no more than a few lines in the local papers, whose pages were full of news about the tragedy surrounding the sinking of the HMS *Thetis* on 1st June. The Cammell Laird built submarine had been undergoing trials off the coast of North Wales when she sank, killing all but four of the 99 people on board.

Busby's second letter was published in the *Evening Express* on 5th June. He wrote that the players had met Harry Morris, who had scored 229 goals in 279 appearances for Swindon Town between 1926 and 1933 and was now coaching in Sweden. Of the match in Gothenburg he described how Arthur Riley had saved a penalty and that it was only some excellent saves by the Swedish keeper in the second half that kept the score down to 2-0.

Before moving on to Borås to play Elfsborg on 6th June captain Tom Cooper presented their tour courier with a silver cigarette case as a mark of gratitude. Against Elfsborg the Reds were beaten 5-2 in a game that Kay had predicted would be Liverpool's stiffest test. Despite the fact three of the five games were lost, it had been an enjoyable tour, with the *Evening Express* and *Liverpool Echo* both publishing a letter from George Kay on 7th June which said: 'All the party are in good health and enjoying the trip of their lives.' The Reds then embarked on the three day journey back to Liverpool, although two of the directors had flown back to London a few days earlier, a seven-hour flight. Kay had prophetically commented in his letter: 'Shades of the future in football, when Liverpool will play games in Copenhagen, Stockholm and others, and return the same day!'

They arrived back in Liverpool on 9th June, the *Evening Express* saying that they all looked fit and that Kay told then they had 'all had a marvellous time.' It was also revealed that the Reds had had several invitations to return to Sweden the next year, but that would go on to prove impossible due to the outbreak of war later that year.

SWEDEN 1951

Due to the Second World War it would be 12 years before Liverpool were back in Scandinavia, with the Reds having made two trips to the USA during the intervening period. The 12 years since their last visit to Sweden had seen air travel become much more economical so that this time the party made their trip by plane for a visit that would see them play five matches.

They set off on 12th May from Speke Airport, with the party consisting of 15 players, manager Don Welsh, trainer Albert Shelley and five members of the Board. Also accompanying them was Ranger, who was still employed by the *Liverpool Echo* and identified as R.W. Prole in the photograph that was in the paper that evening. Pilot from the *Evening Express* was also on the tour, but his identity remains a mystery. The presence of journalists meant that up to date match reports written by local reporters could now be published, rather than relying on telegraphs provided by neutrals or letters that arrived several days later.

Unlike the last time they were in Sweden, the Reds weren't overcome by fatigue from a three-day journey when it came to playing their first game against AIK Stockholm on 14th May, a match arranged as part of the Swedish club's 60th birthday celebrations. They won 7-0 and in the match report that was telephoned to the *Liverpool Echo* Ranger said that Liverpool were never in difficulty and played at only half speed throughout. Remaining in Stockholm, Liverpool then beat Malmö 4-1 two days later in a game marred by left back Eddie Spicer sustaining a broken leg in a tackle made in the centre circle.

Having scored 11 goals in two games at the Råsunda Stadium, the Liverpool side were causing quite a stir in Stockholm and it was hoped that they would play a prestige friendly against Brazilian side Flamengo whilst there. *Evening Express* correspondent Pilot wrote in what would now be seen as shockingly racist tones on 18th May: 'Everyone wants to see Liverpool in action against the coffee-coloured players from South America. It is certain that the match would be a sell out.' However, the next evening the paper reported how the Swedish FA had stepped in and put paid to the game taking place, stating that Flamengo were scheduled to play AIK and it would be discourteous to expect them (AIK) to pull out of the game to make way for Liverpool. Pilot did say though that he had gone to see the Flamengo players train at the Swedish Sports Institute along with Don Welsh and how it was hoped to arrange for the Reds to travel to Rio de Janeiro the following year.

In their next game against Norköpping on 22nd May, Liverpool fought hard to grind out a 1-0 victory against a team who had been unbeaten in their last 13 games against touring English sides. Whilst his team-mates moved on to Gothenburg, Spicer, whose leg was in plaster, flew to London where he was met by his wife who drove him to Liverpool. Spicer told reporters at Heathrow that the fracture was a simple one and he would be back in action in a few months.

The most exciting match of the tour took place at the Gamla Ullevi Stadium on 24th May, the Reds beating a Gothenburg Select XI 5-3 in a game described by Ranger as 'more akin to a vital Football League struggle than a close season exhibition.' Opposition centre forward Granqvist scored a hat-trick and Liverpool were only able to breathe easily when Cyril Done headed in an 88th minute goal to complete the scoring after keeper Charlie Ashcroft had kept the Swedes at bay. On 29th May the tour was completed with another game against Malmö, this time in Malmö, with the Reds going down 2-1 in another hard fought game in which they trailed 2-0 at half-time.

DENMARK AND SWEDEN 1971

The last time that Liverpool had a post season tour to Scandinavia was in 1971. It was a surprising destination at the time, as by then the club tended to go to Spain post season and only play one match, if any at all.

The Liverpool party began this tour two weeks after losing 2-1 to Arsenal in the FA Cup final, flying to Copenhagen on the morning of 24th May from Manchester Airport. They were missing six of the team who played at Wembley. Ray Clemence and Alun Evans were getting married, Brian Hall's wife was expecting a baby, Steve Heighway and John Toshack were on international duty, while Emlyn Hughes remained behind because his brother was injured in a car accident in Barrow a few days before. It meant an opportunity for some fringe players to prove their worth, including striker Jack Whitham and the club's new signing from Scunthorpe, Kevin Keegan. There was no *Daily Post* or *Liverpool Echo* correspondent on this tour, with reports having been obtained from press agencies.

After a brief coach tour of Copenhagen the Reds flew on to Aarhus and checked into the Atlantic Hotel, in readiness for the following evening's game against Aarhus GF. A crowd of 13,000, including 5,000 school children who were given free tickets, saw the Second Division amateur side embarrass the Reds. There was no sign of the upset to come when Jack Whitham gave Liverpool a fifth minute lead but the home side hit back to lead 2-1. Bobby Graham equalised midway through the second half but the Danes' heads didn't drop and they bombarded the Reds goal, eventually winning a penalty four minutes from time which was converted by Kristen Nygaard. A shell-shocked Liverpool could muster no response as AGF held out for a famous victory.

For the next match of the tour, the Reds party had a gruelling day on 26th May, with three flights being needed to reach the Swedish city of Luleå, just 50 miles from the Arctic Circle. They eventually arrived there at 6.30pm having flown via Copenhagen and Stockholm, but when it came to the match the next night there were no signs of tiredness whatsoever. The Reds romped to a 5-0 win against IFK Luleå, who were enjoying their one and only season in Swedish football's top tier. Despite John Toshack not being there four of the Reds goals were headers and Jack Whitham again found the net, scoring twice. Kevin Keegan, the new signing who was desperate to impress, was a livewire throughout and opened the scoring. Whereas the tour may have had an end of season air for many of the other players, Keegan knew it was a big opportunity for him, recalling later: 'I took it seriously whereas to many of the others it was an end of season jolly. At the end of that three-match tour I felt as though I had started to make inroads.'[4]

On 28th May the Reds were on the move again to Sundsvall, which involved flying via Stockholm, where they had to be bussed from Arlanda to Bromma Airport. The game against Second Division GIF Sundsvall wasn't until 1st June though so the players had three full days of relaxation first. Keegan was again in fine form and voted man of the match by Swedish journalists as the Reds proved their class, winning 4-0. After impressing in the first two games though Whitham was disappointing and he was replaced by another youngster, Phil Boersma, at half-time.

The Sundsvall game was the last of the tour but it wasn't time to come home just yet. The party then returned to Denmark, again via Stockholm where they had to be bussed from one airport to the other. They spent three nights at the beach resort of Klampenborg, north of Copenhagen, before returning to Liverpool on 5th June.

3

Italy and Gay Paree

When football returned to normal after the First World War, Liverpool took a different track and headed south in the 1920s rather than to Scandinavia as they had done when going abroad previously. Their only two excursions across the English Channel that decade came after winning titles, although it would be wrong to assume they were both a direct reward for success. The 1922 tour of Italy for example, was organised between the English and Italian Football Associations and was intended to showcase the English game in the country.

However the trips did give the directors an opportunity to give the players some extra comforts for winning the league. In the days of the maximum wage cash bonuses were unacceptable but a tour on top of a mini-break, with generous daily allowances of ten shillings a day thrown in, were not breaking any rules.

The two tours of the 1920s were made in successive years and consisted of some exhausting travel by train, as did the next time they went to France, over 30 years later even though the aeroplane was an alternative by then.

ITALY 1922

At the end of the 1921-22 season Liverpool were invited by the FA to travel to Italy along with Burnley for a trip that would see the two clubs play each other before engaging in a series of friendlies against Italian sides. Each club was paid £100 for their trouble and also had all travel and accommodation expenses paid.[5]

As with some of the other foreign trips before the Second World War, details published in the press regarding the games were very brief, amounting to just a few lines. One of the games, against Pro Vercelli on 5th June, wasn't mentioned at all. Many of the gaps regarding games were filled in later on when letters from players were received. They again provided an invaluable resource in maintaining information regarding this tour but even then not all line-ups from games are known.

The Reds confirmed the title with three games to spare, ironically beating Burnley 2-1 at Anfield on Easter Monday, 17th April. Exactly one month later and a week after the last game of the season they set off for London for the first leg of a gruelling journey that would eventually see them arrive at Lake Maggiore 72 hours later.

They set off from Lime Street station for London on 17th May, spending the night at the Belgravia Hotel close to Victoria station. The next morning they departed for Paris with the Burnley players, with right back Ephraim Longworth describing the journey to Bee of the *Liverpool Echo* in a letter published in the paper on 29th May:

> 'Many of the lads rushed up as soon as the boat was in motion but none were sick. The sea was very choppy and Chambers was the first to be baptised. As he walked along the deck a wave washed all over him and caused all the boys to have a good "cry." In Paris at 6.25 we had a bit of a shock. As a party of our directors were proceeding to a hotel in a motor bus it collided with a lamppost and they all had the wind up, especially our worthy manager!'

The party only had time for dinner and the briefest of looks around Paris before boarding another train for Milan, a journey that would take 26 hours. Despite being in first class compartments, the trip was still an uncomfortable and tiring one, as Longworth went on:

> 'We were unlucky not to have sleepers. We had to sleep the best we could from 9.30 to 8.30. The boys were up earlier that morning than they had been for many a long day. We then had breakfast at Chambery – a roll and a cup of coffee, so you may think the boys had something to say. It would have been very laughable for some of our people to see the sandwiches. They consisted of a roll cut in half and a little ham put in between and a paper cover to stop the ham running away.'

In Turin the players were able to stretch their legs for a period before the train continued and some took the opportunity to get hold of some Italian lira. However Longworth described how Harry Chambers was extremely disappointed when the 30 coins he was given amounted to about three pence. Finally arriving in Milan at 11pm, they stayed the night there before completing the final leg of the journey to Lake Maggiore the next morning. When it came to the scenery though and the beauty of their destination when they eventually arrived there, Longworth was taken aback:

> 'We departed for the Lake District which puts ours in the shade. We thought Grasmere was unbeatable but it is not in the same street as this place. It is impossible to describe such a place with a pen. We travelled through the Italian Alps and the heat was intense – yet all around us the mountain tops were covered with snow.'

Staying at Le Grand Hotel Des Iles Borromees Liverpool and Burnley's players were treated to a reception laid on by the Mayor of Stresa on the afternoon of their arrival, with bouquets being presented to the two chairmen. All the players' needs were taken care of by Signor Antivalli, an official of AC Milan and half back Tom Bromilow couldn't speak highly enough of him, writing to the *Evening Express:* 'He has looked after our every comfort since we left England. We should have been in a very bad plight had we not been accompanied by our guide, interpreter and friend.' They were then treated to a boat trip around some islands and a tour of a palace and its gardens, where Longworth noted there were trees covered in oranges and lemons. The 21st was spent swimming in the lake, where there was an unfortunate incident when midfielder Jock McNab got into difficulty and had to be rescued, which would lead to him being ruled out of the first game with fluid on the knee.

The next day the players took a narrow gauge railway train to the top of Mount Mattarone, which stands 1,491 metres high and from where they were able to see four countries – Italy, Austria, Germany and Switzerland. This was followed by a visit to a casino, but Longworth wrote that none of them chanced their arm on the roulette wheels

On Tuesday 23rd the Liverpool and Burnley players returned to Milan, where a reception was laid on by the Italian FA. They were also taken on motor trips to the cathedral and a cemetery, where they witnessed a funeral and were surprised to see the mourners dressed in both black and white. Of the visit to the cathedral Bromilow wrote: 'Most of the players climbed to the highest step of the highest spire, which entailed the climbing of 475 steps in all. It really is one of the marvels of the world, no words of mine could convey the beauty and grandeur of such a work of art.' Bromilow also wrote how there was quite a lot of bargaining with the hawkers going on, describing: 'For an article which they first offer at 20 lira they eventually sell at about five lira. They apparently imagine that we don't know the value of Italian coinage.'

Reds' Director Mr Cartwright wrote to Bee that there was eager anticipation at the prospect of two English First Division sides facing each other although he personally was concerned at the hot weather, writing: 'The people of Milan, Torino and towns around are going mad over this match. They expect great things from both teams but the heat is bound to affect the play, as no player could maintain his pace for 90 minutes in the heat we are getting.'

Cartwright was not wrong about the match, which was played on 25th May at a slow pace and saw the Reds lose 1-0. The *Daily Mail* carried a brief report of the game the following day, stating that the crowd were not pleased at the fact the players did not exert themselves too much and that some spectators 'showed their disapproval by hooting and booing.'

The Italian fans may have been used to such heat, but it was an entirely new experience for the Reds players, Bromilow saying in one of his letters that it was the hottest he had ever experienced and stuffy at night too. A letter from him was published in the *Evening Express* six days afterwards in which he said of the game:

'Just prior to the time for kick off the temperature reached over 90 degrees and in my opinion it was higher than that at 5pm. Buckets of water were placed around the ground for players to have a dip when necessary. Phew! The heat beats anything I have ever experienced. The onlookers were streaming with perspiration so I leave you to guess what the players had to contend with. The first half was good and even but in the second half the play was a little on the slow side. The sun's rays were a little too much for most of the players and it was only natural that the second half should lack the fire which characterised the first portion. Burnley maintained their opening pace better than our boys and therein lies the reason of their success.'

One thing that surprised the players was the way that this game and others on the tour were officiated. The referee stood on the touchline for the whole game, occasionally running up and down and often changing his mind after awarding a foul, throwing the ball in the air instead. Bromilow wrote that these could be exasperating at times but that the 'peculiar rulings caused quite a lot of amusement for the players.' The match was of such importance in Italy that Burnley's players, who Bromilow said were 'on the very best of terms' with the Reds, having been together since leaving London, were each presented with small gold medals after the game.

After the game in Milan, Liverpool and Burnley's players went their separate ways, with the Reds heading to Modena on the morning of Saturday 27th May, where Bromilow described the weather as 'sweltering and too hot even for cricket.'[6] The players were also having problems with the food and were not keen at all on many of the Italian dishes offered. That evening they had a reception with the Lord Mayor and the next day beat an Emilia Select XI 6-1. This game was given a few lines in the *Liverpool Echo* the next evening, but not mentioned at all in the *Evening Express*. However a week later the *Express* published a letter from Bromilow that had arrived which contained quite a bit of detail regarding the game's events:

'Prior to the kick off at 5pm Wadsworth, as captain, was presented with a bouquet and a book of views of the town of Modena; they were accompanied by three hearty cheers. Our boys played exhibition football of the best kind and won easily by six goals to one, the half time score reading 3-0. The opposition was very keen and energetic but the skill was sadly lacking. Harry Chambers was in his best shooting form and in addition to scoring three goals he almost knocked the goalkeeper through the goal with several other shots of power. They scored their goal in lucky fashion, a long range shot trickled towards Elisha Scott and as he was about to pick it up the ball deflected from a large tuft of grass and rolled into the net. Elisha Scott saved a penalty, we are still wondering why the penalty was given. Tommy Lucas was about to clear when the outside left dashed up and grazed Lucas's face with his boot. The referee instead of giving a foul in our favour immediately pointed to the penalty spot. It was perhaps fortunate for him that he could not hear a word of English or he might have heard a few things about himself of which he was unaware. As Scott saved the shot easily our boys' feelings towards the referee immediately transformed themselves into a smile.'

In addition to getting used to the referee controlling the game from the touchline, the Reds also found out that substitutions were the norm in Italy for injured players. Bromilow wrote:

'It is the custom in Italy that if the player is hurt he can be replaced by a fresh member. They had three players, all ready in battle order behind one of the goals to take the place of a casualty. In the first half, I noticed that their left half did more running than anyone else and did not appear in the second portion, a new man had taken his place. The original left half was apparently tired, but apparently absented himself under the guise of injury.'

The next day the Reds travelled to Pisa, a 10-hour rail journey that took them through 117 tunnels which Ephraim Longworth said were 'not very pleasant.' They drew 2-2 with a Liguria and Tuscany XI on 1st June in a game played in such extreme heat that many fans were fainting and Liverpool's Walter Wadsworth, who wasn't playing, was often administering first aid on the touchline. Despite the heat, it was still an intense and rough game, described by Ephraim Longworth in a letter published by 'Bee' in the *Liverpool Echo* on 8th June:

'It was the worst game I have ever played in. The referee was very poor. One of the Pisa team had the misfortune to have his arm broken. They had no idea of playing football, they were very dirty and it was fortunate that we came off the field without any damage. The crowd were of a similar type; they fairly encouraged their team to play rough. All did as well as could be expected against such a team.'

Tom Bromilow's letter to the *Evening Express,* was along similar lines, as he described how he had 'never played in such a game where so much pushing, kicking and hacking was tolerated,'[7] while the referee would penalise fair charges from the Reds' players. Although the game itself wasn't to the Reds' liking, they were certainly impressed with Pisa itself. In the same letter Longworth said that they had been 'not very much impressed with Modena' but that in Pisa they were given a fantastic reception and that it was 'the finest place we have been on the tour.' His letter continued:

'We have been treated finely by the people of the town and were given a great reception by the Deputy Lord Mayor at the Town Hall.' The players were taken to the cathedral, a country mansion and on a boat trip up the River Arno to the Mediterranean Sea as well as the theatre, but no mention was made by either Longworth or Bromilow in their letters of the Leaning Tower.

The next two games were against the Serie A champions and runners up, Pro Vercelli and Genoa. Bromilow's letter that was printed in the *Evening Express* on 5th June, the day of the Pro Vercelli game, stated that the Reds had been warned they were the best team in Italy and should expect defeat, to which he had responded: 'We shall see.' Pro Vercelli certainly were the crack team of Italian football, having won seven titles but soon afterwards they went into decline and have not been back in the top flight since 1935, only returning to Serie B after a 64-year absence in 2012. The game ended in a 0-0 draw and despite it having been between two of the best sides in Europe there was no mention of it in either the *Express* or *Liverpool Echo*, who instead printed a report on the wedding of Reds outside left Fred Hopkin who got married on the same day. It stated how he had married his bride Annie Gill in their native Darlington before setting off for a Lake District honeymoon, staying in Keswick. Hopkin wasn't the only Reds player getting married that summer, although inside forward Dick Forshaw had decided to go on the tour and his nuptials would take place a few days after the return, with him and his bride honeymooning in Llandudno.

The final match of the tour two days later saw the Reds run out 4-1 winners against Genoa, who were managed by ex Arsenal and Blackburn player Billy Garbutt. The following evening's *Liverpool Echo* carried the details of this game, which was played on a hard ground and the paper implied that the Reds would also be playing games in Paris on their way home. However there appears to have been a change of plan as the Reds arrived back that very evening, barely 24 hours after the Genoa game had finished. The Liverpool party was met by chairman Walter Williams, who had rushed there from Aigburth where he had been watching his son play in a tennis tournament. The *Liverpool Echo's* report of the return the following evening described the players as looking 'tanned and tired' and also a little thinner than usual. It was reported that all of the games were rough with the exception of the Genoa one, where the influence of Garbutt had rubbed off. An unnamed player said: 'There is still a lot of missionary work for the FA to do but I hope they don't expect us to do it. The refereeing is awful, only once did we have a decent referee, against Burnley. Otherwise it was terrible refereeing.'

On the whole though the players enjoyed the trip and had no complaints about the hospitality shown to them or the places they had seen. They were also glad to be returning as a complete party, as the *Echo* reported that Walter Wadsworth had been offered the opportunity to stay in Turin and coach there, although it didn't specify which club.

FRANCE 1923

The few hours that Liverpool spent in Paris en route to Italy in 1922 must have made an impression on the Liverpool staff, as a year later they were back for an extended break, playing two matches there which came at the end of a week of leisure.

In 1922-23 Liverpool had never looked like failing to retain the league title, hitting the top in mid September and never being knocked off it. They were so far ahead that even a loss of form towards the end, when they won only one of their last seven games, didn't prevent them securing the title with two matches to spare.

The season ended with a 1-0 win over Stoke City at Anfield on 5th May and on Friday 18th May a party of 13 players, accompanied by coaching staff and directors, set off for Paris from Lime Street station. That evening's *Evening Express* reported: 'Having finished an arduous season, Liverpool's players are to enjoy a trip to Paris, during which two matches will be played. The tour will therefore be short, but no doubt most enjoyable.'

The players arrived at Paris on the afternoon of 19th May and had no problems on the journey, Ephraim Longworth joking in his letter to the *Liverpool Echo* (published on the 23rd) that 'it must have been calm when even Chambers was all right.' That night some of the directors met boxer Battling Siki, the Senegalese world light-heavyweight champion, who promised to come and see the Reds matches the following weekend. Longworth also wrote in his letter that on the Sunday some of the players went to the races at Longchamps, although were not allowed entry until they had first removed their caps. They refrained from betting though as they were unable to understand the pari-mutuel system, instead admiring the 'lovely sights of the dresses of the mannequins.'

Longworth's next letter was printed on 26th May and had been written two days earlier describing a busy day's sightseeing:

'Yesterday we started on a short tour of Paris. Our first stop was the Pantheon, where we saw some lovely paintings all about French history. We then visited the famous Notre Dame. The history of this church is too well known for me to speak about it, but the work inside is great. We also saw the monument erected to the famous French airman called the "Arc of Aces" Captain Guynemer. We visited the Bastille but saw very little of it because it was in ruins. We saw where the Guillotine used to be erected. We visited the slums of Paris and saw where Victor Hugo lived. We came back for lunch and left again about 2.30. Included in the afternoon's tour were the Eiffel Tower and the place where Napoleon's tomb is. There is one peculiar thing about this, that is everyone who looks upon this tomb must pay a mark of respect because the tomb lies in a sort of pit, so you must bow down to it. The Louvre was the next item on the programme – a wonderful place for pictures. There are three miles of pictures in this building. We had only time to see about half.'

Longworth also revealed that they had toured the ancient city of Rheims, much of which had been damaged in the First World War (then known as the Great War), as well as various battle sites including the German defences at the Hindenburg Line. A charabanc also took the players to the Palace of Versailles, seeing the table on which the treaty that ended the war was signed and they also went to see some of the British trenches. There was sport to watch too, with the Reds players watching Glasgow Rangers, who were staying in the same hotel, beat a combined Paris XI 6-1 as well as attending the World Hardcourt Tennis Championships.

When it came to the games they took place on successive days over the weekend of 26th/27th May and took up just three brief column lines in the *Daily Post & Mercury* and four in the *Evening Express*. The latter wrote: 'On Saturday they met Cercle Athletic de Paris Gallia and were not greatly extended to win by three clear goals, while on Sunday afternoon the FEC Levalis club were beaten by four goals to nil.' The Cercle de Paris club that the Reds faced now play in the lower divisions of the Paris regional league system, while the Levalis club referred to is SC Levallois, who currently play in the fourth level of the French league in a stadium named after their most famous player, Didier Drogba.

There are little details available of the Levallois game, save that it was played in Paris according to a letter from Longworth. A letter from him printed in the *Liverpool Echo* on 30th May though did include some more information regarding the first game, which was played after the players had laid a wreath at the Tomb of the Unknown French Warrior which lies beneath the Arc de Triomphe.

> 'We rested till the match which was billed as Liverpool v Paris. There were only 1,000 spectators due to the match not being advertised. It was played at the Buffalo Stadium, where Siki beat Carpenter. It is set out lovely – everyone is seated. We tried a new centre – Dick Forshaw – but we will not say whether he was a success or not. We managed to win easily, goals being scored by Chambers, Davey Pratt and Forshaw. I think the spectators enjoyed the match.'

On Monday 28th May the party headed back to Liverpool after an enjoyable week, finally arriving back at Lime Street at 9.35pm. It would be over

10years before they would be off to foreign shores again though and more than 30 before they returned to France.

FRANCE 1956

Although the Reds players had thoroughly enjoyed their trip to France in the 1920s, the same could not be said of the next generation to venture there. Liverpool's tour of France in 1956 descended into chaos on more than one occasion, meaning that they came close to abandoning it and coming home.

Perhaps the warning signs were there less than two weeks before departure when it became evident that the players would be going without manager Don Welsh, who resigned on 4th May. After a disappointing season in 1954-55 when they finished 11th in their first season in the Second Division for 50 years, 1955-56 was an improvement and they finished third. However they finished poorly after having a great chance of promotion at Easter and with his contract up for renewal the Board, with whom the *Liverpool Echo* reported he did not see eye to eye over team selection, did nothing to dissuade him from resigning.

Within a few days of Welsh leaving, former captain and current coach Phil Taylor was appointed as a 'liaison official,' his role being to provide a link between the players, training staff and directors. On 14th May, the day before the Liverpool party set off for France, Taylor was named acting manager, reported in the *Echo* as an indication that he would eventually be appointed to the job full time as this was a step up in position from his liaison role. Taylor would still not have overall control on team selection though, he would instead be part of a committee that chose the line-up, to which senior player Billy Liddell was co-opted for this tour.

The following day Taylor, along with16 players, trainer Albert Shelley, director Cecil Hill and chairman Tom Williams set off from Lime Street station for France, where they were to play five games. They were also accompanied by journalist Ranger, who was reporting on the tour for both the *Daily Post* and *Liverpool Echo*, meaning that fans could have up to date reports about what was going on, which proved to be quite a lot both on and off the pitch.

The Reds travelled through the night arriving in Paris on the morning of Wednesday 16th May, where they faced their first organisational problems over the onward transport to Angers, 190 miles away. Arriving at the station, guards refused the party permission to take their skips that were carrying the kit on board and by then the English speaking agent who was sorting out the travel had disappeared. Liddell and Taylor, who could speak a little French, were able to establish that there was another freight train leaving for Angers from a station half a mile away and they were able to summon a taxi to carry the skips there and book them on board.

Liverpool arrived in Angers just three hours before their first match of the tour and found that the hotel they had been booked into was not of the standard required, but others were booked up due to a music festival that was taking place in the town. Given all the circumstances, the Reds did very well to secure a 0-0 draw against SCO Angers, who were flying high in the French Second Division and needed just one win from their last two games to secure promotion (something they would achieve). Liddell didn't look travel weary at all and carved out a number of openings which were well saved as well as hitting the post. It was only late in the game that Angers exerted any pressure and Doug Rudham in the Reds goal was equal to everything. Liverpool's visit hadn't captured the imagination of the locals though with just 5,000 fans attending, which was blamed on the other activities on offer in Angers that week. However, Ranger wrote in the *Liverpool Echo* that prices were four shillings and 10 shillings, so 'cash receipts were not too bad' and that the Reds had been given guarantees about minimum payments they would receive.

The Reds party were meant to stay in Angers until the Sunday 20th May, but were staggered to find out that their rooms had not been reserved for the Friday and Saturday, despite having been given assurances in Paris that they had been. Officials from the Angers club stepped in to help and visited all the hotels in the town in cars, eventually managing to secure rooms for the Reds but spread across three different places. Although grateful for anything given the circumstances, the poor quality of what was secured meant Tom Williams made the decision to take everybody back to Paris a day early on the Saturday instead and seek an urgent meeting with the agent there. Ranger's report in the *Echo* that day stated that they had seen only one person since arriving in Angers, who showed up after the game, took his share of the gate money and disappeared without even saying goodbye. Such was the strength of feeling amongst Reds officials that Williams was seriously considering ripping up the contract and returning home, but he knew doing that would financially penalise clubs through no fault of their own. Instead he chose to receive guarantees about the standard of accommodation that the players would be staying at.

Once back in Paris the players did some sightseeing, which included a tour of the Stade Colombes although this stadium had bad memories for Billy Liddell, who once missed a penalty there for Scotland against France. They also fraternised with Brazilian side Vasco da Gama, who were in the middle of a mammoth 30-game, three-month tour of Europe which had included a game against Everton at the end of April. Ranger fed back to *Echo* readers though that costs in France were far too expensive, with a simple lunch on French railways costing £1 and Roy Saunders being charged £2 for a round of eight orangeades he bought for some English students, then getting asked to pay a supplement as the café was playing music.

Due to the French season still being played there was no opposition available over the weekend and it was six days after they faced Angers that the Reds were in action again. On 23rd May they travelled to Besançon, near the Swiss border for a game with Racing Club Franc Comtois (now known as Besançon RC), who like Angers were in the Second Division, but further down the table in eighth. In a match played under floodlights Liverpool thrashed their opponents 8-1 with a performance described by Tom Williams and Cecil Hill as 'a magnificent display of the finest type of soccer.' Ranger wrote in his match report for the *Daily Post* and *Liverpool Echo* that if the Reds had played like that at the end of the season they would have been promoted, as they dazzled those present with accurate passing and deadly finishing. Racing Club scored first after 10 minutes, but the Reds stormed back to lead 4-1 at half-time and added four more in the second half. Ranger wrote that it could have been a dozen more had it not been for the home keeper and that the Reds players were toying with the opposition by the end of the game.

The next night Liverpool were in action again, travelling 300 miles north to play Rouen, arriving only three hours before kick off after a nine-hour journey by bus and train. As with their previous two opponents, Rouen were in the Second Division and the Reds showed no sign of tiredness as they cruised to a 6-2 victory. Billy Liddell gave them the lead after half an hour and although Rouen equalised Alan A'Court restored the advantage before half-time. Within five minutes of the second half starting further goals from Johnny Evans and Alan Arnell put the game beyond the home side. Rouen pulled a goal back and for a short time the game was a hard physical affair until goals from Evans and Geoff Twentyman restored it to a more amicable pace. The Reds were applauded off by the crowd, which was a disappointing 2,600. This was down to the fact that it was Rouen's third home friendly in a fortnight and at that time the Reds weren't as attractive opposition as the other two visitors – Burnley and Hibernian.

After Rouen it was back to Paris for a few days before another trip out into the provinces on 27th May, this time to Vichy which lies almost 200 miles south. Liverpool's opponents there were St Etienne, a team that would later go down in the club's folklore. Although some way off the formidable side they would be 21 years later, they were still by far the most difficult opposition the Reds would face on this tour. They had just finished fourth in the First Division and a year earlier had won their first honour, the Charles Drago Cup, a short-lived competition for clubs who had been eliminated from the French Cup before the quarter final stage. 'Les Verts,' who included four internationals in their side, took a 13th minute lead but Billy Liddell equalised for the Reds just before the half hour. In the second half Liverpool dominated but couldn't find a winner although it had been a very encouraging performance by them. To put the result into context Stade de Reims, who had finished below St Etienne in the league, had reached the European Cup final that season.

Liverpool's last game of the tour was at Toulouse on 30th May, where they were beaten for the first time on the trip, Jimmy Melia scoring the Reds goal in a 3-1 defeat in which the home side also hit the post twice. Although the game ended in defeat it was no disgrace against a side that had finished seventh in the French First Division. The results, coupled with the organisational abilities shown by Phil Taylor, had done him no harm at all in his quest to become manager on a permanent basis, something that would be confirmed before the next season started. Chairman Tom Williams was pleased with the performances, with Ranger quoting him in the *Liverpool Echo* on 31st May as saying: 'In every town we have visited I have been complimented on the first class displays served up. They have been a credit to English football and I am proud of them.'

Although the football side had gone well, Williams could not say the same about the travelling involved for games and hotel arrangements. With local agents nowhere to be seen, it was often up to the Liverpool party to arrange things and Billy Liddell and Phil Taylor's knowledge of the French language was invaluable. In Toulouse the players were made to leave their hotel at noon even though the game did not kick off until after 9pm. They then had just 40 minutes to make the sleeper train to Paris afterwards and after a quick change and coach journey they got to the station just five minutes before it departed. On arrival in Paris, the party found that their baggage had been left behind in Toulouse, meaning they were stood on the platform in light clothing and sandals carrying pyjamas, rather than the raincoats which were required due to the change in weather.

Another worry was the fact that the passports were in their baggage, which enquiries established would arrive that afternoon with not too long to spare before the players set off for London. Tragic news then came via a telegram for Geoff Twentyman, advising him that his brother had died and the funeral would be that afternoon. Tom Williams offered to have Twentyman booked on a plane to Manchester but given he would not have made it to Carlisle in time anyway he chose to stay with the team and travel home by train. This news made it impossible for the players to forget what had happened regarding various arrangements going wrong in France and enjoy the journey home, meaning that all in all this trip had been one to forget.

4

Entertaining the Troops

Although peace may have come to Europe in May 1945 it didn't mean an immediate return home for soldiers who had been fighting in the Second World War. There was still the task of disarming Germany and setting up the new state, which would involve continued occupation by troops for some time. The onset of the Cold War then meant that a British army presence in the new state of West Germany continued to help defend it from attack by the Soviet Union. This meant that when Liverpool FC played there they were often watched by large numbers of soldiers who were in the crowd.

GERMANY 1945

Germany had unconditionally surrendered on 8th May, a week after Adolf Hitler committed suicide as the Allied armies closed in on Berlin. The British army then occupied much of the north and west of the country, with the rest being split between France, the Soviet Union and United States. Liverpool were the first English team to play matches in Germany after the end of hostilities, which Ranger in the *Liverpool Echo* described as a 'feather in Anfield's cap' as more clubs, including Arsenal and Derby County, were now making arrangements to go there.

The Reds flew from London to Germany, playing their first game against the RAF in Celle on Saturday 28th July and winning 7-0 with Willie Fagan scoring four of the goals. They then travelled 25 miles to Hanover for a match the next day against a team from the 21st Army Group, who had advanced through Normandy, Holland and then the Rhine area of Germany. They provided a much stronger test than the RAF, with their team including Everton's keeper Ted Sagar and Dennis Westcott of Wolverhampton Wanderers. An entertaining game played in front of 35,000 spectators ended in a 3-3 draw with guest player Don Welsh, who would later manage the club, scoring a hat-trick for the Reds. The Reds had hoped to have midfielder Bill Jones, who was in the 21st Army, in their side but he arrived too late to play.

One of those watching the game in Hanover was Liverpool music hall comedian Billy Matchett, who was touring Germany with the Entertainments National Service Association. He wrote to the *Evening Express* saying that he had come across so many Liverpudlian soldiers it was like a home from home and they were thrilled at the team's presence. Despite playing two games in two days and the tiring travel, it was reported in the *Evening Express* that the Liverpool officials were 'entirely satisfied' with the tour and performances in what was a great morale boost for those troops still waiting to return home.

BELGIUM AND SAARLAND 1950

After the disappointment of losing the FA Cup final to Arsenal in 1949-50 Liverpool went on a mini tour at the end of May playing two games in Belgium and the Saarland.

The Reds took on Belgian champions Anderlecht on Sunday 28th May, drawing 1-1. Billy Liddell scored the Reds equaliser in the second half to complete an eventful weekend for him. The previous day he had played for Scotland against France in Paris, missing a penalty but setting up the goal in a 1-0 win. He then took the train to Brussels to join up with his Reds team-mates, scoring his goal from point blank range in the 50th minute.

From Belgium the Reds went on to Saarbrücken, which at the time was the main city of the Saar Protectorate, a nominally independent region of the area of West Germany that was occupied by French troops. In the match against 1FC Saarbrücken on 31st May the Reds went down 4-1, with Herbert Binkert scoring a hat-trick. This was one of a number of friendlies played by the Saar club at that time (the following May they would draw 1-1 with the Reds at Anfield) as due to the political situation they were not part of any league. Later that decade, they re-joined the West Germany league system after the Saar people voted to become part of that country in 1955.

1952 GERMANY AND AUSTRIA

After visiting Sweden in 1951, Liverpool undertook their first multinational tour of Europe since 1936 when they visited four countries at the end of 1951-52, playing matches in three of them. The Reds were away for three weeks in total, playing three games in Germany and Austria before having a few days in Paris, then moving on to Spain for a match in Madrid and a few days in the sun.

Liverpool had an indifferent season in 1951-52, finishing 11th after a late slump saw them pick up just one point from the last four games. As the Reds made their final preparations for the tour, Billy Liddell wished fans a happy summer in his *Liverpool Echo* column on 3rd May but didn't seem over enthusiastic about the impending trip, writing: 'Some may think it's too long a break but to us mortals who live by our feet, it is all too short, especially when you go on close season tour. But however much we grumble and grouse, we will always welcome a game of football.'

On Tuesday 6th May the *Echo* reported that the players were in good spirits as they set off from Anfield by coach to Manchester Airport from where they took a flight to Düsseldorf. The party consisted of 17 players, four directors, manager Don Welsh and trainer Albert Shelley. One notable omission was Bob Paisley who was injured with a broken wrist and his place was taken by Ken Brierley, who hadn't featured for the first team since February.

The first match of the tour was the following day in Essen, a city that had been heavily bombed during the war and where three British airmen were lynched in 1944, leading to two men, including a German army officer, being hanged in 1946. Essen was now part of the British Zone of Occupation and 4,000 British soldiers were in the crowd for the game which was against a combined Rot Weiss Essen/Fortuna Düsseldorf side. Despite being a composite side the Germans showed some great understanding between them and the Reds had to come from behind twice to force a 2-2 draw, their goalscorers being Billy Liddell and Jack Smith. Unusually the home side changed their shirts at half-time, with all the players reappearing for the second half wearing black, including the keeper who was only distinguishable by a red collar. It was suggested by one British spectator, Corporal A. Denny who wrote to the *Liverpool Echo*, that this was a deliberate ploy given the gloomy and darkening weather conditions. Corporal Denny also stated in his letter that the less said about the referee the better but in spite of everything the Reds had put up a 'great show' in a 'classic and sporting' manner.'[8]

From Essen the Reds party travelled to Munich where they spent the weekend, before moving on to Vienna for a match on 14th May against FK Austria Vienna at the Vienna Stadium. This later became the Prater and subsequently Ernst Happel Stadium, which has hosted five European Cup/Champions League finals and the final of Euro 2008. The *Echo* had predicted when the Reds departed that this would be the hardest match of the tour and was proved right as the Reds lost 2-0, although the following day's *Daily Post* report did say that it had been an unfortunate defeat. The Austrians started well with Lukas Aurednik hitting the post twice before scoring in the 14th minute. In the second half the Reds dominated possession but with Billy Liddell closely marked the other players were unable to make it count and wasteful with their chances. Two minutes from time Huber added a second to condemn Liverpool to defeat in a game that had also seen many refereeing decisions favour the home side. However this wasn't used as an excuse for the defeat, with the *Post* reporting that Reds chairman G.A. Richards told the correspondent afterwards: 'Our boys played well considering the standard of refereeing, but Austria deserved to win. It's goals that count in the game.'

The Liverpool party then returned to Germany where they faced BC Augsburg on 18th May. BC Augsburg were a mid-table club in the Oberliga Süd of the German top flight, who in 1969 would merge with TSV Schwaben to form FC Augsburg. In front of a healthy crowd of 36,000 the Reds won 4-1 in a game played in intense heat. Billy Liddell scored twice with the others coming from Jimmy Payne and Kevin Baron, but the Reds didn't have it as easy as the scoreline suggests and the defence had to be at their best to deter the Augsburg attacks.

From Augsburg the Reds players went to Paris for a few days before moving on to Madrid for a game there and some days by the coast, finally returning home on 24th May for a few months rest before training began for the new season. It wasn't over for Billy Liddell though who didn't even return home with his team-mates, instead flying from Madrid to Scandinavia to join up with the Scottish side who were beginning a tour there.

5

Czech-Ing Out the East

Liverpool have twice toured eastern Europe, with both trips taking place in very different circumstances. The first was a jaunt that saw them make a round trip of 3,000 miles by rail over a three week period. The second was made by air to a country under Communist rule.

CZECHOSLOVAKIA, YUGOSLAVIA AND ROMANIA 1936

After venturing further than they ever had before the previous year by going to the Canary Islands, Liverpool again broke new ground in 1936, heading east on a tour that took them through three countries along the River Danube and would take the players away from home for the best part of a month.

As with so many other tours, details in the immediate aftermath of games were very sketchy, with very little information being reported in the press, but more news was provided a few days later when letters arrived from the players. For what was billed in the local press as a 'Balkans tour' Matt Busby wrote letters to the *Evening Express*, while the *Liverpool Echo* received theirs from Ernie Blenkinsop.

Liverpool's season finished on 2nd May and two days afterwards they played a charity friendly at Bristol Rovers before setting off for Prague, taking the train there via London, Dover and Ostend. Ted Savage though, had some problems with his luggage during the early stages of the journey, as Blenkinsop recalled:

> 'One amusing thing during the London to Dover journey. Ted Savage, who had bought a swanky light brown suitcase at Liverpool (costing lots of money so he said) was picking up the case to board the boat at Dover and the handle broke off. He had to pick up a piece of the ship's rope to make a new handle.' [9]

Otherwise the Liverpool party's journey to their destination was trouble free, which couldn't be said about Everton's players who were touring Germany and Austria at the same time. On 7th May the *New York*, on which they were travelling to Hamburg, was involved in a collision with a Dutch steamer off the coast of Belgium. The other vessel, the *Alphard* sank but all 27 crew members were rescued and taken aboard the *New York*, which put them ashore before continuing to Hamburg. It was certainly a case of bad luck for one of the Everton directors George Evans, who had been aboard the Cunard liner *Laurentic* sailing to Quebec when it was rammed by another vessel in fog in the Irish Sea the previous August.

The first match of Liverpool's tour was on 13th May against a Prague Select XI, mainly made up of players from Slavia and Sparta and played at the Letná Stadium, where the Reds played Sparta in the Europa League in 2009-10. The Reds came from 2-1 down at half-time to win 4-2 with the following evening's *Evening Express* describing it as a 'brilliant win' as it was 'practically a national eleven that Liverpool defeated' and that it occurred due to their 'willingness to go that extra yard.'

Liverpool's victory caused shockwaves in Prague, where the select side had never been beaten. Matt Busby's letter to Pilot of the *Evening Express*, which was printed on 19th May, said that locals had expected a four or five goal win and that one official told him if he was a betting man he would now have been without a house. Busby also enclosed a cutting from Prague's German language newspaper *Prager Tagblatt*, which he had had translated into English. The *Express* reported that it said:

> 'It was time that an English club should prove to the continental teams that there is always a possibility of learning from the British how to play football. We are grateful for this lesson from Liverpool. The eleven boys from Liverpool fought from the first to the last for every ball. We admired their perfect poise, their perfect self governing. The spectators were a little disappointed about the result, but had to recognise that the best team won.'

The following evening and a full week after the match, a letter from Ernie Blenkinsop was printed in the *Liverpool Echo*. The paper had not carried any news of the game at all but had since reported on the second match of the tour against HŠK Građanski. Now it was going back and printing a detailed report of the Prague game, which must have been somewhat confusing for fans. Blenkinsop described how the first half of the game in Prague was played in a deluge and the rain was so bad that at half-time abandonment was a real possibility, with drains backing up so much that the dressing rooms were under six inches of water. After a 25 minute delay the referee, who didn't keep up with play but instead stood static about six yards from the touchline, decided to continue after some of the surface water had been cleared from the pitch. Blenkinsop wrote how the conditions suited Liverpool far better once the rain had stopped, saying: 'The heavy ground was now suiting our boys and we were playing with tons of confidence, everyone pulling their weight.' That extended to keeper Alf Hobson, who according to Blenkinsop handled everything cleanly and saved a penalty just after Phil Taylor had given Liverpool the lead with 15 minutes remaining.

The day after the Prague match the Liverpool party took a train to Vienna for a two night break before heading on to Zagreb, now the capital of Croatia but then part of Yugoslavia, a state created after the First World War. There were some language problems on arrival in Vienna, with Busby stating in his letter: 'It was amusing to see trainer Charlie Wilson trying to make the porters in Vienna understand that we wanted a place to dry our togs. At one stage he was making shapes of boilers in the air.' Wilson had already had trouble with German speakers on a train earlier in the trip, as Blenkinsop had explained in his letter to the *Echo*:

'One night through some misunderstanding Charlie Wilson found himself having to occupy the same sleeping compartment with a German gentleman, Charlie did not fancy this and decided to move in on Syd Roberts and Alf Hanson and sleep in their lower berth, Alf and Syd occupying the upper. The conductor, on his early morning survey of the compartment, saw Charlie's original berth empty. After a search he discovered Charlie and insisted that Charlie should return to his proper place. The broken English and Stockport conversation that followed was a scream! Ben Dabbs and I had a real laugh. Needless to say, Charlie won in the end and got to stay with Syd and Alf.'

When Liverpool arrived in Zagreb in the early evening of 16th May after a nine-and-a-half hour train journey, much of which was spent by playing cards, they were met by the Mayor, the president of the HŠK Građanski club and a band that played both national anthems. Many local shops had pictures of the Reds' players too advertising the game, although they were struggling with the correct spellings, with Blenkinsop being referred to as Blackinshop.

There would be no further hospitality though as the following evening the Reds were hammered 5-1 in a game played on heavy ground. On 18th May the *Liverpool Echo* carried a general Reuters report, which dedicated just 17 words to Liverpool's loss, more being given to Brentford's win in Portugal over Sporting Lisbon. The *Evening Express* had a bit more detail, saying that although Berry Nieuwenhuys had equalised the Reds were 2-1 down at half-time. There were protests that the third goal was offside but these were unheeded and Građanski went on to score two more. The hero for the home side was August Lešnik who scored a hat-trick.

By the time the letters from the players had reached Liverpool, the party had moved on to Belgrade and played two more games by the time Blenkinsop's letter was printed in the *Echo* on 27th May. Neither player was complimentary about the gravel pitch or the referee in Zagreb, with the diplomatic Busby being the far milder of the two. He wrote: 'The referee would not listen to our appeal but the goal should never have been allowed. It was not his first mistake as Phil Taylor was deliberately fouled in the penalty area.' Blenkinsop though was more scathing, referring to him as 'the apology for the referee' but both he and Busby did acknowledge the Reds didn't perform to their usual standards and that they were determined to make up for it in their next game in Belgrade. It wasn't just the Reds who were unhappy with the referee however, with Blenkinsop writing that the home crowd were 'giving him the bird' and in one of his later letters he would say that he was suspended by the Yugoslav FA. Despite the result and the unhappiness with the referee, Liverpool had no problems with their hosts at all and later that year returned the hospitality when HŠK Građanski played a friendly at Anfield. The club would eventually be disbanded in 1945 by the Communist government, with Dinamo Zagreb being formed with colours and a crest that bear a striking resemblance.

Before moving on to Belgrade the players watched a Davis Cup tennis match between Yugoslavia and Czechoslovakia. Liverpool's first match in Belgrade was on 21st May against SC Belgrade (known as OFK Belgrade since 1957) and the Reds won 2-0, both goals coming in the first 15 minutes. This was a very good result against a side that had recently beaten Građanski 6-0. The Liverpool Echo carried a report the following night which said that 'the Anfield team had been superior throughout' in a game that was watched by the British Ambassador to Yugoslavia, Ronald Campbell. Three days later the two sides met again in a game arranged at short notice due to the popularity Liverpool's visit had generated. The Reds again took an early lead with Alf Hanson scoring in the third minute but this time they were unable to build on this and Belgrade hit back to lead 3-1. Although Berry Nieuwenhuys pulled a goal back with 14 minutes remaining the Reds were unable to find an equaliser.

There were no more letters forthcoming from Matt Busby but on 27th May Blackstaff in the Liverpool Echo (who appeared to be standing in for Bee Edwards whilst he was on holiday) published two from Ernie Blenkinsop, which given the short time involved were most likely sent by telegraph. Of the game that ended in a 2-0 victory, Blenkinsop wrote: 'We anticipated a real struggle, but, true to form, Liverpool once again surprised the critics and once we had got used to the uneven hard ground our stamina proved too much for our opponents.' Of the game that ended in a 3-2 defeat, Blenkinsop expressed some surprise that the game ended that way given the Reds had won 2-0 a few days earlier. He said: 'We had the usual Continental deluge and thought it would suit us but although our boys fought very hard we had to admit defeat in the end. I would like to say they fully deserved their win and apart from a few bad decisions the referee was very fair.' Blenkinsop also revealed that the players had taken a trip to the top of Mount Avala, a 511 metre mountain that overlooks the city of

Belgrade, as well as visiting the Unknown Warrior's monument.

It was a full week between Liverpool's last game in Belgrade and their first in Romania, the third country of the tour. Their journey to Bucharest began with a twelve hour boat trip down the River Danube, crossing the border at Orsova before having their luggage examined at Turnu Severin, where a horse drawn carriage took them to the nearest train station. This was by far the most unusual form of transport they took on the whole tour and led to more problems with bags, as Blenkinsop recalled in a letter (likely sent by telegraph) that was published on 29th May:

'We were met by the old fashioned carriage and pair. These particular ones must have dated to about 1880. The wheels of the carriages were falling off and the horses were tired and weak looking, we had visions of our baggage dropping through the carriage. However there was only one slight mishap, Tom Bradshaw's team of mustangs were all out, doing a steady six miles an hour through a lovely sloshy part, when Braddy's trunk did a nose dive into about six inches of slush. Tom's trunk seems to be in the wars during this trip. It is a large and roomy one and is coming in very useful for all who have anything that they cannot manage to squeeze in their own bag.'

Once on the train, the card schools started again although this time there was also some playing of the mouth organ to pass time. Although glad to be on the move and away from the poverty of Turnu Severin, Blenkinsop did say they were sorry to be saying goodbye to the Yugoslav hospitality they had received, and that their lapels were beginning to look like pin cushions due to the amount of badges they had received from various clubs as gifts. On arrival in Bucharest, they were met by officials of the Ripensia Timişoara club, who had just won a Romanian league and cup double. Then on arrival at their hotel the thunderstorm which appeared to have been following them around the Balkans struck again.

After a long weekend of relaxing the Reds played their first match on Monday 1st June, beating Venus Bucharest, who had won five titles to date, 4-1 with Fred Howe netting twice. Ernie Blenkinsop was forced to miss the game through an upset stomach but he was still able to write to the Blackstaff at the *Liverpool Echo* that it was the easiest game of the tour and from the tenth minute there was only one team in it.

The following day they were back at Venus's cinder covered ground –described as like a black tennis court by Blenkinsop- to play Ripsensia. The Reds won 2-1 with the decisive goal coming from Alf Hanson three minutes from time. Whereas the previous day's game had been played on a wet surface, the sun had now dried it and this caused a problem for Syd Roberts who damaged his ankle, being forced to have it strapped up for the second half. A representative of the club sent a special telegram to the *Daily Post* concerning the game so they could print a reasonably lengthy report the next day. It was said to have been played in a sporting fashion although at one stage the referee was pelted with lemons, while a letter from Blenkinsop published in the *Echo* a week later said that he was surrounded after the game by an angry mob which had to be dispersed by police. Liverpool had became the first foreign team to beat Ripensia in Romania, the nearest anyone else had come was when an Austrian XI had drawn there 3-3.

The day after the final match the players set off on the long journey home, which took around 72 hours and involved some travel on the Orient Express. The telegram published by the *Daily Post* concerning the Ripensia game stated that some of the players had been troubled by food and would be 'glad to get back to some English cooking' and that was reiterated when they finally arrived at Lime Street on the afternoon of Saturday 6th June. Watcher of the *Evening Express* reported one as saying to him: 'We are jolly well glad to get back to some good old English food.' Matt Busby told the paper that four victories out of six games against some of the best teams on the Continent 'is no mean feat these days' while director George Richards said: 'There were many good players in the teams we met.' This would be Liverpool's last foreign tour before the Second World War and when peace returned Europe was a vastly different place, meaning there would be just one more trip east.

CZECHOSLOVAKIA 1961

Liverpool's first trip behind the Iron Curtain (and only ever one for friendlies) was in May 1961 when they undertook a four match tour of Czechoslovakia. It was the first time that the Reds had gone on tour and a new signing had made a major impact, giving fans plenty of reasons to look forward to the forthcoming season. Bill Shankly chose not to go on what would be an eventful trip, instead leaving Bob Paisley and Reuben Bennett in charge of the team. Fans back home were kept up to date with information courtesy of Horace Yates at the *Daily Post*, who was invited by the club to travel with them.

Just five days after his sensational hat-trick against Everton at Goodison Park in the Liverpool Senior Cup final, new record signing Ian St John was lining up against a South Bohemia regional XI in Tabor on 14th May. In the first half the Reds seemed intent on repaying the hospitality provided by Tabor's fellow countrymen, which began at Prague Ruznyě Airport where they were met by a boys' band. Gerry Byrne scored an own goal when he overhit a backpass after five minutes and then after 16 the defence collectively stood back and allowed Uher to pounce on a rebound and make it 2-0. This spurred the tourists into action although despite good build-up play, their finishing was woeful with Roger Hunt firing straight at the keeper, St John hitting over from six yards and Jimmy Melia dallying with the goal at his mercy. St John though did appear to pull one back but despite the ball being at least two feet over the line before it was cleared no goal was given.

Eventually the Reds pressure paid off, St John heading in a Johnny Morrissey cross on 57 minutes but they had to wait until two minutes from time to draw level when Dick White scored with a header from a Johnny Wheeler free kick. The Scot had again showed why the club had laid out such a large fee for him, with Yates writing in his match report that he 'might easily have scored three or four' in a game watched by 8,000 fans.

From Tabor the Reds then moved on to Brno, ready to face a South Moravian regional XI the next day. This team would be far stronger proposition than their previous opponents, with many players being drawn from the Ruda Hvezda club that had just reached the quarter finals of the European Cup Winners Cup, where they were beaten by Dinamo Zagreb. This was to be one of the last matches the club played, as later that summer they merged with Spartak ZJŠ Brno, later to become Zbrojovka Brno.

There was a much larger crowd than the previous day, 40,000 turning out to see the Reds in the 75,000 capacity Stadion Za Lužánkami, the largest football ground in the country at the time. There was confusion at the start when both sides ran onto the pitch wearing red shirts, causing Brno to hastily change into a white strip. Despite the game's status as a friendly it was a bruising encounter, with Willie Carlin forced off in the first half with a head injury, whilst Brno were forced to make three substitutions due to injuries. Ian St John was bundled over in the penalty area but nothing was awarded and he retaliated soon afterwards with a challenge that led to some finger wagging by the referee.

When they were able to get playing, the Reds performance was far more settled than in their first game and although they went behind after four minutes they took total control, deservedly equalising through Hunt in the 33rd minute. Ian Callaghan was outstanding as the Reds continued to press for a winner and after having a goal disallowed in the 55th minute Hunt scored the winner 12 minutes later. As the Reds coasted to victory the game came to an unexpected end in the 80th minute when the players were ordered by the referee to leave the pitch so television cameras could be positioned there for another major sporting event that was taking place afterwards. The stadium was the finishing point of a stage of the Peace Race, an international cycle race between Warsaw and Prague that was the Eastern Bloc's version of the Tour de France.

It was now six days until their next game and the Reds returned to Prague, where they made use of Dukla Prague's Stadion Juliska, which had only opened a year earlier, for training purposes. There was a blow for Tom Leishman, who had been forced to sit out the first two games through injury when he was declared unfit for the next game with Slovakian side Tatran Prešov on 21st May. Another player forced to miss out was 17-year-old Chris Lawler, taken along for some experience, only for the Reds to be told nobody under 18 was allowed to take part in senior matches in the country. It wasn't all training for the Reds as the party took a solemn trip to the village of Lidice, which was razed to the ground by German forces in 1942 and all adult males shot, with women and children being sent to concentration camps.

The Reds flew the 200 miles to Prešov where St John made all the headlines, scoring the Reds goal only to be sent off near the end for retaliation. His goal opened the scoring after 15 minutes, coming after a free kick was punched clear by the keeper only for Johnny Morrissey to float the ball back into the area, allowing St John to help it into the net. Liverpool dominated against a side that had been unbeaten at home in the league but although chances fell to St John and Roger Hunt, the keeper denied them. Prešov then equalised against the run of play after 33 minutes when Rias scored from what looked like an obvious offside position. In fact Horace Yates wrote in the *Daily Post* that such was the obvious favouritism of the referee towards the home side, that even the crowd were booing plenty of his decisions.

The main talking point of the game came 15 minutes from time when St John was kicked by Ladislav Pavlovič and retaliated mildly, only to be shown his marching orders. The furious Reds striker, who had been hacked down two yards inside the box a minute earlier only to be awarded a free kick instead of a penalty, pointed at Pavlovič gesturing that he should go too, but the referee was having none of it. Eventually only the intervention of Reuben Bennett, who escorted a dejected St John from the field, enabled the game to continue. Sensing victory was in their grasp, Prešov sent on star player Martinček as a substitute. The striker had scored six goals in a league game the previous week but was carrying a slight injury and the Reds rearguard stood firm and held on for a draw. The Reds were then delayed on their way back to Prague when their plane touched down at Brno where it was found to have a faulty engine. After an hour was spent carrying out repairs they continued on their way.

In the *Daily Post* on 23rd May, a lengthy piece appeared written by St John outlining his side of the story regarding the sending off and reassuring fans about his temperament:

'In view of this startling event in my football life, I thought Liverpool FC supporters might like to know what happened. They have no need to fear that their club may have bought a firebrand centre forward and a player looking for trouble and accepting it with both hands. I will tell you the story and let you judge for yourself. Had the series of events leading up to my dismissal taken place with an English referee in charge I am convinced I would never have been subjected to the indignity of having to leave the field before my colleagues. Yesterday I was receiving treatment from trainer Bob Paisley for the most revealing bit of evidence for the treatment to which I was subjected at Presov. From my hip down almost to my knee there are scars left by a set of football studs. This injury was received within half a minute of me being dismissed, I was kicked and felled yards inside the penalty area. The referee awarded a free kick at the outer edge of the penalty area, I could hardly believe my eyes, but there was no point in arguing. It was from the free kick that one of the Presov forwards took two deliberate kicks at my foot. The first I might have dismissed as an accident but when it was followed almost immediately by another I saw red. Who else would not? My immediate reaction was to hit back and I admit raising my foot in retaliation, but my better senses prevailed even in this situation and I stubbed my toe into the ground short of the player who had attacked me. The referee immediately ordered me off the field, I was staggered but there was no mistaking his pointing finger. I indicated my opponent and tried to ask the referee if this player was going off with me. The referee could not understand English so I went across to my opponent, grabbed him by the arm and turned towards the dressing room with him. I thought that was clear enough, but the referee came up and quickly showed that I was to go off alone. I think it was the most exasperating moment of my life in sport. What happens now is out of my hands but I have a clear conscience. Even now I can find nothing with which to reproach myself and I can only hope that even at this stage justice will be done.'

Liverpool's next game was on 24th May against Město Most, arranged to mark the opening of the home club's new stadium. Captain Dick White was ruled out after badly bruising his tibia against Prešov, an injury that was expected to prevent him from walking for a fortnight. Ian St John did recover from his injury, but almost got sidelined instead by a stomach bug, which also struck keeper Bert Slater.

The game against a side in the middle of the Second Division of the Czechoslovak league was Liverpool's easiest of the tour. Horace Yates wrote that Most were no better than an average English Fourth Division side and that 'at times Liverpool moved the ball superbly with magnificent direct football but this was little more than a practice outing for them.' St John was warmly applauded by the crowd, his performance covering every inch of the pitch including plenty of darting runs and headers and on several occasions he evaded opponents with ease. The Reds ran out comfortable 4-1 winners, St John and Jimmy Melia scoring one apiece in each half and Most's consolation coming after an error by Slater. Although it was not a dirty game there were injuries for each side, Johnny Morrissey losing a tooth in a challenge and Most's keeper Uher being taken to hospital after a challenge from St John.

Although the tour had now come to an end the players enjoyed a few days in Prague for sightseeing after the club's offer to arrange a fifth match was declined due to the Czechoslovakian league season being about to end. There was a scare on the flight home however, on which the Reds were joined by Nottingham Forest who had also been in the country. The 'Saint' recalls in his autobiography: 'Someone had forgotten to lock the rear door of the plane and there was a tremendous thump as we climbed into the sky. The cabin staff all threw themselves at the door, finally wrestling it closed'.

When the squad arrived home safely, it was clear the highlight of the tour had undoubtedly been the form of St John, who had shown in the all the games why Bill Shankly had been so keen to sign him. When the new season started he wouldn't disappoint, helping the Reds back to the top flight for the first time since 1954 along with someone else who would arrive before the end of the summer, Ron Yeats.

6

Across the Ocean Waves

In 1946 Liverpool ventured outside of Europe for the first time with a trip to North America, sailing across the Atlantic, something they would then repeat in 1948 and 1953. Eleven years later Bill Shankly's title-winning side also went to North America but by plane. All of the tours were mammoth by today's standards with the number of games being played reaching double figures and the players being away for a month.

NORTH AMERICA 1946

In the summer of 1946, prior to the start of the first Football League season since the end of the Second World War Liverpool were invited to undertake a month-long tour of the United States and Canada. The tour came about as authorities there sought to develop the game further, in light of many returning soldiers having watched it regularly whilst stationed in Europe during the war. As a club carrying the name of a city that was so well known in America due to emigration and also where many of its forces personnel passed through and were stationed nearby in Burtonwood, Liverpool were a natural choice.

With chairman William McConnell also being a friend of Belfast-born Joe Barriskill who was General Secretary of the United States Soccer Association, there were not too many difficulties in making the arrangements, with the tour being confirmed in January. It was decided to stick primarily to the east coast with the Reds declining invites to play in California, although there would be games in Chicago, St Louis and Toronto.

The last match of the season was scheduled for Saturday 4th May at Bolton, but due to the tour this was brought forward to the Monday and the Reds lost 1-0. It had been suggested by some fans that form in the second half of the season was poor due to the fact the players had one eye on their tour, although in reality they had been inconsistent all season. The best part was a run of four wins in September and October, but from then on they couldn't string two victories together until April and eventually finished 11th in the Football League Northern Section, which was won by Sheffield United.

With many Cunard liners still being used for troop shipment and some having been sunk during the war, the Liverpool party had to sail from Southampton aboard the *Queen Mary*. The 16 players, manager, trainer and four Board members left Liverpool by coach on Friday 3rd May for the journey south in readiness for the ocean crossing which would begin the next day. One key player missing was Billy Liddell, who was unable to secure his release from the RAF. Charlie Lambert was on a forces team tour of Scandinavia while keeper Cyril Sidlow had been selected by Wales for a Victory Championship match against Ireland. The Reds were only the second English team to visit America, the first having been Charlton Athletic in 1937 and correspondent Stork in the *Liverpool Echo* described them as ambassadors for English football, writing: 'They realise their responsibilities and they will go with every confidence that they will do well.' The *Echo* also reported that several hundred American G.I.s and Canadian soldiers with their brides would be on board the *Queen Mary* and en route to New York the vessel would be calling at Halifax in Nova Scotia.

On arrival in Southampton the party was met by officials from Southampton FC and FA Secretary Stanley Rous. They spent the night before the sailing on board the ship, where rumours began to spread that Cyril Sidlow had joined them. The Welsh international was supposed to be in Cardiff at a time when withdrawals from international squads were not an option. Under the headline LIVERPOOL FC MYSTERY the *Liverpool Echo* reported that no information could be obtained about him and that manager George Kay was refusing to discuss the matter. The fact that Plymouth's Bill Shortt played in goal for Wales instead seemed to point to Sidlow's presence but it wasn't confirmed until arrival in New York. His inclusion meant last minute heartbreak for Charlie Ashcroft, who had been named as the keeper for the trip but was ultimately left behind.

The party arrived in New York on 10th May and chairman William McConnell sent a cable to the *Echo's* Ernest 'Bee' Edwards saying: 'All is well, grand passage, everybody happy.' Edwards had been invited to accompany the Reds but was unable to do so due to other commitments, but readers would be kept informed of goings on by special correspondents assigned on the other side of the Atlantic to send reports over, as well as letters sent by airmail from manager George Kay. In an indication of how different the game in England is now to then, Edwards wrote that there would be novelties in the USA for the players, which involved night games, playing on Sundays and using a white ball.

The first match was on Sunday 12th May against a New York All Star XI at the Triborough Stadium in Randall's Island, once the joint home stadium of the New York Yankees and also where Jesse Owens had competed in the Olympics trials in 1936. A near capacity 20,000 crowd which included several United Nations delegates witnessed the Reds get off to a winning start with Jack Balmer scoring twice and Willie Fagan, captain for the tour, scoring the other. The New York side was made up of players of various nationalities, including players of Irish, Italian, Scottish and Syrian origin. The most unusual feature of the game was that spectators were given a running commentary over the loudspeaker as it took place so that the crowd could be kept updated as to what was going on.

The Reds then moved on to Baltimore for a game the following Wednesday, where there wasn't so much interest in seeing the Reds face a Baltimore All Star side, made up mainly of players from the Baltimore Americans who had won the American Soccer League in 1945-46. Just 5,801 turned out at the 31,000 capacity Municipal Stadium for a game that was played under floodlights, kicking off at 8.15pm. The Reds romped to a 9-0 win with Balmer scoring four and Fagan also hitting a hat-trick. The other goals came from Cyril Done and Bob Priday. The *Liverpool Echo* report into the game was provided by American journalist Milt Miller, who had been assigned the role of following the Reds and he described them as a 'well oiled combination' that displayed 'superior speed, generalship and staying power.' White balls were used for this game and changed frequently, with George Kay saying afterwards that one of the things they had to learn to contend with was the flashlights of the photographers, which were going off every time a player got to the penalty area and was ready to shoot.[10]

Liverpool's party returned to New York for a reception given at City Hall on 17th May, where city council president Vincent Impellitteri recalled that he had spent three months in Liverpool during the First World War while his ship was being repaired. He then thanked the city for entertaining American servicemen in the most recent conflict. In return chairman William McConnell gave thanks for the hospitality shown and expressed a wish that an American team would visit England so it could be reciprocated. At the reception George Kay was interviewed by Milt Miller concerning the tour's progress so far. The following day's *Liverpool Echo* reported the interview, in which Kay pointed out that the Reds had been fortunate as the turf had been softened by rain which made it ideal for their style of play and were also aided by superior fitness. After the reception the players watched a boxing bout at Madison Square Garden where Doncaster's British Empire Heavyweight Champion Bruce Woodcock was stopped in the eighth round by local hero Tami Mauriello.

On Sunday 19th May the Reds were back at the Triborough Stadium to face an American Soccer League XI. Although this was the national league in the country, most of the teams came from the north eastern area. Cyril Done hit his second hat-trick of the tour in a 5-0 win, the other goals coming from Bob Priday and Jack Balmer in front of 16,000 fans.

The crowds for the two Triborough games raised eyebrows and there looked to be a real possibility that Liverpool's visit was raising the stakes as 'soccer' sought to challenge baseball in the popularity stakes. Such a thought would seem ludicrous, but baseball authorities were worried enough to put pressure on newspapers to limit their coverage of this new competitor, while servicemen who had been in Europe were keen to continue watching the game. There were over 50 leagues thriving in the USA and Bee Edwards wrote in his *Echo* column: 'Liverpool FC are oiling the wheels of progress and nothing can stop the challenge of soccer to baseball.'

The only American player to appear in both games at the Tribororough Stadium was Brooklyn Hispano goalkeeper Gene Olaff, who Kay had identified as the one player who could hold his own in the English First Division. According to the *Liverpool Echo* report into the second game, only his brilliant goalkeeping had prevented the Reds winning by a far greater score than 5-0. The son of a Swedish seaman who jumped ship in New York, Olaff was a former navy diver whose day job was as a policeman in New Jersey. Kay actually admitted he would have signed him but had no chance of persuading him to give up a career that offered a pension at the age of 50.[11] Olaff played for the USA against Scotland in 1949 but his career got in the way of him playing in the 1950 World Cup as he was unable to secure leave. In July 2013 he was still alive and residing in Florence Township, New Jersey.

The fourth game of the tour was against a New England Select in Fall River, Massachusetts, but due to a waterlogged pitch on 21st May it had to be put back 24 hours. Like the game in Baltimore it was played under floodlights, although Kay believed that they were too low and affected the sight of the players. The Reds went 3-0 up thanks to a brace from Robert Priday and one from Jack Balmer. However New England, whose side were composed mainly of Portuguese players hit back with goals from Ed Souza and Joe Chapiga and the game finished 3-2. The home players' goal celebrations surprised Kay, given at that time it was customary for a simple handshake and trot back to the halfway line to suffice. Kay's letter to Ranger of the *Liverpool Echo* said: 'Joe and Ed flung their arms around each other, waited in the centre circle, and it needed only a banjo to make it a real hill-billy show. The other players of their side gave individual step dances in their joy.'[12] It was clear that in addition to enjoying the good results, the players were having a good time on the tour, being given excellent hospitality and taking full advantage of the range of ration-free food on offer and hotel facilities. George Kay described how things were going in an airmail letter that was published in the *Liverpool Echo* the night after the New England game:

'The terrific hospitality we are receiving is the only thing likely to beat us. Apparently the Americans, in an effort to repay some of the hospitality extended to their servicemen, are being exceptionally lavish during the entertaining line – and they were never behind in that even before the war. We are feted here, there and everywhere, are being taken to see everything and everybody while the life in the cafes and drugstores is amazing. You can get all the dishes everybody could possibly desire in the eating places and naturally we are taking advantage of the opportunity. All the party is in good shape but the heat is so terrific that you get free and involuntary Turkish baths in the hotels, which still have the central heating on. Fortunately there is a swimming pool in our hotel where the players spend most of the little spare time which the day's full programme leaves them.'

Kay's letter also shed light on some of the problems Football League clubs were facing just having the most basic of facilities back at home, as he wrote: 'British clubs, harassed by the difficulty of getting gear and balls will envy the Americans, where there is apparently no shortage.' In another letter he also described how Anfielders would laugh if they could see the team arriving at matches in America, writing: 'The motor coach we travel in is escorted by police cars and motorcyclist police wave ordinary traffic out of the way for our priority.'[13]

Liverpool's next game was in Philadelphia on 26th May, where they faced a Philadelphia Select XI, made up of players from the city's two American Soccer League sides – the Americans and Nationals who had finished second and third bottom of the league. The game was played at Frankford Stadium, home of the Frankford Yellow Jackets who had been NFL champions in 1926. The players travelled by train on the morning of the game but this did them no harm whatsoever as they stormed to a 12-0 victory, with Cyril Done getting four goals and Jack Balmer also managing a hat-trick.

The Reds then took to the skies, flying to Missouri for a game on 31st May against a St Louis All Star side, representing the St Louis Municipal League. The Reds won 5-1 in a match that took place in the Walsh Stadium, which was normally used for speedway and attracted a crowd of 12,493, one of the biggest soccer attendances the city had ever seen. A match report was cabled over to the *Liverpool Echo* by Herman Wecke of the *St Louis Post-Dispatch* and it described how the Reds had an early scare when Joe Spica hit the post after five minutes but from then on their teamwork and ability to pass the ball was the decisive factor.

As Liverpool continued to win games with ease, George Kay stated that he felt it would be better if two English teams toured to give American fans a real taste of what football was about. In a letter published by the

Liverpool Echo the day after the match in Philadelphia, he wrote how the American spectators weren't keen on any of the game's physical elements:

> 'They certainly do not stand for any rough tactics on the field, as I have heard them booing any ungentlemanly conduct, so the rough guy we imagine the Yank to be does not exist, so far as we have experienced. Personally I think a tour of two English teams here would be beneficial, to let the folk see a real battling game where a breath of wind hardly divides the teams, giving them soccer at its real best. I think we can go through the tour without defeat, although we play on grounds not turfed, but simply dirt and cinder, which will not be to our liking.'

Liverpool were making enough headlines in the USA to receive offers to extend their stay over the other side of the Atlantic and play matches in Costa Rica and Mexico, but the offers had to be declined due to lack of time. In all the players were away from their families for six weeks, but Kay knew how they could smooth it over on their return, writing: 'We have some nylons as peace offerings.' Baseball chiefs were also admitting that the crowds at games meant that instead of trying to fight 'soccer' they had to embrace it and try to find a way of blending the two games together. This was largely down to Liverpool's tour and Ernő Schwarz, manager of the American Soccer League team who was travelling with them wherever they went, told correspondent Milt Miller that 'everywhere Liverpool went it was lauded as the finest soccer team that has ever visited this country.'[14]

From St Louis Liverpool flew to Chicago where on 2nd June they played Chicago Maroons, a team of university students who were one of five teams that made up the North American Soccer League. The Reds won 9-3 at Soldier Field, a venue which hosted games in the 1994 World Cup and is now home of the Chicago Bears American football team, but was in 1946 tenanted by the Chicago Rockets. In a game that the Reds led 6-3 at half-time then failed to score for 18 minutes of the second period, Jack Balmer got four and Willie Fagan also got a hat-trick. After Chicago, the Reds crossed the border to Canada where they played Ulster United, a side formed in 1914 by Ulster-Scots migrants, at the Maple Leaf Stadium. In front of a capacity crowd of 13,746 at the baseball venue, Fagan and Robert Priday both hit hat-tricks in an 11-1 rout on 5th June.

From Toronto the Liverpool party flew to New York where they would play the last two games of the tour. For many of the players it would have been their first time on an aeroplane and in the *Liverpool Echo* on 7th June Milt Miller's cable, in which he described them as the 'rampaging Reds' said: 'Flying's the method of travel was the unanimous opinion. The Britishers made the trip from Toronto in less than two hours. They recounted how they utilised the travelling time saved to see the sights of the cities visited.'

Miller also described how the Reds players, who had now been in America for almost four weeks, looked 'happy and as fit as a fiddle.'

For the penultimate game on 9th June the Reds would have to make do without leading scorer Jack Balmer due to a sprained ankle sustained in Toronto. The game against Kearny All Stars, made up of players from Kearny Celtic and Kearny Scots of the American Soccer League, turned out to be one of the closest of the tour. The Reds were 2-0 up in the first five minutes thanks to goals from Willie Fagan and Cyril Done, but in the end they tired due to the baking hot sun and would have to be content with a 3-1 victory in front of 11,000 at the High School Stadium.

The match against Kearny meant the Reds had played select sides representing all four of the main centres of the ten team American Soccer League – Baltimore, New York City, New Jersey and Philadelphia. To round off they would be playing another game against a league select XI on 11th June, this time at Ebbets Field, home of the famous Brooklyn Dodgers baseball team that had been American League champions in 1941 and would also win the title in 1947. Branch Rickey, general manager of the Dodgers was one of the baseball moguls who realised that 'soccer' may well be something that the game had to live with so sought to profit from it. As such he intended to use Ebbets Field for games during baseball's off season and was hoping for a 25,000 turnout for the Reds appearance there. The American Soccer League selected their strongest players available but were no match for the Reds, for whom a fit again Jack Balmer scored in a 10-1 win. Cyril Done was the star of the show getting four, while Willie Fagan also hit a hat-trick in front of a disappointing crowd of 8,000, a thunderstorm that evening discouraging many from attending.

It meant the Reds had an unblemished record, winning all ten games scoring 70 goals in the process and they had been fine ambassadors for the game. Despite the ease of Liverpool's victories George Kay believed that soccer still had a future in America, even though many of the players the Reds had faced in the 'all star' teams were of European origin. The *Liverpool Echo* reported on 19th June that the Reds manager had written to them saying that the game could do well providing it was played in schools and the right coaching was applied.

It wasn't straight home for the Reds though, as the players had a week at leisure in New York during which they took in a baseball game at the Yankee Stadium where the attendance of 67,000 showed which sport was still tops in America. George Kay wasn't impressed though, writing to the *Echo*: 'The game lasted two and a half hours, very tiring and not a lot of action in the whole affair. Soccer has it licked a mile for a continuous game in which there is always something doing.'[15] He also said that he hoped to have a rest somewhere 'far from the madding crowd' on his return, but that they were suitably impressed with the way the tour had gone and they may well be back in America the following year.

Kay believed that the Americans were surprised at just how superior the Reds were and as they headed home the *New York Times* summarised their play perfectly, reporting: 'Liverpool came to the States for a crack at our teams and our vitamins. It was a clean sweep. The Britons swept all ten of their matches and, like Jack Spratt and his wife, they also swept the platter clean.' The paper also made reference to how well fed the players were compared to home, saying: 'Away from the British austerity program, they plunged zestfully into our steaks, eggs, milk and other vittles. Not only was there a perceptible gain in strength on the playing field, but the squad averaged a gain in weight of seven pounds a man.' The American soccer authorities were also appreciative of the Reds and on 18th June, two days before they set sail for home, the American Soccer League and United States Soccer Association co-hosted a farewell dinner at the St George's Hotel in Brooklyn.

Liverpool's party finally arrived back at Anfield on 26th June, some 54 days after they had first left. Around 200 well wishers were there to greet the players, who were described by Bee Edwards in the *Liverpool Echo* as 'bronzed, bow-tied and a little jaded.' Kay told Edwards that not too much should be written into the results due to the standard of the opposition but he couldn't play down the importance of the lack of rationing, which he believed increased the players' performances by 50%.

After a rest the players were raring to go when the new season started and with Billy Liddell available for selection, along with the record signing of Albert Stubbins from Newcastle, the Reds won their first title since 1923. It was said that the visit to America played a key part in that title triumph, as it built up their strength and helped foster a team spirit amongst a side that had been fragmented during the war years. When it came to preparing the next summer's tour, a return to America wasn't the only offer the Reds had, as they were also invited to visit Palestine. However neither was feasible due to the Football League season being extended after a severe winter caused several postponements, with Liverpool playing their last league game on 31st May.

The Reds were back in 1948 though when they undertook an 11-game tour, winning them all. As in 1946, games were played in Baltimore, Fall River, New York, Philadelphia, St Louis and Toronto, with Montreal being the only city they hadn't played at previously. Whilst in Toronto Billy Liddell was presented with a suitcase, which he used to carry his belongings on all his subsequent travels and is now on display in the club's museum. In a game against the New York All Stars the Reds came up against Joe Gaetjens, who went on to score the goal for USA against

England in the 1950 World Cup. George Kay also signed a player, with Scottish centre half Joe Cadden, who emigrated to America after the war, impressing against the Reds.

1953 NORTH AMERICA

After a five year absence the Reds were back in North America in 1953, undertaking a 10-game tour and playing at many of the venues they had been to in 1946 and 1948. This was a very different Reds side however from those that had visited previously. They were far from championship material, having only avoided relegation on the last day of the season and many of the players were nearing the end of their careers. They were now managed by Don Welsh, who had guested for Liverpool during the Second World War and won the FA Cup with Charlton in 1947. He had taken over from George Kay, who had been forced to retire through ill-health in 1951.

Before the party sailed for America the club was rocked by the sudden death of vice chairman Ralph Milne, who died at home aged 70 shortly after watching the FA Cup final between Blackpool and Bolton on 2nd May. Milne had first taken ill only four weeks earlier while the Reds were in London to play Arsenal on Easter Saturday, but he refused to return home and instead travelled on to Cardiff for the game there on the Monday. After a spell in a nursing home he appeared to be on the mend and he had been intending to go to America so his death came as a great shock.

Milne's funeral took place at 12.30pm on Tuesday 5th May at Landican in Wirral and was attended by all those who were going on the tour – 16 players, Don Welsh, trainer Albert Shelley, chairman George Richards and director James Troop. They then returned to Anfield where they boarded a coach for Southampton, sailing from there aboard the *Queen Mary* for New York. On board the players kept fit with a five mile run around the decks every morning along with work in the gym and swimming pool. This type of training was not normally the most popular but Billy Liddell had no problems with it given how luxurious the voyage was and hospitable the Cunard staff were. He had been on an ocean voyage having gone to America in 1948 but this was a whole new experience for younger members of the squad. His letter back home said:

> 'The sight of the vast ship as you approach the dock is enough to rouse the interest of anyone and the remarks of wonder and surprise from the younger element in the team was as understandable as their amazement when viewing the ship from inside. After you have come to your bearings you begin to realise how wonderful the ship is and marvel at the feat of engineering which is really a floating hotel with its vast dining rooms, lounges and entertainment rooms. It is a marvellous holiday travelling on such boats, but the real reason of our voyage was not forgotten and

manager Don Welsh soon had us all lapping the promenade deck and doing our physical training in the open and gymnasium. Usually there are grumbles about the routine of training but there was not a murmur on this occasion for the boys realised that with all the extra food they needed the exercise to keep their trim figures. The most pleasing part of the training however was the dip in the swimming pool to finish off the morning's work. The boss was always well to the fore in the pool but did not expect the dip he got when some of us threw him in with his training togs on. We spent a few hours at the "Pig and Whistle" with the crew, another night at the engineering officers' ward room and we discovered some talented darts throwers. We were well looked after on board and things moved smoothly due to the wonderful efficiency of the Cunard Line. The entertainment side of the trip was divided between deck games such as quoits, tennis quoits and shuffleboard, table tennis, the cinema and dancing. But much as the boys have enjoyed their sea voyage they looked forward to getting to New York and getting their land legs before they tackled Ireland in Brooklyn.'[16]

The Reds arrived on 11th May, when Welsh told reporters he believed that two games against an Irish all star side, made up of players from the Irish League, would provide the Reds with their toughest test. Whereas Liverpool had been the only European side to tour in 1946, they were no longer a unique attraction. Since then Fulham, Manchester United, Newcastle and Tottenham had all crossed the Atlantic although the Reds were the first English team to make three visits and were the sole Football League team there in 1953. There were other Continental sides touring though, with Liverpool set to face Germans 1FC Nuremburg and Swiss side Young Boys Berne as well as the Irish side, who themselves would be playing Young Boys.

The first match took place on 14th May against the Irish All Stars at Ebbets Field. The Reds were far more acclimatised and fresher than their opposition, who had only arrived in Montreal the previous day and then had to travel on to New York. This showed in a game that Liverpool led 3-0 at half-time, the first goal coming from Louis Bimpson in just the fifth minute. Billy Liddell, dubbed 'Cannonball Liddell' by the American press, added two more before the break and Bimpson got another in the second half but had to go off injured with a sore knee, when he was replaced by 19-year-old Ronnie Moran. The Reds' victory merited just four brief paragraphs in the Liverpool Echo, whose roundup also reported that Bolton had lost 2-0 against a West German Select XI in front of 55,000 fans in Berlin. Far more detail was given to an FA XI losing 3-1 in Argentina to a combined Buenos Aries side in a game played before 120,000 fans at the River Plate Stadium.

While the Irish side returned to Canada, Liverpool stayed in New York where they faced an American Soccer League XI three days later at the Triborough Stadium. Kevin Baron, replacing the injured Louis Bimpson, gave the Reds the lead only for the Americans to equalise from a penalty kick but Baron restored the lead before half-time. Bill Jones got two in the second half to complete a 4-1 win with one American paper referring to Liverpool as the 'Red Raiders', while the home goalkeeper Cecil Moore was described as the 'cage guardian.' The Liverpool party then moved on to Fall River to play a New England select side, made up of teams from what was now a New England regional division of the American Soccer League. The Reds won 4-0, with Bill Jones again grabbing a brace with the other two goals this time coming from Sammy Smyth.

Despite what Don Welsh had said at the beginning the next game of the tour, against 1FC Nuremburg in New York on 24th May was arguably the hardest that the Reds would have to contend with. The German side had won all four of the games they had played on their tour so far, scoring 34 goals in the process. They had won the Oberliga Süd in 1951, one of five regional leagues that made up the top division in Germany prior to the formation of the Bundesliga in 1963. An indication of the strength of German football was that in 1950 and 1951 Liverpool had played two friendlies against Saarbrücken, drawing 1-1 at Anfield and losing 4-1 in Germany. Such was the interest in the game that a stadium record crowd of 23,562 turned out at the Triborough Stadium and this would have been higher had police not closed roads leading to it when the car parks became full. Liverpool won a closely fought contest 4-3, in which Charlie Ashcroft put in a brilliant performance in goal to help the Reds on to victory.

Liverpool then flew with Trans-Canada Airways to Montreal for a game on 27th May at the Delorimier Stadium (home to the Montreal Royals baseball team), where they had beaten an All Star side 4-2 in 1948. This time they hit double figures, winning 10-0 in a game that saw Bill Jones get a hat-trick with Billy Liddell, Joseph Maloney and Jimmy Payne each getting a brace. The other goal was scored by 18-year-old Alan A'Court, on as a substitute for Kevin Baron and he was described by the following day's *Montreal Gazette* as showing 'surprising speed and ball control as well as shooting power.' The local paper believed the scoreline flattered the Reds, who were far more suited to the slippery conditions caused by a pre-match shower and it was also critical of the home side for trying to pass the ball about too much when a 'boot upfield' may have done Liverpool more harm. Whilst in Montreal the Reds players met ex Everton star Sam Chedgzoy, who had settled there after leaving the Blues in 1926, managing the Montreal Carsteel side in the 1930s. Although he was now 64 Billy Liddell still described him as looking 'fitter than ever.'[17]

The Reds then moved on to Ohio where they hit double figures again, beating a Toledo All Star side comprising players from Ohio, Michigan and Ontario 10-3 in front of just 3,000 fans at the Glass Bowl American football stadium on 31st May. The following day's *Toledo Blade* described how Liverpool had toyed with their opposition in the first half and led 7-1 at the break, before slacking off in the second period. Billy Liddell was described as putting in an 'outstanding offensive demonstration' by scoring two goals but one of the Toledo goals was an own goal from Ronnie Moran, whose misdirected header to Ashcroft went into the net. The fact that Liverpool had a settled team was clearly an advantage in every game they played, as the representative sides they faced consisted of players who in addition to holding down full time jobs had not had much chance to practice together and establish a team pattern.

Back at home, celebrations for the Coronation of Queen Elizabeth II on 2nd June were in full swing, which meant the matches in Montreal and Toledo were given minimal coverage in the Liverpool press, which was dominated by the royal event and also the ascent of Everest by Edmund Hillary and Tenzing Norgay on 29th May. In Liverpool, the Coronation was marked by services at the Anglican Cathedral, a concert at the Philharmonic Hall, a fireworks display in Walton Hall Park, a march by the King's Liverpool Regiment and the planting of trees by the Lord Mayor on Utting Avenue near Liverpool FC's Anfield ground. The Coronation was even marked by a special football tournament, the Coronation Cup. The eight-team tournament was held in Glasgow and won by Celtic, who beat Hibernian 2-0 in the final on 20th May, much to the surprise of many football supporters on the other side of the Atlantic who asked the Reds party how none of the four competing English sides had managed to reach the final.

Next stop for Liverpool was Chicago where they played an All Star team at Hanson Field on 7th June, Billy Liddell scoring a hat-trick in a 4-2 win. The Chicago side was made up of players from the Chicago-centred National Soccer League, which is still in existence today and the longest continually running league in the USA, having been founded in 1928. Their trainer was Charlie Hurry, who hailed from Bolton and the game was promoted by league secretary George Fishwick, an ex resident of Wallasey who attended St Francis Xavier school in Everton and would later become president of the United States Soccer Federation. Whilst in Chicago members of the Hansa club looked after many of the Reds players' needs and Billy Liddell was surprised to meet Bill Dunn, who he had played alongside in the 1930s when he was at Scottish junior side Lochgelly Violets.

Two days later the Reds were in St Louis where Sammy Smyth scored a hat-trick as they won 5-1 against an all star side selected from players of the four teams that made up the St Louis Major Soccer League. By now the Reds had been away for five weeks and as much as they were enjoying themselves, Liddell confirmed in a letter to the *Liverpool Echo* that was published a week later that they were now 'yearning for home.'

The tour was rounded off with two games in two days over the weekend of 13th/14th June. The first was in Toronto where the Reds faced the Irish All Stars for the second time on the tour, winning 3-1 at the Varsity Stadium thanks to two goals from Kevin Baron and one from Sammy Smyth. The following day at the famous Yankee Stadium in New York, the Reds' 100% record in America finally came to an end. Tiredness caught up with them against Young Boys Berne, with the *New York Times* reporting that the game ended in a '1-1 deadlock'. In front of a crowd of 11,085 the Reds trailed 1-0 at half-time before Billy Liddell got a second half equaliser but they couldn't find a winner meaning the 30-match winning run was over. The next day's *Liverpool Echo* described the end of the tour as an anti-climax and suggested that the Swiss side wasn't what its name had implied, with the report stating: 'Whether the name is a true indication of their strength, average age and experience of their team is something here we do not know. It may be wrong to assume that it was only a youth eleven.'

The Liverpool party set sail from New York on 17th June, arriving back in Liverpool on the 23rd. Manager Don Welsh reported that all the players were well, but that there were still concerns over Louis Bimpson's ankle. There were no reports of anybody getting married this time, instead it was National Service which was on the players' minds, with both Bimpson and Ron Moran being expected to report for duty in early July.

Unlike the 1946 tour this trip to America didn't inspire the Reds to glory over the coming season. Instead the mainly ageing team finished bottom of the league, never seriously looking like they could avoid relegation. This would be the last time the Reds would go to America by cruise liner, as the next time the jet age was well and truly here.

1964 NORTH AMERICA

It would be 11 more years before Liverpool, newly crowned as league champions, were back on the other side of the Atlantic, during which time there had been significant changes both at Anfield and in terms of travel. Since their last trip the Reds had spent eight long years in the Second Division, from where they were rescued by Bill Shankly, who went on to deliver the club's sixth league title in just their second season after promotion.

The Reds clinched the title on 18th April with a 5-0 win over Arsenal at Anfield and their season came to a close on the 29th when they lost 3-1 at Stoke. A week later on 6th May, kitted out in new dark grey club suits, they boarded a British Overseas Airways Corporation jet at Manchester for a flight to New York. The airline, which would go on to merge with British European Airways in 1974 to form British Airways, had acquired their first jets capable of flying non-stop across the Atlantic in 1956. They made such an impact in sea travel that Cunard began cutting crossings and moving towards cruising instead and it meant that although the players may not have got to America in such luxurious fashion, it took them just one day to get there instead of six. Liverpool weren't the only local side taking advantage of this as Everton had decided to venture even further and undertake a five-week tour of Australia, which made them the first English club to play on all six continents.

There were some big names missing on the Reds trip however. Roger Hunt, Gordon Milne and Peter Thompson were selected by England for their own trip across the Atlantic, which would see a friendly against the United States followed by participation in a four-team tournament in Rio and Sao Paulo that commemorated the 50th anniversary of the Brazilian FA. It meant youngsters Tommy Smith, Chris Lawler and Gordon Wallace would have the chance to impress Shankly while veteran Alan A'Court, who hadn't featured at all in 1963-64 was also included in the party. They were joined by a new face, striker Phil Chisnall, who had completed his £25,000 transfer from Manchester United the previous month.

Ian St John was looking forward to the tour and would provide updates in his *Daily Post* column. The Reds would be facing some sterner opposition than previously, with three games arranged against Meidericher SV (now MSV Duisburg) and one against Hamburg SV. Plans for a match against Brazilian opposition though failed to materilaise. 'The Saint', who was always willing to get stuck in and never one to shy from a scrap on the pitch did have one confession to make though when it came to the preparations. One thing that did scare him was needles and he wrote the day before departure: 'Last week we had our vaccinations. It is amazing what a little needle will do. I admit quite frankly the sight of it scares me stiff. On the field I will face anybody without a quiver, but not that needle and I am not alone, believe me.'

Along with Ronnie Moran, A'Court was the only player who had gone on the last American trip in 1953 although trainer Bob Paisley had been on that tour as a player. Paisley was in charge of team affairs for the start of this tour, as manager Bill Shankly opted to stay behind as he continued with his plans for the next season although he did see the players off from the airport. The weekend before the tour began Shankly was in Scotland watching games in the Summer Cup, with his target believed to be a full back to replace Moran who was coming to the end of his playing days.

The *Liverpool Echo* reported on 4th May that an initial approach for Hearts Under-23 international Chris Shevlane had been turned down but the Edinburgh club may be willing to sell for £30,000.

On arrival at John F. Kennedy Airport the Liverpool party, headed by chairman Tom Williams and captain Ron Yeats were met by officials of the American Soccer League and taken to the Governor Clinton Hotel (now the Affinia) at Seventh Avenue and 31st Street in Midtown Manhattan, just a few blocks from the Empire State Building. After trying to get over jetlag they spent the 7th May sightseeing and also attended the World's Fair, a major international exhibition at Flushing Meadows. One of the attractions on show there was a six-a-side football tournament, which wasn't of the best standard and led Bob Paisley to rue the fact he and Reuben Bennett didn't have Bill Shankly and Joe Fagan there with them to enter a team.[18]

The next day the party travelled to Boston for the first game of the tour that evening against Boston Metros at the Everett Stadium. The Reds showed no signs of jetlag or tiredness as they cruised to an 8-1 win in a game that saw Ian St John give them a third minute lead. The Reds did take their time to get going though after St John's opener and it wasn't until the 28th minute that they added to their lead, Phil Chisnall getting his first goal for the club and Alf Arrowsmith made it 3-0 before half-time. After the break the squad was utilised to the full with Tommy Smith, Chris Lawler and Bobby Graham coming on as substitutes and all finding the net, with the other second half goals coming from Arrowsmith and St John. To their credit the home side never gave up and Ron Yeats and Tommy Lawrence had to be at their best to deny them, but a deserved consolation eventually came with eight minutes remaining when Oscar Sapia fired in from close range after a free kick was played into the box.

In 2012 the *Boston Globe* ran a feature on the game, bringing together four players who had played against the Reds. Midfielder Frank Mirisola described how the score may not have been so high had a Boston player not dribbled the ball through the legs of a Liverpool player, which led to them 'really starting playing.' The Metros were not quite at full strength, with some players being rested ahead of a crucial top of the table league game against Ukrainian Nationals in Philadelphia a few days later, but on the other hand the Reds were also missing some key players. The crowd for the match was a healthy 10,000, which included four seamen from Liverpool, who had paid $90 (about £30) to fly from New York and managed to meet the players. It was the largest soccer crowd that Boston had seen and even more impressive considering that local baseball side the Boston Red Sox only averaged a little over 11,000 that year.

The Reds headed straight back to New York after the Boston game, in readiness for a game against New York All Stars on 10th May at the

Downing Stadium in Randall's Island. This was the stadium where the club had played their first game in America in 1946 and had been renamed from the Triborough Stadium in 1955, in honour of John J. Downing, a Director of the city's Department of Parks and Recreation.

The New York match again saw Liverpool start slowly before winning convincingly. Phil Chisnall opened the scoring in the fifth minute but after a quarter of an hour Paul Soane equalised from a corner. The Reds regained the lead on 34 minutes through Ian St John who got another four minutes later in very fortunate circumstances when he jumped and missed a header only for the ball to drop on his heel and bounce into the net as he landed. By now New York's confidence had dropped and Willie Stevenson added another on the stroke of half-time. Alf Arrowsmith got a brace in the second half and the squad was again utilised, with Tommy Smith coming off the bench to get the seventh goal two minutes from time.

After the game Liverpool's players were whisked to the CBS television studios where they watched a live recording of the Ed Sullivan Show, on which Gerry and the Pacemakers were guests, performing *I Like It* and new single *Don't Let the Sun Catch You Crying*. It may seem surprising that they didn't perform the song with which the group and Liverpool FC had become associated, but at that time *You'll Never Walk Alone* hadn't been released in America and when it was in 1965 it only reached 48 in the charts. The Ed Sullivan Show, which was ranked at No 15 in the TV Guide's top 50 shows of all time in 2002, was broadcast from coast to coast at 8pm and ran from 1948 to 1971. Five months earlier The Beatles had appeared on the show and generated a record American television audience of 73 million although this broadcast, which included the Reds players taking to the stage, wasn't quite as popular. Whereas the Reds were only just starting out their American tour Gerry and the Pacemakers were coming to the end of theirs and a week later lead singer Gerry Marsden was back at his home in the Dingle area of Liverpool. In an interview for the 22nd May edition of music magazine *Merseybeat* he said of meeting the Reds in New York: 'It was nice to have a chat with them about our home town – though most of the players seem to hail from Scotland!'

The next day the Reds party flew by TWA to St Louis, with Ian St John taking time to write his *Daily Post* column whilst on the flight. He said that the standard of football wasn't even as good as the Lancashire Combination or Cheshire League and that 'if only this was the standard of football we had to worry about at home. I could promise you the championship, the cup and anything else you want thrown in for good measure.' Of most concern to St John was the oppressive heat, which he felt was more worrying than the opposition and made the players feel as if they had done a day's training by only walking a few blocks. St John also described how the Reds were a popular attraction and subject to plenty of media coverage, which captain Ron Yeats dealt with aptly, never turning a hair. The only downside was the theft of cine cameras from St John and Yeats, which had included plenty of film of New York and Boston.

Despite the fact his players were enjoying America and had begun the tour with a crushing win, Bill Shankly was not bothered in the slightest that he had opted to stay behind. A *Daily Post* reporter asked him on 8th May if he had made the right decision and he replied 'without any doubt' as he told how he had taken coach Joe Fagan with him on his latest spying mission to Scotland.

At St Louis the Reds checked into the newly opened DeVille Motor Hotel, one of a wave of new hotels with parking spaces springing up across America. Chairman Tom Williams though had an embarrassing incident that made quite a mess of the new rooms in their third day there, prior to a match against a Catholic Youth Council (CYC) XI. Williams had been struggling with constipation ever since arriving in New York and turned to Bob Paisley for help. After eating fruit salads for breakfast didn't work Paisley gave him a tablet and was eventually called to Williams' room as a matter of urgency, where he described the scene as 'wall to wall. It was everywhere.'[19] To increase the embarrassment, Williams had only taken one pair of trousers with him and had to borrow a pair off Ron Yeats, who was of a similar height but much broader in frame, meaning he had to wear a raincoat over them so nobody could see.

The foundations of the St Louis CYC, which is still running today, go back to 1910 when Christian Brothers wanted to provide sport and recreation for youngsters in the Archdiocese. They ran soccer leagues in the area and regularly sponsored visits by touring professional teams so that the best local youngsters could test themselves against top quality opposition. St John's comments in his newspaper column came back to haunt the Reds players as they nearly had a humiliating defeat in this game. In front of 6,000 fans the home players, who were all amateur, equipped themselves well in defence and prevented the Reds forwards from finding a breakthrough. They also got forward on occasions and Chris Lawler, deputising for Ron Yeats who had an injured knee, put in a solid performance keeping them at bay. However he couldn't stop Pat McBride twice hitting the bar before they took a sensational lead with six minutes remaining when Reds defender Phil Ferns turned the ball into his own net during a goalmouth scramble. Liverpool, who were termed the 'Red Devils' by the local press, had their blushes spared two minutes later when Willie Stevenson converted an Alf Arrowsmith cross.

The Reds spent another couple of days in St Louis before flying to Chicago on 15th May, where the tour would begin to take a step up in terms of quality and there was no room for complacency. Their opponents at Soldier Field on 17th May would be CF Monterrey, who had just finished third in the Mexican league and been runners up in the cup final. There were plenty of Mexicans in the 12,384 crowd who added some atmosphere to the occasion by setting off fireworks, which only added to the 80 degrees heat. The Reds though coped with the conditions and the partisan fans were quietened down in the 18th minute when Ian St John opened the scoring. Tommy Lawrence was a virtual spectator in goal as Liverpool took complete control of the game, St John adding two more in the second half to complete his hat-trick.

The following day the Reds returned to New York and the Governor Clinton Hotel, where they had a week's rest before the next game against Hamburg SV at Randall's Island. Some of the players took in a baseball game, which Ian St John wasn't impressed with, bluntly stating: 'What they find in that game to get excited about I cannot grasp.' It was during this week that Bill Shankly joined the tour and his arrival was eagerly awaited by all, especially the American press who had heard so much about his charisma and enthusiasm for the game. Ian St John described his arrival as 'like a breath of home to have him with us again' and that 'I don't think he will ever talk himself out of football topics and the Americans must have learned a lot from him.'[20]

Although Shankly's arrival was welcomed, the man himself did not appear to adapt too well to American ways and some of his antics on this tour have become the stuff of legend. Those there have recalled how he refused to change his watch to American time, saying: 'No bloody Yank is telling me the time.' This led to team sheets being pinned up on the hotel noticeboard at 6am and when he fulfilled a lifelong ambition of visiting Jack Dempsey's bar in New York, he stayed for 20 minutes before leaving at 9pm much to Bob Paisley's surprise. In Shankly's mind though, it was 2am and way too late. In his autobiography *The Saint*, published by Hodder & Stoughton in 2005, Ian St John recalls that on one evening the players went out for a drink and returned to the hotel at midnight, only to find Shankly up and about wanting to chat to anybody. This led to the players slipping away one by one until the boss was on his own and 'awake but with nowhere to go in a heathen place that had never heard of Tom Finney.'

Shankly certainly had mixed feelings over America and although he would have been glad to see Dempsey's bar, he could not have been pleased to arrive and see Ron Yeats with his knee in plaster. However with the extent of the injury being unknown and him being the captain, he remained with the party and relied on Ian St John to help him get dressed. Yeats was in the stands as the Reds lost 2-0 against Hamburg, bringing to an end their proud record of remaining unbeaten in America which had stretched back 34 games. In temperatures of over 90 degrees the Reds were obviously hindered by the absence of their captain and England internationals and Hamburg were a strong side. Their star player was centre forward Uwe Seeler, a one club man who in 1970 would become the first player to score in four World Cups (Pele joined him a few minutes later).

On the same day the Reds played Hamburg there was tragedy in South America when 318 were killed in Lima at the end of an Olympics qualifier between Peru and Argentina. Rioting erupted when a late Peru equaliser was disallowed and as many fans tried to escape after tear gas was fired into the crowd, they found the gates to the stadium were locked and many women and children were amongst those trampled to death. It was a shocking example of failings by the authorities to maintain fans' welfare. The day after the Hamburg defeat the Reds party flew to Detroit and took up residence at the Sheraton Cadillac Hotel. Just a few hours after Liverpool's touring party left New York, the England international squad arrived in readiness for their game against USA, which would take place on the same day that the Reds played in Detroit. Before playing their game, Bill Shankly agreed that the players could give a coaching clinic to local youngsters, although he was not impressed when he saw posters advertising the match. He believed that the team name alone was enough to sell the match and the fact they came from the same city as The Beatles shouldn't have come into it. However one of the match promoters Len Morgan, a Liverpool exile living in Detroit told the *Liverpool Echo:* 'Unfortunately we in football are the poor relations and have to take the crumbs from the table, so to speak.'

Liverpool's game against Meidericher at the University of Detroit stadium on 27th May was the first of three that they would play against the German side over the next nine days. It ended in a convincing 4-1 win for the Reds, who led 3-0 at half-time thanks to a double from Gordon Wallace and one from Alf Arrowsmith. After the break there was little chance of Meidericher getting back into the game with Ronnie Moran, who captained the side in Yeats' absence and Gerry Byrne outstanding in defence. Arrowsmith got Liverpool's fourth with 14 minutes remaining and Meidericher's consolation didn't come until the last minute when they were awarded a penalty which was converted by Ludwig Holden. The attendance for this game was 7,000, which despite appearing to be low has to be put into context with the fact that tickets were priced at $3-5 compared to the cheapest baseball seats of $1. Also, on the same day, there were just 5,062 at Randall's Island in New York to watch Reds striker Roger Hunt score four goals in a 10-0 victory for England. Three days earlier Liverpool and Hamburg had attracted 13,000 to the same stadium, an indication of just how popular the foreign tourists were.

The following day it was back to Chicago on an American Airlines flight, but before leaving Shankly found he had a problem over breakfast. Being up at 6am the hotel restaurant wasn't open, but he insisted on taking two journalists from the *Daily Express* and *Daily Mail* for a walk to find some rather than wait. After eventually finding a café and ordering a full English and tea for three, Shankly was told by the huge proprietor that it was hot dogs or burgers only. When they got back to the hotel they found that all the players had eaten and were ready to set off for the airport.

On arrival in Chicago they again stayed at the Sherman House Hotel. It was not just the hotel that was familiar to the players, but also the stadium and opposition as the Reds took on Meidericher at Soldier Field on 29th May. Beforehand though, they were ordered by Shankly to take part in an impromptu five-a-side game on the very spot where Gene Tunney had successfully defended his world heavyweight title against Jack Dempsey in 1927. When it came to the match proper against Meidericher, it was a much less open affair than two days earlier and ended in a 0-0 draw.

The Meidericher game included another solid display from Chris Lawler at the back and he was doing a good job of convincing Shankly that there was no need to enter the transfer market. At the start of the tour the *Liverpool Echo* had speculated that Shankly was looking at signing a full back but the form of Chris Lawler in America, where Shankly watched him deal more than capably with Uwe Seeler, was making such a move unnecessary. Ian St John's column in the *Daily Post* on 30th May had a great deal of praise for the young defender, saying that he had been 'splendid as Ronnie Yeats' deputy' and that 'he could not have discharged his duties better' against Seeler. St John's thoughts regarding Lawler did prove to be correct as he went on to play over 600 games for Liverpool, being one of only three players to win the league title in both 1966 and 1973.

Chicago may well have been Shankly's favourite place on the tour, given he visited the scene of the bout and also because of his love of the gangster movies. After the game the Reds flew west to San Francisco, while chairman Tom Williams returned to England with the Football League's Annual General Meeting looming. By arriving on the West Coast, Liverpool FC had now gone further than they had ever done before, a total of 5,171 miles from Anfield. They had three nights there at the Richelieu Hotel prior to the match on 3rd June against a San Francisco Select XI at the Kezar Stadium, then the home of the San Francisco 49ers American football team and made famous by the 1971 film *Dirty Harry*. Despite the vast distance, there were no signs of homesickness as the Reds racked up their best ever victory in any type of fixture, running out 14-0 winners in a game that Alf Arrowsmith and Ian St John both scored four goals. Such was the Reds dominance that they were 8-0 up at half-time and in the second half San Francisco keeper Zig Ottoboni was singled out by the press correspondent as their best player for making several spectacular saves. At the opposite end of the pitch, Trevor Roberts, who replaced Tommy Lawrence after he injured a foot in training, touched the ball just once in the first half. Lawrence's injury had meant an unexpected transatlantic dash for third choice keeper Bill Molyneux, who was flown out in the few days before the game and came on as a second half substitute.

The day after playing in San Francisco the Reds party flew to Vancouver in British Columbia, Canada for the last leg of the tour, where they would spend a week at the Devonshire Hotel and play two games. All around America they had met British immigrants but there was someone special in Vancouver for Willie Stevenson as his sister was living there. The first of the games was on 6th June against Meidericher, but as the players were getting up that morning, 4,708 miles away in London (which was eight hours ahead) chairman Tom Williams was at the Football League Annual General Meeting at the Café Royal in Regent Street. The most important thing on the agenda for Liverpool FC was the presentation of the Football League Championship trophy. Despite having been confirmed as champions six weeks earlier on 18th April the Reds still hadn't received the trophy, the Football League refusing an offer by deposed champions Everton to hand it over then and instead insisting on the presentation having to wait until the AGM.

As the trophy prepared to be returned to Anfield for the first time in 17 years, the Reds played out a bad tempered game against Meidericher. The match was played at the Empire Stadium, venue for the 1954 Commonwealth Games and attracted a crowd of 19,600 who saw all the game's main talking points occur within a four minute spell in the first half. In the 28th minute Manfred Mueller badly fouled Ian St John who retaliated by knocking him to the ground, leading to both players being sent off by referee Dan Kulak with Mueller having to be helped due to the blow he had received. Two minutes after the sending offs, Alf Arrowsmith burst through the defence and lobbed the keeper to put the Reds 1-0 up, but within a minute Meidericher were level when Meinz Versteeg scored from the rebound after Tommy Lawrence could only parry a free kick.

During the second half the game sometimes descended into a farce as neither looked willing to attack, play was at walking pace and officials of both sides went on to the pitch to remonstrate with the referee after challenges. Boos rang out from the spectators on several occasions and at the end of the game the Meidericher players lined up as was their custom to wave to the crowd only to be jeered. In his autobiography St John recalls about his sending off: 'The German centre half decided to kick me for just about the entire first half. Eventually I snapped and gave my marker a crack. When I reached the touchline I sat next to Ronnie Yeats and told him he had been fortunate to miss the game.' The match also saw some gamesmanship from both benches who were pumping up and letting air out of the ball every time it went near them and on the whole it hadn't been the best advert for Anglo-German relations on the 20th anniversary of the Normandy Landings.

The Meidericher match would be the last action that Bill Shankly would see on the tour as he returned home prior to the next and final game, which was four days later on 10th June against the Vancouver All Stars at the same stadium. This game, which the Reds won 2-0, was a far better spectacle than the locals had been subjected to against Meidericher and Ian St John atoned for the sending off with a brilliant deep lying display in which his passes created a succession of chances for Gordon Wallace and Alf Arrowsmith. The goals both came from Arrowsmith, one in each half and the Reds also hit the post twice.

The victory in Vancouver meant that the Reds had won six, drawn three and lost one of their 10 games and scored 40 goals. They had again been extremely popular in America breaking attendance records in several cities. The day after playing in Vancouver the Reds party flew to Toronto, where they spent the night, then took an overnight flight to Manchester via Glasgow. Ian St John ran into trouble at Customs though and had a watch confiscated as well as receiving a fine of £20. Bob Paisley, a much more experienced traveller told him that the best place to hide things was used jock-straps as 'they don't dig around too much when they see those.'[21]

When the players got through Customs, they were greeted by Bill Shankly and one fan, 45-year-old Bill Strange from Wavertree who had been seeing his wife off on a flight and decided to stay behind to see the Reds arrive. Shankly was fairly dismissive of the tour itself, telling the Liverpool Echo: 'They're coming home from the tour and that's all, there is nothing special in it. Everyone knows about it.' Vice-chairman Sid Reakes was much more positive though, saying that it had been 'wonderful' and they had played first class opposition, but were glad to be getting home. After five weeks away, another holiday may have seemed the last thing that was wanted but many of the players had family commitments to keep, with St John taking his wife and children to a caravan in Morecambe.

The legacy of this tour though was twofold. Firstly there would be no more tiring end of season jaunts, no matter how lucrative they could prove due to the negative impact they could have on the players' fitness. When it came to defending their title for the following season the Reds were jaded and started very badly, sinking into the relegation zone when they lost 4-0 against Everton at Anfield on 19th September. It was not until December that they began to pull away to safety and they eventually finished seventh. The second legacy came in Liverpool's cup success. What the poor start did do was ensure the Reds concentrated on the cups more than ever and they went on to win the FA Cup for the first time as well as reach the semi-finals of the European Cup. In future though, any end of season games would come in the form of a one-off friendly against a local side at a sunshine destination, where they players would be taken to enjoy a break to unwind with minimum travelling.

7

Costa Capers

Although the Reds went on their fair share of end season trips that involved a lot of travelling to, from and around their destinations in the USA, northern and eastern Europe, they have also indulged in plenty of trips abroad to Spain and other holiday destinations. The earlier tours were structured, but many of the later ones were much more ad-hoc, the club giving the players a holiday to show appreciation for their efforts. In the mid 1960s no games were involved in the end of season holidays but that later changed and to recoup the costs the players were asked to play a low key game against a local side.

Many of the games that were played on those end of season trips went unreported or were only mentioned very briefly in the press. This is probably not surprising as the likes of secretary Peter Robinson and board members did not travel. Tommy Smith recalls the none too serious nature of the games: 'We would never see a Barcelona, Real Madrid or even one of the lesser Spanish League sides. Our big summer confrontation usually entailed nothing more than a clash with the local waiters.'[22]

CANARY ISLANDS 1935

Before the days of jet travel Liverpool undertook their longest journey to date, making the long sea voyage to Gran Canaria at the end of 1934-35 for a tour that saw some relaxation in the sun and games against three local sides in Las Palmas.

The players set off on Wednesday 8th May aboard the *MV Adda* which was ultimately bound for Calabar in Nigeria, Las Palmas being the second of six stops en route. One player missing was record scorer Gordon Hodgson, who was spending the summer as the professional cricketer for Forfarshire in Scotland. On 13th May the ship called at Madeira, from where Tom Cooper posted a letter to Bee Edwards at the *Liverpool Echo* describing their experiences so far:

> 'The first day was very quiet, but the second day there were a few missing faces from the table. Tiny Bradshaw was the first to fall ill. Some others followed and left about five at the table. The next few days they all got their sea legs and joined in a few deck games. There were some needle games between Riley and Nivvy against Vic Wright and myself, and they

were always on top but we called it luck. They insisted it was skill, so we will leave it to you. Most of the time is passed away by playing solo or bridge. We are just beginning to strike warm weather. Some of the lads are doing some sunbathing; Nivvy and Savage were practising baseball but it was not long before the ball was overboard.'

The Liverpool party arrived at Las Palmas on Tuesday 14th May, the same day that a freak snowfall fell back home. They checked into the Metropole Hotel where author Agatha Christie had stayed eight years earlier with her daughter and secretary, having decided to move on from Tenerife as there were no white sandy beaches there.

The players spent a few more days relaxing before their first game, which was against Marino at the Campo Deportes on 19th May. The Liverpool newspapers were able to receive fairly detailed reports regarding all the games from press agencies which were published on the day after the match. For the Marino game, the *Liverpool Echo* and *Evening Express* carried an identical report, which stated that the Reds struggled to adapt to playing on hard ground with a light ball in the first half, leading to them trailing 2-1 at the break. In the second half though they became more accustomed to the conditions, with Berry 'Nivvy' Nieuwenhuys adapting particularly well as they were similar to what he was used to in his native South Africa. Cheered on by members of the crew of the White Star liner *Lancastria* which was in port, Liverpool stormed back to lead 4-2 and although Marino made it 4-3 they added a fifth near the end to run out 5-3 winners.

Four days later Liverpool were back at the Campo Deportes to play Victoria. This time the Reds had to be content with a 2-2 draw, Victoria's equaliser coming three minutes from time. The final game of the tour was on 26th May against a team from another island, CD Tenerife, but the game was still played in Las Palmas. The *Liverpool Echo* reported that the Reds had won 4-2 and dominated the game, having scored three goals in the first half hour.

The following day, a Monday, the party headed home, boarding the *MV Accra* which called at Madeira and Plymouth before finally arriving at Liverpool on Sunday 2nd June. The *Daily Post* reported that all of the players 'presented a bronzed appearance' and that they felt the tour was a success with the opposing players having been fast but lacking skill and ability in defence. Most of the Liverpool team had brought back appropriate souvenirs of their time in the Canary Islands – canaries in cages.

Due to the six-day sea voyage between Liverpool and Las Palmas which considerably slowed down the mail, no letters home had been published by the papers during this tour as on previous occasions. However a photographic record of the tour was kept by defender Ben Dabbs, whose family donated pictures to the club museum in 2002. They included a squad photograph with the players all in suits despite the high temperatures, another of a group having a beer in the shade and another of Miss Spain greeting the players before one of the games.

The only other time Liverpool were in the Canary Islands was in May 1968 when they visited Gran Canaria, drawing 1-1 against UD Las Palmas, who had been formed in 1949 as a result of a merger between 1935 opponents Marino and Victoria. Chris Lawler scored Liverpool's goal in a game that was played on the same night that Manchester United were crowned European champions with victory over Benfica at Wembley. The following day Bill Shankly returned home leaving the players in Gran Canaria to enjoy a well earned break at the end of the season.

SPAIN AND SOUTH OF FRANCE 1958

In the summer of 1952 the Reds played a one-off friendly in Madrid at the Bernabéu Stadium, losing 3-1 against a combined city side. This was the last match of a gruelling tour that had also seen them visit Germany, Austria and France. The next time Liverpool went to Spain for an extensive visit was in 1958 when they went on a five-game tour that saw them away for nearly three weeks, playing games all over the country as well as one in France on the way home.

Whereas the 1935 trip to the Canaries involved a leisurely sea voyage the same could not be said of this trip which was much more arduous in reaching its destination and although it contained visits to coastal areas also involved a lot of travelling. The Reds party of 15 players, along with manager Phil Taylor, trainer Albert Shelley and three Board members set off from Lime Street station on the midnight train to London on 8th May.

There were some notable players missing from the squad due to the looming World Cup, which saw some Reds involvement despite the club having been in the Second Division for four years. Keeper Tommy Younger had been called up by Scotland and winger Alan A'Court was in the England squad. Also unavailable were Johnny Wheeler who had been named in an FA party that was visiting Nigeria and Jimmy Melia, who was undergoing his National Service. This meant that there were some opportunities for youngsters and fringe players to shine, with 18-year-old winger Johnny Morrissey being included along with Alan Arnell, Louis Bimpson and Roy Saunders, whose opportunities had all been limited in the preceding season. The latest appointment to the coaching staff was also missing, with assistant trainer Joe Fagan not due to take up his position until the beginning of June.

After arriving in London early in the morning the party continued on to Paris by train and boat, spending the evening there before taking another overnight train to Irun where they were met by Spanish officials and taken the final seven miles to San Sebastián by bus. It meant the total time spent travelling had been 30 hours and the first game against Real Sociedad was to take place the following day, on Sunday 11th May. Sociedad had finished ninth in the Primera Liga in 1957-58 and the match had the potential to be a stern test for the Reds, who came out 1-0 winners thanks to a goal from Billy Liddell. The next match was on 15th May 50 miles away in Pamplona against Osasuna, who had finished above Sociedad in fifth place. However the Reds again were not daunted by strong opposition and ran out 3-1 winners, a very good result considering their Second Division status and the fact that Osasuna's compatriots Real Madrid were two weeks away from playing their third successive European Cup final.

In contrast to some previous trips, there were little details made available to fans back home regarding this tour. The *Daily Post, Evening Express* and *Liverpool Echo* didn't send any reporters and on occasions some papers did not even publish any details of the matches. When they did, they were no more than a few sentences long and there were no letters home from players detailing their experiences.

It had been hoped to arrange a game against Atlético Madrid but this didn't come off so the Reds next match was on 20th May against Elche, 414 miles from Pamplona but near to the coastal resorts that were being developed on the Costa Blanca. On paper this was the Reds easiest game of the tour so far as Elche had just been promoted from the Tercera (Third) Division but the home side ran out 1-0 winners. Liverpool then made their way back up north along the coast to Barcelona for a match against another Tercera side, CE L'Hospitalet, on 25th May. Again the Reds lost out against supposedly inferior opposition, going down 2-1 with Louis Bimpson scoring the goal against a side that had only been formed a year earlier from the merger of three other teams.

The long and slow journey homewards continued as the party crossed the border from Catalonia into the south of France for a game against Perpignan on 27th May. The Reds arrived in a country that was in the midst of political chaos following the seizure of government buildings by troops in their North African colony of Algeria. Just three days before the Reds played Perpignan a military coup was a real possibility after the island of Corsica was seized by paratroopers but this was averted after political leaders agreed to the return of former Prime Minister General de Gaulle as an emergency measure prior to the creation of a new constitution and elections. Given all this was going on, it's probably no surprise that none of Merseyside's newspapers on 28th May reported that the Reds had won 4-0. It is known that Bobby Campbell, Billy Liddell and Johnny Morrissey scored three of the goals, but the scorer of the other remains unknown.

SPANISH COASTAL RESORTS 1960S AND 1970S

If nearly getting caught up in a military coup in France wasn't enough, the Reds were up against guns twice during the 1960s in Majorca. First some of the players ran into trouble in a bar in 1966 and in 1969 there was a farcical incident involving trainer Bob Paisley, who was escorted to the dressing rooms by armed civil guards during a game.

After winning the league in 1966 the players went to Majorca where they soon started attracting crowds on the beach by putting on displays of head tennis. One night however, defender Gerry Byrne was accused of putting on an exhibition of a different sort, as Tommy Smith remembered in his 1998 autobiography *Over the Top*:

> 'There we were sitting in this bar-cum-restaurant and enjoying a good session. Gerry had gone off to the toilet and the next thing we know, one of the club bouncers was standing over us, pointing to the door and saying "OUT!" Apparently, Gerry had been having a pee in the toilet cubicle when the door accidentally opened. It probably didn't have a proper lock. This bouncer was claiming Gerry had done it on purpose and that he was some kind of exhibitionist.'

After reluctantly leaving following the appearance of more bouncers, Smith vowed to return to sort the bouncer out the next night but at the hotel captain Ron Yeats decided it couldn't wait until then and they took a taxi back to the club, as Smith continues:

> 'Ronnie banged on the front door and we barged our way in, stepping across to the bar where we demanded a couple of beers. The barman suddenly recognised me. "No beers", he said "We no serve HIM." As Ronnie continued to argue for the drinks, I said I was going to look for the bouncer who sparked all the trouble. As I moved away from the bar, I saw the big man picking the waiter up by the collar and repeating his request, this time in Spanish although the Scottish accent must still have bemused the barman ... "DOS CERVEZAS!". I suddenly spotted the bouncer and he was shocked when I stepped in front of him and grabbed him by the collar. It all happened in a matter of seconds. I had a firm grip on the fella. And big Ronnie was still holding the barman off the ground when there was a tap on my shoulder. I turned round and there was the manager, complete with little Spanish moustache and dickie bow. He said "OUT!" I said "NO". The next thing, he produced a gun. "Big man," I shouted, "He's got a GUN!" Yeatsy let the fella he was holding fall to the floor. Even a 6' 2" Scot who was fearless in any situation knew when to back down. We edged towards the door and, in the twinkling of an eye, we were OUT! Just like the man said.

That wasn't the end of the matter however. Despite having been faced with a firearm, Smith recalls how the Reds skipper had an immense attack of bravery and decided to head back for more:

> 'We went to walk away but something came over Yeatsy. I don't know if it was the cocky look on the bouncer's face or the simple fact that he had not been given those two beers. He wheeled round and kicked the door just like kicking the centre forward on a Saturday. The barman turned with a surprised look. He was a fat lad and he went down like a sack of potatoes as big Ronnie hit him with a punch Muhammad Ali would have been proud of. I hit the bouncer, finally getting my revenge, and all hell broke loose. Ten waiters were trying to get through the same door to help their mates. It was like something out of the Wild West. Chairs were flying. Fists were flying. I don't know where the manager was with his gun. Suddenly we heard the sound of a police siren in the distance. We ran out and disappeared into the night air before the local constabulary arrived.'[23]

It had certainly been an eventful first Spanish trip for Smith, who had been forced to miss the 1965 holiday due to an England Under-23 tour and the birth of his first child. He also got to witness the drinking qualities of trainer Reuben Bennett, who liked to drink Cointreau. Smith remembers that on seeing Bennett drinking it Gordon Milne quipped that it was like lemonade and decided to join him on it. A few hours later Milne fell off his stool causing Bennett to laugh 'lemonade, eh'. Another brush with trouble came when Smith, Byrne and Milne were thrown into jail after the hotel night porter took exception to the excessive noise. Milne demanded to see the manager or British Consul after the police knocked on his door, but soon changed his mind when the militia poked a gun in his ribs. After three hours in Palma's main police station they were released at 6am and on hearing of the incident the hotel manager sacked the porter on the spot.

The next time Liverpool were up against guns was in 1969, this time in the stadium itself. The Reds set off for Majorca on 19th May two days after the end of a season that had saw them achieve their highest ever points haul but still fail to land the title as Leeds United set a new record of 67 points to win the championship. Writing in the *Daily Post* on the day of their departure Horace Yates wrote that the trip would allow the Reds to combine 'business with well earned pleasure.' Fourteen players made the trip but some had to remain behind for solely business reasons and forego the pleasure. Alun Evans and Emlyn Hughes were included in the England Under-23 squad for games in Belgium, Holland and Portugal while Ian St John opted instead to attend a coaching course at Lilleshall. In addition two players were forced to stay at home due to impending nuptials, with Ian Callaghan and new signing Larry Lloyd both due to get married on 31st May.

The Reds were staying in C'an Pastilla for 12 days, with a game against Real Mallorca scheduled for Thursday 22nd May. News of the match made the front page of the following evening's *Liverpool Echo* following a bizarre incident that saw Paisley escorted to the dressing rooms by gun-toting civil guards. Despite the home side having made 10 changes at half-time, a local adjudicator refused to allow Paisley to send on a second substitute 15 minutes from the end of the game. As Paisley stood up to try and wave Brian Hall off the pitch, two civil guards abruptly arrived and grabbed an arm each to carry him to the dressing room, from where he was unable to see Bobby Graham score the goal that gave Liverpool a 2-1 win. Despite the shock of the incident, Paisley made it clear it was best forgotten about when he spoke to the *Echo's* Reds correspondent Chris James by phone from the hotel the following day. James quoted Paisley as saying:

> 'It's pointless doing anything about it. It's something best forgotten. They had an adjudicator there and when I got up to wave Brian Hall off so that we could substitute Phil Boersma all of a sudden he waved police to me and all of a sudden they were dragging me off to the dressing rooms. There was no interpreter so there was nothing I could do. I just went off quietly and when they saw I wasn't going to give any trouble they just left me sitting there. It had nothing to do with the referee or anything that happened on the pitch. It was all so silly.'

Liverpool's other end of season matches in Spain over the next few years passed off without incidents and brought nowhere near as much coverage in the press. In fact the friendly with CF Benidorm on 11th May 1972, who the Reds beat 3-0 in front of 1,750 fans, was not mentioned at all by any journalist and instead referred to in a matter of fact way by Kevin Keegan in his *Liverpool Echo* column a week after it was played. Keegan paid more attention to the fact the hotel was 20 yards from the beach and there was plenty of lying about in the sun, but also revealed there were some language difficulties especially when it came to the Spanish words jamon and jamona – which mean 'bacon' and 'buxom middle-aged woman' respectively!

The Reds had initially been set to undertake a tour of Greece in 1972, arranged as a thank-you gesture after the Reds had allowed Panathinaikos to use the facilities at Melwood prior to their European Cup tie with Everton in 1970-71. However those plans had to be abandoned after the Football League rescheduled a postponed game with Arsenal for two weeks after the season ended and new dates for the Greek trip couldn't be agreed. Another cancelled sunshine trip was at the end of 1973-74 when a planned friendly with Alicante was shelved due to five players being away on international duty and a number of others unable to travel for personal reasons. Club secretary Peter Robinson explained to the *Liverpool Echo:* 'We could not raise a representative team and we did not think it fair to British fans on holiday there to pay high prices to watch the game.'

The Reds were back in Spain in 1975 and 1976, holidaying on the Costa Blanca on both occasions. On 29th May 1975, a day after Leeds had lost the European Cup final against Bayern Munich, the Reds beat CF Benidorm 2-1 thanks to two goals from John Toshack. This game had taken place more than a month after the Reds' final league game of the season, although they had played at Anfield against a Don Revie XI for Bill Shankly's testimonial, as well as away friendlies at Plymouth and Rosenborg in between. The following year however, the players jetted off to Spain just a few days after the second leg of the UEFA Cup final against Bruges. They also faced a far sterner test than CF Benidorm of Spain's fifth tier had provided with Hercules, who had just finished sixth in the Primera Liga, providing the opposition and the Reds went down 3-1.

8

Mainland Europe – Tests of Physical and Mental Strength

Towards the end of Bill Shankly's managerial reign and for much of Bob Paisley's nine years in charge, Liverpool began a pattern of preparing for the new season by spending a week away playing two or three tough games in readiness for the new campaign. This was a move away from the traditional pre-season preparation of in house practice matches or behind closed doors friendlies. The change in track gave the managers a chance to try out formations and new signings for the coming seasons against top class opposition whilst also not travelling too much. It may be more than just a coincidence that the club's title successes of 1973, 1976 and 1977 came in the aftermath of this new type of tour.

WEST GERMANY 1967

After spending two summers at home following the month-long slog to America in 1964, Liverpool were on their travels again in August 1967 playing three games in West Germany, two of them against familiar opposition. It was a break from the normal pre-season routine for the Reds, but Bill Shankly felt it was in the club's best interests, saying:

> 'I know it is no joyride, that is one of the reasons we are here. I think this is the nearest approach to football of our own standard that we could have got anywhere. After all it is part of our training, we are only halfway through our preparations. I believe the games will apply a competitive edge that will not otherwise have been achieved. There will be challenge, talent and atmosphere. What more could we ask?'[24]

In June Shankly had broken Liverpool's transfer record when he signed Tony Hateley for £96,000 to provide some added power in attack. In the days before setting out for Germany though the striker's fitness provided cause for concern when he injured his ankle in a behind closed doors game against Tranmere on 1st August. However after coming through training on the morning of 3rd August Hateley joined the travelling party on the plane that afternoon as they flew to London with Shankly continuing to express caution. He told Horace Yates, who was covering the tour for both the *Daily Post* and *Liverpool Echo*, that a final decision on whether he would feature in the first game against Cologne would be made the next day.

At Heathrow Airport the Reds' connecting flight was delayed for an hour due to technical difficulties, leading to a replacement aircraft having to be found. When they did arrive in Cologne, it was without chairman Tom Williams and secretary Peter Robinson, who instead headed to Frankfurt to attend the following day's draw for the Inter Cities Fairs Cup, where the Reds ended up being paired with Swedish side Malmö in the first round. Whilst the draw was being made, the players were having a final training session before the game, after which Shankly decided it was too much of a gamble to risk Hateley. The *Liverpool Echo* that night reported the boss as saying: 'He is practically fit and I dare say he could have played but it would be foolish to take risks with him.'

Given the question marks over Hateley's fitness, it was probably best that he hadn't played in this match as it was a friendly in name only, with Cologne giving the Reds a stern physical test. The German side won 1-0, gaining some revenge for Liverpool's European Cup quarter final victory over them two years earlier. The most controversial incident came after 16 minutes when Emlyn Hughes was sent off for retaliation after he had been kicked in the shin and went down injured. After several minutes of treatment Hughes was carried off on a stretcher, but not before the referee had pointed to the touchline in a manner that indicated he would have been leaving the field anyway. Shankly and Reuben Bennett tried to protest, while even Cologne's Wolfgang Overath was speaking up on his behalf, but the referee was adamant and signalled Geoff Strong, who was preparing to come on as a replacement, to sit back down on the bench. Bizarrely no action was taken against any Cologne player and when play resumed it was with a Liverpool free kick.

Despite their setback, Liverpool were the better team, only to be beaten by a well worked free kick in the 72nd minute. Horace Yates wrote that although they had lost there were plenty of encouraging signs, with Gerry Byrne coming through the game after almost a year out through injury, the defence remaining sound, Hughes performing well in his 16 minutes of action and not being as badly injured as feared and Hateley still to come into the side. This tour was realistically the first foreign trip that fans had been able to go on and around 50 Reds were in the Müngersdorfer Stadium. The *Liverpool Echo* reported the next evening that they had been as big an attraction as the team itself, stopping the traffic when they saluted the coach that brought the players to the stadium. One Cologne official said: 'We thought our followers were enthusiastic but these men are fanatics. Liverpool must be the luckiest team in the world to have followers such as those'. [25]

The Reds remained in Cologne until Monday 7th August, staying at a quiet country hotel where business rather than pleasure was the order of the day, the players fully aware that they were not on holiday. By staying in this type of accommodation, Shankly was replicating the preparations for normal league games as much as possible with the closest the players got to leisure being a round of golf, which some of them including Hughes embarked upon the day after the Cologne game but they had to undergo a training session in baking hot sun as well.

With respect to the Hughes dismissal Horace Yates reported that the club just looked at it as one of those things, especially as other English clubs were having similar problems. The following day Leicester's David Nish was sent off in a friendly against Kaiserslautern and earlier in the week Plymouth had a player dismissed at Kiel. In each circumstance, no action was taken against any home players but with Leicester's chairman Len Shipman also being president of the Football League, Yates expressed the opinion in the *Liverpool Echo* that the issue looked certain to be raised and English observers present at friendlies in future.

The only disappointing aspect of the stay in Cologne came on the final day when the dressing room was broken into during training and several players had money taken, with Gerry Byrne ending up worst off losing £40. Whilst that was happening back at Anfield somebody who would become one of the most important men in the Liverpool success story in the coming years was beginning his new job. Geoff Twentyman, who had played his last game in 1959-60, was the club's new chief scout, replacing Norman Low who was moving to America. He would go on to unearth numerous great players from less fashionable clubs including Alan Hansen, Steve Nicol and Ian Rush.

From Cologne the Reds moved on to Hamburg for a match with SV Hamburg on Tuesday 8th August. The game would be played at the impressive Volksparkstadion, which translates as 'people's park stadium' and could hold 72,000 including 30,000 seats with spaces for 15,000 cars. It was one of the reasons why West Germany had been awarded the 1974 World Cup and Peter Robinson was impressed, saying: 'Where on earth could we put a motorcade like that? If 15,000 motorists came to Anfield some of them would have to leave their cars in the city centre.'[26]

Liverpool and Hamburg had met in New York three years earlier, when Hamburg became the first side to beat Liverpool in 35 matches in America. In that game a teenage Chris Lawler played at centre half due to Ron Yeats being injured, marking West German international forward Uwe Seeler, who played in the 1966 World Cup final against England. Now he was established as the club's first choice right back, with Yeats remaining a colossus in the middle. Defender Willi Schulz had also played in the final so the Reds could expect another tough game although on paper Hamburg were not as strong as Cologne. They had finished 14th in the Bundesliga in 1966-67 compared to Cologne's position of seventh.

Tony Hateley was declared fit for this game and made a good impression in a 2-2 draw, setting up the second equalising goal for Ian St John as well as laying on another chance for Roger Hunt, who headed over. The goal, which came in the 63rd minute, was a classic example of what he had been bought for, as he headed the ball down for St John to lash it past the keeper. Yates wrote in his report for the *Daily Post* that it must have been a 'wonderful moment for Shankly' and that 'at last he has a big man in the attack that can head down those balls which have been going to waste for far too long.' There was one note of caution though as he wrote: 'More than once he was taken unawares by St John's quick thinking football brain' but overall he was positive, concluding: 'I am convinced the reward will be well worth waiting for.'

Once again the Reds were followed by a small band of supporters in Hamburg, around 20 of whom were allowed in for free after they were found milling around the players' entrance seeking complimentary tickets. Yates described it as a 'handsome gesture' as many of the fans' funds were running low and they still had to travel further away from home if they were to complete the tour, which was to end on Saturday 12th August with a match against Hanover 96. With tickets for the matches costing up to 25 shillings, compared to a maximum 10 shillings at Anfield, the travelling fans were glad of any help they could get.

The day after the Hamburg game the players were given their first day off of the tour but there was a blow for Tony Hateley, who had a knock to his thigh during the game and required treatment. With his ankle also causing him problems, the decision was taken to send him home on the first flight the next morning, as the electrical equipment required for the injuries was only available at Anfield. Shankly explained that there was no point keeping him in Germany when he couldn't train fully and getting him fit for the start of the league season, just over a week away, was the priority. On Friday 11th August the Liverpool party travelled to Hanover where they again received excellent hospitality, the home club allowing them to train on the pitch at the 74,000 capacity Niedersachsenstadion. Hanover had finished ninth in the previous season's Bundesliga but were expected to give the Reds their sternest test of the tour as they were by far the fittest side they would come up against, having taken part in the Intertoto Cup. They had also made several additions to the squad over the summer, including Yugoslav international forward Josip Skoblar and 22-year- old Jupp Heynckes, who the Reds would become familiar with the following decade as he scored twice for Borussia Mönchengladbach in the second leg of the 1973 UEFA Cup final.

A crowd of 25,000 was expected for the game with many British servicemen stationed in the region, but heavy rain restricted it to 10,000. Hanover were without Skoblar due to injury and offered little up front as the Reds tore them apart, winning 4-1 thanks to goals from Ron Yeats, Willie Stevenson, Ian St John and Roger Hunt. The win was extremely satisfying given Tony Hateley was back on Merseyside but there was still plenty of potency with Emlyn Hughes showing great creative qualities and Willie Stevenson, whose place was one of the most under threat, also giving Shankly plenty to ponder. Between 30 and 40 Reds fans were in the stadium and despite being completely soaked to the skin sang 'We Are the Greatest' as the game drew to a close.

On returning home Bill Shankly expressed his satisfaction that the tour had achieved what it set out to. He told Michael Charters of the *Liverpool Echo* on 15th August, four days before the season started: 'Our players were under pressure all the time by the three teams we met. It was what I wanted and I think the boys have benefited by the change from our routine in previous years.'

Although Shankly had been happy with the tour, it didn't bring Liverpool success in 1967-68, as they had to settle for third place, three points behind champions Manchester City. It was still an improvement on the previous season's fifth place although Tony Hateley didn't quite live up to expectations. He got a respectable goals tally of 27 goals in all competitions but many of these were against lower quality opposition. Horace Yates' match report from the Hamburg game, in which he had suggested that at times Hateley wasn't in tune with Ian St John rang true and he was sold to Coventry early in 1968-69.

WEST GERMANY AND HOLLAND 1972

After their 1967 sojourn Liverpool mainly stuck to the British Isles for their pre-season preparations for the next four years, although there were one-off matches in 1969 and 1971 against Feyenoord and Hamburg respectively. However after going agonisingly close to the title in 1971-72 the Reds were off on a mini-tour again as they got ready for 1972-73 with a trip to West Germany and Holland.

In one of the closest ever finishes to a Football League season just one point separated the top four sides at the end of 1971-72. Liverpool finished in third, denied the title by a late disallowed goal at Arsenal in their final game that finished 0-0. It extended the club's trophyless run to six years but Bill Shankly's second great side was coming together nicely, it just needed some extra firepower up front. This was initially expected to come in the shape of Huddersfield striker Frank Worthington but when his medical revealed abnormally high blood pressure the deal was called off and the Reds turned to Nottingham Forest's Peter Cormack instead, signing the attacking midfielder for £115,000. Another close season addition was Tranmere's Trevor Storton, signed for £25,000 and brought in to provide defensive cover.

After three weeks of training at Melwood and two behind closed doors practice games against Chester and Tranmere the Reds flew to Düsseldorf on Tuesday 1st August in readiness for the first game against Bochum the following evening. As well as reporting the departure the *Liverpool Echo* also speculated on who would make way for Cormack who seemed certain to start, reporting that Brian Hall, Steve Heighway and John Toshack were the players whose places were most under threat.

In the end Shankly surprised everybody by starting with Storton and naming Cormack as a substitute as he sought to demonstrate that expensive fees don't necessarily mean a first team place was guaranteed. In a high tempo game that saw Bochum employ a rigorous man marking system the Reds won 2-0, with Cormack coming off the bench to score one of the goals in the second half, but he then had to be withdrawn after twisting his knee. He had shown during his half an hour on the pitch though why Shankly had signed him, as the Reds had been seriously lacking in goals from midfield the previous season.

The Reds took very few supporters to this midweek fixture, with air fares being prohibitive for many. One fan who did make it was Chris Wood from Upton (near Chester), who was then working for British Rail in London and could take advantage of huge travel concessions available to staff. Once over there, he recalls that one way of saving money was to buy food from vending machines, which could not distinguish between an English 5p piece and one German mark, which was worth about 25p. In addition to the Reds fans that had travelled from England, many British soldiers based in the locality were also at the game although they weren't always welcome, Wood recalling that many went simply to rile the locals, with the Second World War being fresh in the minds of many.

The day after the Bochum game, Cormack's knee injury was deemed serious enough to rule him out of the next game with Utrecht, so he was flown back to Liverpool for further treatment, with Phil Boersma flying out to replace him. On 4th August the Reds party took a short flight to Amsterdam then transferred to a hotel in Utrecht to prepare for the match there that would take place the following evening, a Saturday. There were now just seven days to the start of the season and although the squad was reduced through injuries Shankly wanted nothing less than 100% in this game against a side who were stronger than Bochum. Although the players needed an early night, the same didn't need to be said of the coaching staff and Shankly entertained journalists in the hotel bar, having them in stitches on one occasion when he told the barman that the miniature train which delivered drinks around the horseshoe-shaped bar was late. There was plenty of football talk as well though, with Shankly saying that Cormack would be part of his first eleven with Brian Hall making way. He said he expected his new signing to net 10 goals in the coming season, whereas Hall had managed just one in the league in 1971-72.

On the morning of 5th August the Reds players trained at the Stadion Galgenwaard, with Chris Wood being one of a number of fans who managed to watch them. With this game being of a weekend and Utrecht being easier to reach than Bochum there were more fans there, but still few enough to be sorted out with complimentary tickets by the players. Liverpool won the game 1-0 thanks to a goal from Steve Heighway in the first half, scored after one of his trademark mazy runs. They needed to be grateful to Ray Clemence who made five top class saves in the second half, as well as captain Tommy Smith who organised the defence well. Utrecht had been a far better side than Bochum, the Reds having deliberately chosen to make their hardest match of the pre-season their last one. Bill Shankly was extremely pleased with the workout they had given his side, saying afterwards: 'We will be properly fit by the end of the week and it will be a case of maintaining that fitness throughout the season. We will be very difficult to beat, we finished last season as the form team, losing only one of our last 17 games.'[27]

After the game many Reds fans took full advantage of the fact Dutch bars stayed open well into the early hours, whether it was in Utrecht or Amsterdam. Chris Wood remembers not booking any accommodation due to this, knowing there was a dormitory establishment near the station where a bed for a few hours could be secured for around £1.

The following week Cormack was still injured so Hall retained his place in the side and scored the opening goal as the Reds won 2-0 against Manchester City at Anfield on the opening day of the season. When he returned to fitness Cormack did establish himself in the side, with Hall, Boersma and Toshack being rotated depending on the opposition. Liverpool went on to win the title and also secured their first European trophy when they won the UEFA Cup in Mönchengladbach, less than 50 miles from Bochum where all the pre-season plans had first been put into place.

HOLLAND AND WEST GERMANY 1975

Bob Paisley took over from Bill Shankly as manager in 1974 and kept the new routine going, although plans for his first pre-season had already been made by the time of Shankly's shock resignation on 12th July.

The Reds were set to play two games in West Germany in 1974 but their participation in the Charity Shield against Leeds on 9th August meant a planned game against Rot Weiss Essen that day had to be cancelled. They did play the other game though, beating Kaiserslautern 3-1 on 6th August. Kevin Keegan was sent off for fighting in this game but Peter Cormack, who had a similar build and hairstyle claimed he had thrown the punch to try and deflect some negative publicity from the high profile player. It was only years later that the truth was admitted, although there was no way Keegan could hide from his sending off three days later against Leeds, when television cameras showed him and Billy Bremner trading punches before throwing their shirts to the floor.

Paisley's first full summer in charge in 1975 started with the usual end of season wind down trip to Spain, but for the pre-season tour of Holland and West Germany it was clearly business not pleasure. The Reds played three games although Paisley found himself coming home early to try and sort out some transfer dealings.

The Reds flew out to Holland on Friday 1st August but three days before they travelled there was a blow when captain Emlyn Hughes was injured in a behind closed doors game against Chester. There was a surprise when Bob Paisley announced his replacement with 18-year-old Colin Irwin, who hadn't even featured regularly for the reserves the previous season, being included in the 15-man party. Paisley confirmed on departure that every player would get a chance at some point, which meant an opportunity for young striker Jimmy Case and new left back Joey Jones, signed from Wrexham for £110,000 during the summer, to stake a claim. Like Shankly, Paisley saw these games as a way of bringing the players to peak fitness, with tour reporter Michael Charters quoting him in the *Daily Post* on 2nd August, the morning of the Utrecht game:

'The system of part training at Melwood and playing games in Europe has served us well over the past decade. We choose our opponents carefully so that they approach the games in the same spirit as us, as a means of bringing their players to peak fitness. Yet because there is some prestige at stake there is just enough competitive edge in the games to make the players play hard.'

Despite arriving in a country that was in the middle of a heatwave with temperatures in the 90s Paisley was not concerned, believing it helped keep the players' weight down and he put them through a session on the morning of the Utrecht game. Utrecht were familiar opposition, the Reds having played there three years earlier and again they came out on top, coasting to a 2-0 win thanks to goals from John Toshack and Peter Cormack. Cormack's came about 30 seconds into the second half and Chris Wood, one of the small band of Reds' followers, remembers missing that goal and only finding out about it when he saw the scoreboard. He recalls:

'At a lot of foreign stadia, just as at British stadia at the same time, you could walk uninterrupted around almost the whole arena. Having watched Liverpool score into the goal behind which we were standing in the first half, myself and a few friends walked behind Utrecht's Main Stand at half-time so that we could continue standing behind the goal which Liverpool were attacking. But either we started that walk too late or were distracted en route. As we reached the opposite terrace, a glance at the scoreboard told us that we had extended our interval lead to 2-0 ... and that we had missed Cormack's goal which had been scored in the opening seconds of the second half!'[28]

Paisley felt the Utrecht game was too easy but believed the next game on 5th August against Borussia Dortmund, who had beaten the Reds in the European Cup Winners Cup final nine years earlier, would be a much sterner test. He warned the players against picking up cautions though, as new rules meant a sending off triggered an automatic one game ban with no appeal. It was as if the home side knew this, as the Reds players were given a tough time with Kevin Keegan and Ian Callaghan being singled out. Both were booked for innocuous looking fouls but no action was taken against any Dortmund players. Eventually the Reds' class prevailed though as they won 2-0 and toyed with their opposition so much that the home crowd of 30,000 started jeering. The opening goal came from Joey Jones, which capped what Charters described in the following day's *Post* as a 'brilliant individual display' that was part of a 'top class exhibition of teamwork.'

Although the next match on 8th August was against Dutch side Roda JC the Reds stayed in West Germany, travelling by coach the day after the Dortmund game to Aachen which was just 10 miles from Kerkrade where Roda are based. Despite the impressive performances Paisley was not resting on any laurels and informed the local press that he would be returning to Liverpool the day before the Roda game along with chairman John Smith, to prepare for a possible transfer raid in Scotland. With the deadline for signing players who were eligible to play in the UEFA Cup just eight days away, the coming weekend was the only chance to personally watch any targets that had been recommended by scouts beforehand. The players that they were believed to be interested in were Dundee United's Andy Gray and Motherwell's Willie Pettigrew, joint top scorers in Scotland the previous season.

The heatwave was continuing and the Liverpool supporters who made the week-long jaunt were enjoying themselves. With three days between games and relatively little distances to travel, Chris Wood recalls how time was spent enjoying the sun, drinking beer, watching the team train and trying to find other matches to go to. When it came to finding somewhere to stay, the exceptionally warm weather also meant that some didn't even bother checking into hotels:

'It was a long, hot summer or at least the week when Liverpool were in Holland and Germany in 1975 was. These pre-season trips tended to be "booze cruises" on land and although that's not really my thing it's easy enough to get caught up in it, especially if you are trying to cool down. The team trained at Utrecht's Galgenwaard Stadium in 1975 but we weren't allowed in to see it which was unusual because normally these morning-of-the-match training sessions were not closed to the general public and it was pretty easy to get in to see them. In Dortmund we had more luck because the team trained on a practice pitch right by the side of the Westfalenstadion. We always went to the stadium on the morning of a match and more often than not there was a training session that we could watch. Even a small town like Kerkrade had a few bars but the bulk of us used the bar of the Hotel Juliana where most of our group was staying. Dortmund was much bigger of course so it was just a question of wandering around, seeing a bar you liked the look of and going in there for a few drinks before moving on somewhere else. A few of the lads could not afford a hotel in Dortmund and therefore booked themselves into what they called The Park Hotel and that's all it was, a park with no hotel. But the nights were warm so trying to kip down in a park was not a major problem, not on a warm night and not after several beers had been sunk in local bars. On days when we weren't travelling from one venue to another, we slept in, watched the team train when possible, organised games amongst ourselves, did a little (and it really only was a little) sightseeing and spent a lot of time pre-match and post-match in local bars. I was always on the lookout for another match to see and the new German League season started the day after we played at Roda in 1975. We played Roda on a Friday evening and instead of returning to England the next day, I went with a few of my railway colleagues to watch Duisburg play Fortuna Düsseldorf on the Saturday afternoon.'[29]

With Paisley gone Joe Fagan took over team affairs for the game against Roda, which celebrated the installation of the Dutch club's new floodlights. Peter Cormack was a casualty due to a foot injury, meaning Brian Hall was given a chance to impress, with Jimmy Case coming into the attack in place of Kevin Keegan. He had suffered bruising to his back in the Dortmund game and flew home with Paisley and Smith after it was decided a short period of rest was best for him. For 21 year old Case it was a good opportunity as he had not looked too comfortable in midfield against Dortmund and he seized it, scoring the Reds' goal in a 1-1 draw. Liverpool were not quite as sharp as in the two previous games, the heat and gruelling training schedule seemingly taking its toll in the second half and they also looked to have missed the creativity of Cormack and Keegan. Roda's goal was scored by their captain Dick Advocaat, who later managed Rangers to a treble and a double in successive years in 1999 and 2000 and then won the UEFA Cup in 2008 with Russian side Zenit St Petersburg.

Although it had been a slight disappointment not to return with a 100% record, there were plenty of reasons to be happy with this tour and they were summed up by Michael Charters in the *Liverpool Echo* on 11th August, five days before the first game of the season away to Queens Park Rangers. Youngsters Phil Neal and Joey Jones had been impressive as full backs, Kevin Keegan was outstanding, Ian Callaghan showed no signs of ageing, John Toshack and Ray Kennedy gave alternate options in attack and Tommy Smith was a capable deputy anywhere along the back four if a regular was injured.

There would be no further signings that summer though, with Paisley deciding not to pursue any further interest in Andy Gray or team-mate David Narey after watching Dundee United play St Johnstone at Tannadice. The failure of the moves to materialise didn't have any implications, as like three years earlier some tough games against Dutch and German opposition got the players ready for the season ahead and the Reds again completed a Football League Championship and UEFA Cup triumph.

HOLLAND 1976

After the successful tour of 1975, Liverpool again chose to have a three-game programme prior to the 1976-77 season, which also ended in success. The tour gave some players a last chance to prove themselves and like that of the previous year was carried out amidst rumours of another new signing.

The Reds had to restrict themselves to Holland this year due to the beginning of the West German season on 7th August. As such they chose some of the toughest opponents, with two of the three teams they would face being in European competition for the coming season. On 3rd August the *Daily Post* reported that although the club had financial guarantees to cover costs, the tour would not be a lucrative one. However that was seen as unimportant to the Reds given the support they commanded at home and that there was no better place to sharpen the players' reactions in time for the new season.

Bob Paisley initially named 14 players, but on the morning of 3rd August Steve Heighway felt a reaction to a thigh strain he had picked up in a friendly against Southport the previous week and it was decided to leave him behind and not call up any replacement. His absence meant that teenager David Fairclough, who had made such a sensational impact as a substitute towards the end of the previous season, would be given far more minutes on the pitch than he may have expected. Also missing was Tommy

Smith, who was in America playing for Tampa Bay Rowdies and would not be back until the fourth game of the league season. Smith had finished the previous season as the first choice left back after a loss of form by Joey Jones and injury to Alex Lindsay, but this tour gave those two players an opportunity to regain their places while he was away.

The build-up to the first game against Feyenoord on 4th August was overshadowed by some dramatic transfer developments, as Bob Paisley broke off from a training session on the morning of the game to travel 30 miles to the Dutch national team training headquarters at Zeist with chairman John Smith. Once there they met manager Bobby Robson and two directors from Ipswich Town, who were also on tour in Holland, to discuss the possible transfer of David Johnson. However with Ipswich seeking £200,000 for the former Everton striker, some £75,000 more than Liverpool valued him at, there was still plenty of hard bargaining to be done. Although it wasn't used as an excuse, Paisley's absence from training and Heighway's injury did the Reds no favours when it came to the match, in which Feyenoord beat Liverpool 2-0 at the Stadion De Kuip. The Reds were overrun in the first half by a far fitter side who were playing their third pre-season game, and although they rallied in the second Fairclough and Jimmy Case were not getting their shots on target. Paisley felt the defeat, Liverpool's first on the Continent since losing at Red Star Belgrade in the European Cup in 1973, would do the players a lot of good, saying afterwards that it: 'Would bring their heads down from the clouds after the celebrations last season'[30] and that 'we came on this tour for the major reason of sorting out the faults that we saw.'[31]

The day after the Feyenoord game the players had their first day off of pre-season, then on Friday 6th August had a gruelling training session in hot sunshine before travelling to West Germany even though the next game was in Holland against Roda JC. As with the previous year, it was decided to stay just over the border in Aachen rather than in Kerkrade itself. It was hoped that Heighway would be able to fly out to join the squad but his thigh was failing to respond to treatment and he remained at home to Paisley's disappointment. Thankfully, there were no other injuries to report apart from a spate of mosquito bites. While the Reds travelled to Aachen, John Smith and secretary Peter Robinson returned to England to attend a meeting chaired by Dennis Howell, the Minister of Sport and attended by representatives from all eleven British clubs competing in Europe in the coming season. The behaviour of fans was an increasing concern but there had been no incidents involving the Reds. Smith prepared a dossier detailing the arrangements made for transporting Liverpool's fans to the UEFA Cup final in Bruges the previous May, which was distributed around all other clubs. He then told Charters who reported in the *Echo* on 6th

August: 'We have more experience of European competition than any other major club in England and have offered the benefit of that experience to other clubs.'

Against Roda Paisley was looking for a much improved performance than against Feyenoord, a game in which he believed the right mental attitude was lacking. On the day of the game, Charters reported in the *Echo* what he had said:

> 'I'm not worried about their fitness, I know that will be right at the right time. I'm not worried about their ability – they have proved themselves as League Champions and UEFA Cup winners. But I am concerned that their mental attitude must be right. They have been showered with praise these last couple of months and rightly so. Now the time has come to forget all the back slapping and get on with the job. That job is to defend the title and keep it because winning the championship is always the priority for us.'

Paisley made it clear that Alec Lindsay was one of the players who he felt needed to sharpen up, saying:

> 'We all know what he can do, his skill on the ball is obvious but he didn't show it against Feyenoord. He played as though he did not have the confidence to show his ability. That is all in the mind and it is up to him to snap out of it. I have spoken to him and if he can regain his confidence as well as his form then he has a place in the first team. That is why these tour games are so important for him particularly.'

On the day of the Roda game Ian Callaghan was forced to pull out due to an infected foot. He was replaced by Terry McDermott who seized his chance to shine, scoring the opening goal in the 14th minute and having another tremendous shot turned around the post by the keeper. He also set up a number of attacks which the Reds failed to convert and with less than a minute remaining some sloppy defending allowed Roda an equaliser they barely deserved. This game was played on a Saturday evening, meaning that there were a fair number of Reds supporters present compared to the game against Feyenoord. Chris Wood was one of those who travelled, remembering that he and many others did so having been made to feel so welcome the year before.

The last game of the tour was the following Tuesday, 10th August against Twente Enschede, who would be without their star player, midfielder Frans Thyssen, due to a hamstring injury. Callaghan had recovered from his injury, but the performance of McDermott against Roda had made it impossible to leave him out and Paisley instead played both of them in midfield, moved Jimmy Case into attack and dropped Fairclough, who had been struggling in front of goal. There was a warning to McDermott against consistency though, with the *Echo* on the evening of the game that Paisley had said: 'One swallow doesn't make a summer, I'm waiting to see how he shapes in the next few games.' Steve Heighway was still not quite fit enough to fly over to take part but it was hoped that after an extra day's rest he could play for the reserves at St Helens Town the following evening to prove his fitness in time for the Charity Shield the coming Saturday.

Twente were potentially the hardest opponents the Reds would face on this tour, having led the Eredivisie for much of the previous season only to finish fourth after six key players got injured in the run-in. Every player was a full or under-23 international and they had won all six of their pre-season games so far, scoring 17 goals and conceding just three. Preparations for the game took on a much more familiar feel to games at home, with the players staying in a quiet country hotel with no distractions. However this failed to inspire them to a first win and the Reds went down 2-0, with Horace Yates confirming in the *Daily Post* that Twente were the best side they had faced. After sitting tight in the first half the Reds got more adventurous after the break which left them exposed at the back and they succumbed to two breakaway goals, meaning that they had endured their worst pre-season since they started to tour in Europe nine years earlier. The game saw a disappointing performance by Lindsay, who was substituted in the second half with Jones taking his place.

The following day the Reds party flew home from Amsterdam with Paisley asking fans not to read too much into the defeats, saying that they would be ready for the start of the season. He also gave a key indication into the psyche that helped Liverpool dominate football for so long over the next 10 years, in that it was drummed into the players that you are only as good as your last season. Michael Charters quoted him in the *Liverpool Echo*:

> 'We don't like losing at any time but it is better getting it out of our system in friendly games rather than in the real matches. We've learned a lot from these games. The mental attitude and application of some of the players has not been right and they will have to realise that the adulation from their success last season is over. It means nothing now. You can't sit back on what you did in the past. Now they have to achieve it all over again and if the disappointing tour results teach them that, then it will have been worthwhile.'

To ensure the players were on their guard, by the end of the week Paisley had dipped into the transfer kitty, meeting Ipswich's £200,000 asking price to bring David Johnson to Anfield after Tottenham had indicated they were ready to move for the player. Despite the size of the fee, Johnson was still not included in the squad for the Charity Shield, in which Liverpool beat

Southampton 1-0 at Wembley. For that game McDermott was left out to make way for Heighway, but he would seize his chance when it came later in the season and cap it with a goal against Borussia Mönchengladbach in the final of the European Cup, which Liverpool won for the first time. They also retained the league title as Liverpool's players didn't look back, Paisley's assessment of pre-season and what was needed to get things right having been spot on.

BELGIUM/DENMARK/WEST GERMANY 1980

Liverpool continued the pattern of playing tough warm up games in Holland and West Germany in 1977 and 1979, although in both cases they involved playing in tournaments. In 1978 they played three tough friendlies in a six-day period, but spread out over three countries against Basle, Bayern Munich and FK Austria. A change to their regular routine did no harm the following season, when the Reds were formidable and broke points and defensive records as they romped to the league title, but a similar style tour in 1980 led to Bob Paisley deciding that maybe it wasn't the right way to prepare.

The Reds began their pre-season preparations for 1980-81 with a friendly in Dublin against Dundalk on 30th July, before flying to Brussels to take on Anderlecht at the Stade Emile Verse, where they had been beaten 3-1 by the Belgian side in the European Super Cup in December 1978. It may have been a case of familiarity breeds contempt as just 10,000 turned out, but those who stayed away missed an entertaining game in which the Reds came from 2-0 down to lead 3-2, only to concede two goals in the last 10 minutes and lose 4-3. The first two Reds goals had been scored by David Fairclough, who was in the side in place of the injured David Johnson and desperate to prove his worth, given that at the end of the previous season Ian Rush had arrived from Chester for £300,000, a huge sum for a teenager. Paisley had opted not to take Rush or his fellow new signing, defender Richard Money, on this tour as he believed they would be better off training at Melwood and getting a feel for the club.

From Brussels the Reds moved on to Denmark, where they faced Danish Cup winners Hvidovre IF in Copenhagen two days later. The game ended in a comfortable 3-1 win for Liverpool, with Paisley taking the unusual step of making four substitutions due to the low key nature of the game. It was not the kind of test that he normally demanded, with Liverpool's players having no difficulties in terms of stamina or fitness against a team of part timers.

Paisley would have no such worries about the demands the opposition would place on his players in the final game of the tour, against VFB Stuttgart on 5th August. They had reached the semi-finals of the UEFA

Cup the season before and contained three of the West German national side that had won the European Championships that summer. Despite controlling the midfield defensive mistakes cost the Reds in this game, as they went down 3-2 after taking a first half lead through Kenny Dalglish. Paisley acknowledged that things would be better by the time the season started though, saying afterwards: 'We gave away three silly goals but we still have a fortnight to sort it out. If we learn our lessons from this defeat we can still anticipate better things.'[32]

On returning to his office at Anfield, Paisley again stressed that pre-season tours are about conditioning exercises and in terms of getting the players right mentally that had been achieved. However he did concede that perhaps they had done too much travelling, the *Daily Post* reporting on 7th August that he had said: 'Perhaps this tour wasn't exactly the right way to go about our preparations. We've had four games in seven days and a lot of travelling in between. At half-time in Stuttgart we knew the players were very tired.' The travelling also took its toll on fans, with Chris Wood recalling how with over 500 miles between each venue his time was spent either on trains or watching the games. He also found that by now 5p coins didn't work in the German vending machines.

Also on 7th August, Michael Charters wrote in the *Liverpool Echo* that the Reds had looked 'anything but champions in style and effect', a potentially worrying sign for the season ahead. In the end, the Reds triumphed in Paris to win a third European Cup and also won their first League Cup, but they were sadly lacking in the league. Their fifth place finish was their lowest since 1971, they lost at home for the first time since 1978 and got knocked out of the FA Cup by Everton. The following year, it was back to the one place, as the Reds prepared for what turned out to be another title-winning season with three games in Switzerland.

SWITZERLAND 1981

In preparing for the 1981-82 season Liverpool went back to what had served them so well before, arranging three games in relatively close proximity against fairly strong opposition, allowing them to do some training in between games. As with some other tours, this one was also dominated by transfer activity although it wasn't just incoming transfers that were making the headlines.

Liverpool's first game of the pre-season was a friendly at Scunthorpe on 4th August, arranged as a gesture to give the home club, from whom they had signed Kevin Keegan and Ray Clemence, a much needed financial boost. The day before the game Clemence stole the headlines as he was reluctantly transfer listed by the Reds, sparking a race for his signature between Southampton and Tottenham. The keeper had made his desire to leave the club known a month earlier but his request was initially refused. However, faced with an unhappy player Paisley eventually relented but it was made clear that only realistic offers would be considered, with the asking price set at £300,000.

Despite being transfer listed Clemence was still allowed to make an emotional return to Scunthorpe and was included in the Reds side that won 2-1 thanks to goals from David Johnson and Terry McDermott. Clemence was given a standing ovation by the home fans and described his return as 'really tremendous', while Craig Johnston, signed from Middlesbrough for a club record £600,000 at the end of the previous season was lively on his first performance in a red shirt.

The transfer listing of Clemence left Bob Paisley with a transfer headache regarding the goalkeeping situation, as the deadline for registering players for the European Cup was 15th August, less than two weeks away. Bruce Grobbelaar had been signed for £250,000 from Vancouver Whitecaps and now had a chance to show that he could be pitched straight into first team action without the usual grooming process in the reserves. If he didn't look ready, Paisley would have to buy as reserve keeper Steve Ogrizovic had declined the offer of a new contract. The games against teams that were just a week away from their new season were the perfect opportunity for Grobbelaar, but on 7th August as the Reds departed it was not clear whether he would even be allowed into Switzerland due to his Zimbabwean citizenship. Both his and Australian Craig Johnston's passports were held up in the post having been sent to the Swiss embassy to secure visas and secretary Peter Robinson explained to Ian Hargraves of the *Liverpool Echo* that it was a case of getting there and hoping some discretion would be shown by the immigration authorities. On arrival special dispensation was given to allow the two players into the country, meaning Clemence didn't have to fly out as an emergency replacement. The Reds also arrived without Graeme Souness, who was left behind after suffering a knock in training and his place was taken by Jimmy Case, another player who was being linked with a move away from Anfield having been linked with Everton the previous month.

The following day the Reds preparations were given a further blow when the match against Swiss champions FC Zurich was postponed due to a late thunderstorm. It was rearranged for 24 hours later but this would have a knock on effect on training, as it meant just two days between this and the next game. Despite this Paisley resisted the urge to go into the game with the aim of making substitutions just for the sake of it, telling Ian Hargraves: 'The aim is to get our best side into the best possible condition.'

The Reds beat Zurich 3-0 with the only change being an enforced one, Ronnie Whelan replacing the injured Johnston in the second half.

Grobbelaar had the sort of performance that would go on to typify his Reds career, making three outstanding saves, one of which was described by Hargraves as 'resembling Clemence at his best' but also fumbling a cross. Grobbelaar himself knew there was room for improvement, saying afterwards: 'I got myself into one or two difficult situations but I think that sort of thing will soon be ironed out.'[33] Johnston also put in a good performance before he was forced off and the Reds goals came from Kenny Dalglish, Ray Kennedy and Phil Neal, who converted a penalty just as he had done in the European Cup semi-final in the same stadium four years earlier. There was no news from home regarding bids for Ray Clemence, but an offer by Swansea of £320,000 for Colin Irwin was turned down by Paisley, who believed his versatility made him far more valuable.

The Reds then moved on to Geneva, although 10 fans remained in custody in Zurich after being arrested and held to appear before the courts on suspicion of theft. The *Daily Post* reported on 10th August that a police spokesman confirmed they had been seen on overcrowded boats on a lake and on questioning found to have in their possession wallets and gold bars, valued at £2,800. Although the behaviour, which had come to light by pure chance, can't be condoned it was still far less than some Swiss newspapers had claimed had gone on with reports of assaults, rioting, smashed windows and looting. The police though confirmed that they had had no complaints of any of this occurring.

Terry McDermott flew out to join the squad for the match against Servette Geneva on 11th August, which was a boost with Craig Johnston still suffering the effects of a knock to the knee received in the Zurich game. On the evening of the game the *Echo* predicted that Servette would pose no more difficult a test than Zurich but the Reds lost 2-1, exactly the same scoreline that the Swiss side had beaten them by ten seasons earlier in the European Cup Winners Cup. McDermott gave the Reds a sixth minute lead but Servette, who were more advanced in their preparations and used five substitutes to keep fresh, seized on an error by Phil Thompson to equalise and then hit the winner 11 minutes from time as the Reds tired. Their determination to claim the scalp of the European champions in front of a crowd of 16,500, their biggest gate for many years, was shown when Howard Gayle was clean through only to be rugby tackled to the ground. Grobbelaar again had a good game, making a brilliant save in the first half described by Ray Kennedy as one of the best he'd ever seen but the keeper was again self critical, believing he could have done more to stop the winning goal. Ian Hargraves also predicted he would become a popular figure with the Kop due to his 'constant ball juggling, long accurate throws and razor sharp reflexes.'[34]

As Liverpool moved on to Neuchâtel for the final match of the tour two nights afterwards Paisley's injury problems mounted. Jimmy Case was barely able to stand after injuring his foot in the Servette game and there was news from Melwood that Graeme Souness had broken down in training and may now miss the start of the season.

Liverpool's visit to the small lakeside city that has a population of just 30,000 was a big event locally, with guests at the game including the president of the Swiss Confederation and British ambassador. To commemorate the fact that 1981 had been designated International Year of the Disabled by the United Nations the game was kicked off by a fan in a wheelchair. The crowd of 6,800 was twice Neuchâtel's average but the Reds gave their worst performance of the tour in what should have been the easiest game. Although they were territorially dominant and never looked like losing they couldn't convert this to chances, with the midfield being particularly weak without Souness.

The following day, 14th August, the Reds party flew to Heathrow but whereas the players continued on another plane to Liverpool Bob Paisley and chairman John Smith remained in London to conduct some transfer business. They went to a nearby hotel to meet Mark Lawrenson and officials from his club Brighton and a fee of £900,000 was agreed to secure the services of the player, who finally arrived at Anfield at midnight for his medical after delays caused by heavy traffic.

The versatile Lawrenson's arrival also opened the door for Colin Irwin to talk to Swansea, the Reds having accepted an increased £350,000 bid and the *Daily Post* reported that Jimmy Case also looked set to be moving to Brighton. It had initially been proposed for him to go there as a makeweight in the Lawrenson deal but with him wanting time to think things through and Arsenal hovering, the Reds decided to put the money up to secure Lawrenson's signature first and deal with Case's departure separately. The funds for Lawrenson's transfer were made up in part by the £300,000 that was received on the same day from Tottenham for Ray Clemence, the Reds having successfully held out for a fee that Spurs had been reluctant to pay due to his age. A boost was also received when Steve Ogrizovic agreed to stay at the Reds for another year and fight for his place, meaning Paisley did have some relative experience to register for the European Cup.

The legacy of this tour was that the Reds went on to secure a 13th league championship, although they did it the hard way having been 12th in the table at Christmas. However some of the characteristics that would highlight the season were demonstrated on the tour. Bruce Grobbelaar was both brilliant and erratic and Phil Thompson struggled defensively, having the captaincy taken off him during the season. The Reds were weak in midfield due to the absence of Souness and during the campaign Paisley tried many midfield combinations, with Ronnie Whelan eventually coming into the side in place of Ray Kennedy.

Ultimately the harsh economic reality meant this tour to Switzerland was the last of its type, save for two games in 1984 within a few days against Borussia Dortmund and Charleroi. Crowds at Anfield were falling as Merseyside suffered badly during a recession that left over 20% of the local population unemployed. It meant that if the Reds were to continue to be able to sign the best players, they had to take the money to play in tournaments that may not have been the best preparation in the cases of ones played in the height of the Spanish summer, but could guarantee gate receipts equivalent to two or three home games.

9

The Irish Kop

For many years Liverpool has drawn a significant amount of its support from Ireland. With the standard of football there not being so high and the best players playing in England, it is only natural that fans have done the same when it comes to supporting teams.

Liverpool FC's success, coupled with its location on the west coast which makes it easily accessible for fans, has led to the club having a very large following in Ireland. After visiting in the 1960s for the first time since the beginning of the 20th century, they became frequent visitors in the 1980s and 1990s for short tours and one-off friendlies, many of them in mid-season. However the increasing globalisation of the game since the Millennium has seen them neglect Ireland, travelling further afield instead.

1962 DUBLIN AND LIMERICK

At the end of 1961-62 Liverpool visited Ireland for the first time since before the First World War, their short tour coming at the end of a season when they had finally managed get out of the Second Division.

The Reds clinched promotion on 21st April with a 2-0 win over Southampton at Anfield but there were still five more games to play before the end of the season. The last of these was a 4-2 defeat at Swansea on 4th May then the Reds beat Everton 1-0 in the Liverpool Senior Cup final at Goodison Park on the 8th before heading over to Ireland for the first match with Bohemians which took place on 14th May at Dalymount Park.

Perhaps inevitably given the fact the game came so soon after the end of a long season it was a lacklustre display by the Reds, who won 1-0 thanks to an Alan A'Court goal after 10 minutes. To ensure a more competitive game, Bohemians had some guest players including Irish international Ambrose Fogarty, who had been with them between 1953 and 1955 and was now playing for Sunderland. Although he showed some neat touches some of his team-mates weren't of the same standard, while he was already a familiar opponent to the Reds defenders who knew what to expect of him. The news accounts of the game weren't favorable though, with the *Liverpool Echo* stating that the 10,000 crowd had expected a more positive display from the Reds and were critical of them.

Two days later Liverpool faced Limerick, managed by Ewan Fenton who was a member of Blackpool's FA Cup winning team in 1953. In conditions that were made difficult by high winds they again put in a below par display, winning 5-3 in a game that could have gone either way until Kevin Lewis got the fifth with three minutes remaining. Two of the Reds' goals came due to goalkeeping errors and their own keeper Jim Furnell was far busier than had been expected. The *Daily Post* concluded that if they were to make a mark on the First Division the next season they would have to perform far better than this.

After a shaky start Liverpool did enjoy a steady season in 1962-63, finishing eighth. They were back in Ireland too due to the severe winter that led to several postponements. With Ireland not being as badly hit the Reds took on Drumcondra at their Tolka Park ground on 6th February, winning 5-1 with Ian St John hitting a hat-trick in a match that helped the players maintain their fitness.

1968 AND 1969 BELFAST

Liverpool's first visits to Ulster after the partition of Ireland in 1924 were not until the late 1960s, when they played matches in successive years against Linfield at Windsor Park. Both games marked the start of Liverpool's pre season preparations and gave Bill Shankly an opportunity to give some youngsters a run out, although in the first case his hand was somewhat forced due to injury.

Two days before the 1968 game the Reds suffered a blow when left back Gerry Byrne was forced to withdraw from the squad after suffering a reaction to a long standing cartilage injury in a behind closed doors practice match. Byrne hadn't played since March due to an injured cartilage and this fresh injury was a major setback as he entered hospital for another operation on 25th July, the day before the Linfield game. The *Liverpool Echo* reported that that it wasn't a serious matter and he could be available again in September, but in the end Byrne would play just three more games for the Reds. It meant a call up to the squad for Peter Wall, who had played nine games towards the end of the previous season.

The Reds set off for Belfast minus Bill Shankly, who was laid up in bed with a chill, but he was still able to telephone Bob Paisley with his preferred team selection, which was effectively the strongest available side, with Wall at left back. Despite their superior quality they were still given a shock after just two minutes when future Everton player and Northern Ireland manager Bryan Hamilton finished off a neat move by lobbing the ball over Tommy Lawrence. For half an hour the part timers resisted everything the Reds threw at them as they dreamed of a famous victory, but in the 34th minute Roger Hunt equalised in fortunate circumstances. His shot from 20 yards rebounded off the post against keeper Robert McGonigal who was prostrate on the floor and bounced into the net.

Early in the second half Tony Hateley, who had a point to prove as it was widely acknowledged that Shankly was on the lookout for another striker, fired the Reds 2-1 up and Hunt added another in the 72nd minute. The second half saw Ray Clemence, still two weeks away from his 20th birthday, make only his second appearance for the club (the other was a friendly in Porto the previous May) and although he didn't have much to do, he acted confidently when called into action. The game had proved a useful exercise for the Reds as any quality Linfield lacked was made up for with sheer determination. At the end of the game the players knew that they had been in a competitive game as they prepared for the season ahead. The match, played on a Friday night, had attracted 16,000 fans to Windsor Park which at that time had a capacity of 58,000.

The following year Liverpool again went to Belfast in the last weekend of July although on this occasion the match took place on a Saturday afternoon. With Gerry Byrne's Anfield career now looking over Bill Shankly was still struggling to find a solution to his left back problem, as during 1968-69 Peter Wall hadn't been able to make the position his own meaning utility man Geoff Strong had worn the number three shirt for much of the season. Shankly took a full strength side to Belfast and also included youngsters Brian Hall and John McLaughlin in the party.

Just like a year before, Liverpool were left reeling by an early goal as Alan McGraw headed Linfield ahead after just 90 seconds. This time though the Reds hit straight back, levelling almost immediately through Emlyn Hughes and Ron Yeats made it 2-1 after 36 minutes. The second half was played at almost walking pace and the Reds were guilty of some woeful finishing. Linfield were nowhere near as competitive as the previous year, with many of their players having not yet trained after only returning from holiday the day before.

The month after Liverpool's second visit sectarian violence exploded across Northern Ireland leading to the deployment of British troops in the province at the request of the Unionist government. It would be several years before Liverpool visited Belfast again and the following summer they played in Dublin, beating a League of Ireland XI 2-1 at Dalymount Park.

1981 DUBLIN AND BELFAST

In 1981 Liverpool played in Belfast and Dublin within a few days of each other for the first time since 1903, with a game against Home Farm arranged as part of the deal which saw Ronnie Whelan join the Reds, then a match with Crusaders to celebrate the opening of the Irish League club's new stand.

Despite the game in Belfast being the most likely to attract any attention due to the political situation, it was actually at Tolka Park in Dublin where protesters hit. Officials arriving at the ground on the morning of the game, 22nd August, found that vandals had climbed in from the banks of the River Tolka and carved a 20 yard 'H' into the pitch. This was a direct reference to the H-Block of the Maze prison in Belfast, where ten Irish Nationalist prisoners had died whilst on hunger strike in the previous four months, the most recent death being just two days before this game. It meant some emergency returfing had to be carried out but the Reds were assured before they flew out that the pitch was playable. The H-Block Committee themselves denied any involvement in the vandalism while Reds manager Bob Paisley said he hadn't even been told about it, telling the *Liverpool Echo* on departure: 'I am surprised but as far as I am concerned we are going.'

As the name implies Home Farm, now dissolved after being known as Dublin City from 2001-06, were a club that put a special emphasis on developing youth talent. Ronnie Whelan had joined as a six-year-old in 1967 and played for the Republic of Ireland at junior and amateur levels before joining the Reds in September 1979. He was on target in this match against his former club, with Terry McDermott also grabbing a brace as the Reds won 5-0. The match marked Graeme Souness's first start of pre-season and was another opportunity for new keeper Bruce Grobbelaar, defender Mark Lawrenson, signed over the summer for a club record fee and forward Craig Johnston, who had joined towards the end of the previous season to impress. Although Liverpool had been intent on rising above politics and playing the game, some Reds fans who attended did run into trouble with the hunger strikers issue being prominent. Phil Rimmer remembers standing on the terraces and being subjected to verbal abuse for much of the game, with the comment of 'Your Queen's a whore' sticking in the memory. He was also told to watch his back after the game as people would be waiting for him at the exits, causing him to move about as much as possible.

Two days later Liverpool made the three-hour coach journey to Belfast for their first friendly since 1969. The Reds had faced Crusaders in the first round of the European Cup in 1976-77 winning 2-0 at Anfield and then 5-0 at Seaview. That was the most high profile fixture in Northern Ireland for several years after UEFA banned the Province from hosting matches between 1971 and 1975 due to the Troubles. Now they were back for the friendly, even though England had refused to play in Belfast in the previous May's British Championship. Crusaders' chairman Derek Wade expressed 'thanks and appreciation' to Liverpool for fulfilling the fixture in his programme notes, while his Reds counterpart John Smith wrote: 'We are pleased to visit Belfast again, particularly in the light of reaction at another football level so far as Belfast overtones are concerned. We are here for the broad sake of sport; we are happy to do so.'

Liverpool finished their pre-season preparations in style, winning 5-0 just as they had done in 1976. David Johnson was given the opportunity to stake a claim for his place after Johnston's arrival and he was on the scoresheet just as he had been in the European Cup game. Terry McDermott also found the net as he had done five years earlier while the other goals came from Kenny Dalglish (2) and Mark Lawrenson, who put in a fine performance at centre back having played left back against Home Farm. Liverpool were delighted with the reception they had received in both Dublin and Belfast, secretary Peter Robinson telling the *Liverpool Echo* the following day: 'It was marvellous. We were told in both the North and the South that we are now the number one club in Ireland. We now get upwards of 1,000 people travelling to watch us every Saturday. That is good for the club and good for the city.'

To reaffirm their commitment to Belfast despite the Troubles, Liverpool played Glentoran later in the season on 19th April in a game that was part of their centenary celebrations. Although it was Liverpool's first visit to The Oval and the first time the two sides had met, they did have one thing in common that season as both had been knocked out of the European Cup by CSKA Sofia. In the game Mark Lawrenson got Liverpool's goal in a 1-1 draw. The following year the Reds were back at Windsor Park but not to play Linfield. Instead they played Manchester United in a testimonial arranged for Irish FA secretary Billy Drennan. 30,000 attended a game that United won 4-3.

Liverpool played Home Farm again on 20th August 1984, this time as part of a deal that took Brian Mooney and Ken De Mange to Anfield. Both youngsters played as guests for Home Farm, with Ronnie Whelan, now an established player at Anfield, again being on target for the Reds against his old side in a 3-0 win. In between the two Home Farm games, Liverpool's only visit to Dublin to play a club side was on 23rd November 1982, when Ian Rush scored the Reds goal in a 1-1 draw with Shamrock Rovers, a game that marked the switch on of new floodlights at their Glenmalure Park ground.

1986 CORK

In the late 1970s and early 1980s Liverpool played three friendlies against Irish representative sides in Dublin. However in 1986 there was a change of scenery as the Reds played in Cork, honouring an invitation that had first been made two years earlier.

Liverpool agreed to play a pre-season friendly in the Republic of Ireland's second largest city back in January 1984 and it was hoped to stage the game in 1985 to coincide with its 800th birthday celebrations. However the ban on English clubs playing anywhere outside of England after Heysel soon put paid to that and instead the national side played a friendly against Spain in the city. With the ban being lifted in 1986, a new date was arranged which was five days before the start of the new league season and the Reds were certain to be a big attraction given they had just completed the league and FA Cup double.

After playing Everton in the Charity Shield at Wembley on 16th August, the Liverpool party flew straight to Cork that evening on a scheduled Aer Lingus flight from Heathrow, taking the Canon League trophy and FA Cup with them so they could be displayed at the offices of the *Cork Examiner*. That night the Lord Mayor of Cork hosted a civic reception for Liverpool's players and officials, giving them a good opportunity to unwind after a busy pre-season build-up. Included in the Liverpool party as a guest of the club was Franco Barratine, the secretary of Juventus as links between the two clubs continued to be forged in the aftermath of Heysel. Barratine was no doubt keen to see Ian Rush in action, the Liverpool striker having signed for the Italian side the previous month before being immediately loaned back to the Reds for the 1986-87 season.

The following day was a leisurely one for the players, some of whom went to kiss the Blarney Stone whilst others played golf or snooker, or did some sightseeing in Kinsale. There would be no liberties taken however, with a 10pm curfew being demanded even though the match would not kick off until 6.45pm the next day, Monday 18th August.

The venue for the match against an Irish International XI was Flower Lodge, which was then home of Cork City but is now owned by the Gaelic Athletic Association and named Páirc Uí Rinn (Ring Park). Most of the players in the Irish side came from the League of Ireland, with national boss Jack Charlton explaining in the match programme that it was unfeasible to expect English sides to release players so close to the start of the season. One English-based player involved though was future Liverpool midfielder Ray Houghton, then with Oxford United, while Kenny Dalglish also gave permission for Reds reserves Ken de Mange and Brian Mooney to play for the Irish side.

In front of 16,000 fans the Reds fell behind on 24 minutes when Mike Hooper, standing in for Bruce Grobbelaar who had torn a stomach muscle at Wembley making him doubtful for the start of the season, spilled a shot and Houghton smashed the ball into the roof of the net. In the second half though, the introduction of Jan Mølby for John Wark helped turn the game. The big Dane converted a penalty on 56 minutes after Rush had been fouled in the box and then Kevin MacDonald got the winner with 10 minutes left after being cleverly set up by Dalglish.

After the match there was a further opportunity for the players to unwind as a celebratory banquet was held at the Jury's hotel attended by 250 guests. Many of the players then headed off to CoCos night club, finally retiring to bed well after midnight. The following day though it was an Aer Lingus flight to Manchester and the serious business of preparing for the new season, which was now only four days away.

1995 DUBLIN AND BELFAST

In the early 1990s Liverpool were in great demand for friendlies in Ireland and those that they played were not necessarily only at the beginning or end of a season. An early FA Cup exit in 1993 led to a hastily arranged match against Shelbourne on the weekend of the fourth round ties. Due to the game only being arranged at a few days notice it was not ticketed, leading to chaotic scenes with the gates of Tolka Park locked an hour before kick off with thousands locked outside. When the teams took to the field, most of the attention was focused on under fire Reds boss Graeme Souness, who still managed a smile for the cameras situated near the dugout. His mood would have relaxed even further when goals from Jamie Redknapp and Mark Walters gave the Reds a 2-1 win.

In May 1994 the Reds were facing Shelbourne at Tolka Park again, with Roy Evans now in charge following Souness's departure the previous January. The Reds romped to a 5-0 victory, all the goals coming in the first 20 minutes of the second half. In between the two Shelbourne matches, Liverpool played a League of Ireland side at Lansdowne Road in October 1993 to mark the installation of the stadium's first floodlights. 28,000 turned out to see the Reds win 2-1.

At the end of 1994-95 the Reds faced University College Dublin (UCD) at Lansdowne Road in a game to mark the centenary of the only university side in western Europe to play in their country's top division. The game was moved as UCD's 3,000 capacity ground was nowhere near big enough, as 22,816 fans attended and saw a 2-1 win for the Reds, Jamie Redknapp and Robbie Fowler (2) scoring the goals.

1995 marked a new era in Irish friendlies though as it was the first of six years running when the Reds would spend a few days there playing two games each time. It also marked their first visit to Belfast for 12years due to the reduction in security fears there. Despite the absence of the first team from Ulster for some time, Liverpool youth sides often took part in the prestigious Milk Cup tournament, winning it in 1988 when they beat Motherwell 4-0 in the final. Reserve manager Sammy Lee also took an under-21 side there in 1993 when they played matches against B Division teams Dungannon Swifts and Limavady. The hospitality afforded on that visit, alongside the declaration of ceasefires by paramilitary groups in 1994 no doubt played a part in Liverpool's decision to play in Belfast again.

The first of the two 1995 matches in Ireland came on 12th August against Shelbourne at Tolka Park in a game that marked the Irish club's centenary. The Reds were just a week away from the start of the new season and nearing peak fitness, but Roy Evans took no chances and left Stan Collymore and Robbie Fowler at home to nurse minor injuries. Irish international Phil Babb though did manage to recover from a sore knee to be included for the trip and he managed an hour of the match before being replaced by Dominic Matteo. This was the Reds' seventh pre-season game and their superior fitness and quality showed, with only keeper Alan Gough standing between them and an avalanche of goals. Despite Liverpool dominating from start to finish, Steve McManaman's eighth minute goal was all that separated the two sides at the end of the game.

Two days later Liverpool were in Belfast for their first match against Linfield since 1969. A capacity crowd of 25,000 turned out to see Ian Rush score the only goal after 37 minutes in a game where the Reds were again repeatedly thwarted by a home keeper in outstanding form. Rush's goal no doubt went a long way to helping Roy Evans make his mind up as to who should start the season in attack alongside record £8.5 million signing Stan Collymore, who shook off his earlier injury to take part in this game but Fowler still had to miss out.

The pattern of playing two games in three days on either side of the border continued for the next two years, although further Troubles including the IRA revoking its ceasefire did lead to some speculation that the Reds would be seeking to make other plans in 1996. This proved unfounded however and in a game that marked the end of the Kop at Windsor Park, which had been there since the 1930s, the Reds needed a late equaliser from Robbie Fowler to draw 2-2 with Linfield. Two days later there was nearly another embarrassing scoreline, with Steve McManaman's goal three minutes from time giving Liverpool a 1-0 victory over Dundalk at Oriel Park. That game was arranged to celebrate the 70th anniversary of Dundalk joining the Free State Senior League.

In 1997, all eyes were on 17-year-old Michael Owen who was now staking his claim for a first team place after being given some chances towards the end of the previous season. He did his cause no harm in Belfast on 26th July, scoring both the Reds goals in a 2-1 win, the first game to be played in front of the new 5,000 seat stand that had been built to replace the Kop. However he sat out the game in Dublin, where Liverpool beat a combined UCD/Shelbourne side 6-0 at Tolka Park.

THE DUNDALK CONNECTION

Liverpool's match against Dundalk in 1996 had been the latest in a long line of friendies between the Reds and the Irish side, who hailed from County Louth halfway between Dublin and Belfast near the border. Links between the sides were first established in 1969-70 when they met in the Fairs Cup, with Liverpool winning 14-0 on aggregate, hitting ten at Anfield. By the time they were drawn against each other again in the European Cup in 1982-83, the friendship had already developed and was only cemented even further.

The first friendly between the sides was on 30th July 1980 at Lansdowne Road in Dublin. This was Liverpool's first pre-season game of 1980-81 and they won 2-0 in front of 20,000 fans thanks to goals from Kenny Dalglish and Phil Neal. The game had come about after the Reds had signed three teenagers – Synan Braddish, Derek Carroll and Brian Duff – from Dundalk for a combined fee of £50,000 in 1978. Despite Duff especially showing promise, scoring 28 goals for Liverpool's 'A' team (a modern day under-18s), all failed to adequately make the step up in level and returned back to Dundalk midway through 1979-80 before the friendly had even taken place.

In October 1990 Liverpool signed young player of the year Tony Cousins from Dundalk, which led to the Reds visiting Oriel Park the following July. Liverpool's general secretary Peter Robinson wrote in the match programme of the links between the clubs and the Reds' following in Ireland:

> 'We are delighted to start the new season with a match against Dundalk as we have so many friends and supporters in Ireland. No doubt many of the supporters attending tonight's match will have travelled to watch us play at Anfield as we regularly enjoy a large following from Ireland at all our home games. For a lot of young supporters however, this may be their first opportunity to watch our players in the 'flesh', although they may have seen us on many occasions on television.'

Cousins himself didn't feature in the game although Steve Staunton, another ex Dundalk player, did play at left back. Speaking of his excitement of the return in the programme he said: 'It will seem strange going back to my home town to play at Oriel Park. Yet in a sense I will feel proud to be going there with Liverpool and proud that it was the place where I started my senior football.' The game marked the debuts of Mark Wright and Dean Saunders, a double capture from Derby County in the summer and the latter a British transfer record. However they were unable to inspire Liverpool to a victory as the game ended in a 0-0 draw. Cousins, whose transfer had led to the game taking place, failed to make a single appearance in three injury-ravaged years at Anfield and left in 1993 on a free transfer to Middlesbrough.

Johannes Gandil, who represented Denmark at both athletics and football in the Olympics and hosted a dinner for the Liverpool party in 1910

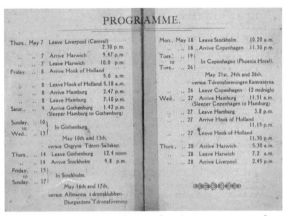

PROGRAMME.

Thurs., May 7	Leave Liverpool (Central)	2.30 p.m.	Mon., May 18	Leave Stockholm	10.20 a.m.
" 7	Arrive Harwich	9.47 p.m.	" 18	Arrive Copenhagen	11.30 p.m.
" 7	Leave Harwich	10.0 p.m.	Tues. " 19	In Copenhagen (Phoenix Hotel).	
Friday, " 8	Arrive Hook of Holland	5.0 a.m.	to		
" 8	Leave Hook of Holland	5.18 a.m.	Tues. " 26	May 21st, 24th and 26th.	
" 8	Arrive Hamburg	2.47 p.m.		versus Tdrottsföreningen Kamraterna	
" 8	Leave Hamburg	7.10 p.m.	" 26	Leave Copenhagen	12 midnight
Satur., " 9	Arrive Gothenburg	1.42 p.m.	Wed. " 27	Arrive Hamburg	11.31 a.m.
	(Sleeper Hamburg to Gothenburg)			(Sleeper Copenhagen to Hamburg)	
Sunday. " 10	In Gothenburg		" 27	Leave Hamburg	3.8 p.m.
Wed. " 13			" 27	Arrive Hook of Holland	11.15 p.m.
	May 10th and 13th.		" 27	Leave Hook of Holland	11.30 p.m.
	versus Orgryte Tdrott-Sällskap.		Thurs. " 28	Arrive Harwich	5.30 a.m.
Thurs., " 14	Leave Gothenburg	12.4 noon	" 28	Leave Harwich	7.2 a.m.
" 14	Arrive Stockholm	9.8 p.m.	" 28	Arrive Liverpool	2.45 p.m.
Friday, " 15	In Stockholm.				
to					
Sunday. " 17					
	May 16th and 17th.				
	versus Allmanna i drottsklubben				
	Djurgardens Tdrottsförening				

Itinerary issued to players for the 1914 tour of Scandinavia. Liverpool FC continuned to issue cards like these right up to the 1970s

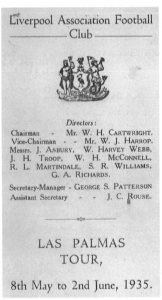

Liverpool Association Football Club

Directors:
Chairman - Mr. W. H. CARTWRIGHT.
Vice-Chairman - - Mr. W. J. HARROP.
Messrs. J. ASBURY, W. HARVEY WEBB,
J. H. TROOP, W. H. McCONNELL,
R. L. MARTINDALE, S. R. WILLIAMS,
G. A. RICHARDS.

Secretary-Manager - GEORGE S. PATTERSON
Assistant Secretary - - J. C. ROUSE.

LAS PALMAS TOUR,

8th May to 2nd June, 1935.

Itinerary card for the 1935 Canary Islands tour (courtesy Sarah Howe)

Top: Le Grand Hotel in Maggiore where Liverpool stayed in 1922 prior to playing Burnley in Milan (courtesy Aaron Logan).
Below: The Hotel Eggers in Gothenburg where Liverpool stayed in 1914 (courtesy Ezeu Wikicommons)

MV Adda on which the touring party sailed to Las Palmas in 1935

Players taking a break in Belgrade, 1936

THIRD MATCH OF TOUR

LIVERPOOL A.F.C. V. BELGRADE S.K.
YUGO SLAVIA.
MAY 21 1936.

Autographs collected by Ernie Blenkinsop against SK Belgrade in 1936, courtesy of his grandson Bob Blenkinsop

USA 1946 tour, 12th May 1946 before the match against New York Allstars at Randalls Island. From the collection of Jim Donnelly

A menu from a farewell dinner from the 1946 USA tour, held at the St George Hotel in Brooklyn. From the collection of James Cotton

The squad on board the Queen Mary en route to America in 1953

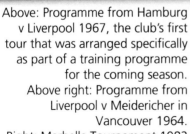

ESTADIO MUNICIPAL DE HOSPITALET
GRAN PARTIDO INTERNACIONAL
Mañana lunes, a las 6 de la tarde:

LIVERPOOL-HOSPITALET

3.er clasificado en la Liga de   (Reforzado con varios ases
Inglaterra, vencedor del Real   azulgranas)
     Sociedad y Osasuna
DISPUTANDO EL V TROFEO SASTRERIA VICENTE
Comunicaciones con el Estadio Municipal de Hospitalet
METRO TRANSVERSAL: Estación Santa Eulalia
     AUTOBUSES: Plaza España - San Feliu
Entrada General, 15 Ptas. Socios Hospitalet, 8 ptas.

Advert in the Spanish press
for Liverpool's match against
Hospitalet in 1958

Above: Programme from Hamburg
v Liverpool 1967, the club's first
tour that was arranged specifically
as part of a training programme
for the coming season.
Above right: Programme from
Liverpool v Meidericher in
Vancouver 1964.
Right: Marbella Tournament 1982
programme

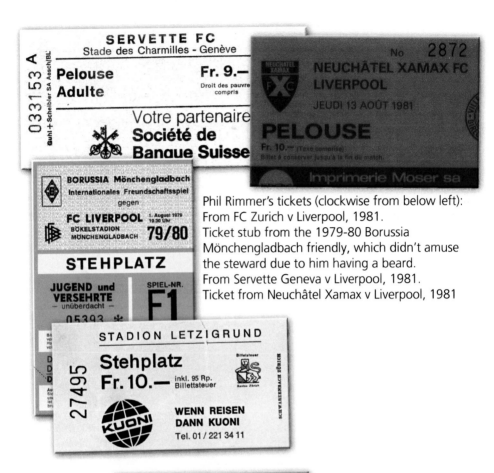

SERVETTE FC
Stade des Charmilles - Genève

033153 A
Guhl + Scheibler SA Aesch/BL

Pelouse
Adulte

Fr. 9.—
Droit des pauvres
compris

Votre partenaire
Société de
Banque Suisse

No 2872

NEUCHÂTEL XAMAX FC
LIVERPOOL

JEUDI 13 AOÛT 1981

PELOUSE
Fr. 10.— (Taxe comprise)
Billet à conserver jusqu'à la fin du match.

Imprimerie Moser sa

BORUSSIA Mönchengladbach
Internationales Freundschaftsspiel
gegen
FC LIVERPOOL 1. August 1979
19.30 Uhr
BÖKELSTADION
MÖNCHENGLADBACH **79/80**

STEHPLATZ

JUGEND und
VERSEHRTE
— unüberdacht —
05393 *

SPIEL-NR.
F1

Phil Rimmer's tickets (clockwise from below left):
From FC Zurich v Liverpool, 1981.
Ticket stub from the 1979-80 Borussia
Mönchengladbach friendly, which didn't amuse
the steward due to him having a beard.
From Servette Geneva v Liverpool, 1981.
Ticket from Neuchâtel Xamax v Liverpool, 1981

STADION LETZIGRUND

27495

Stehplatz
Fr. 10.— inkl. 95 Rp.
Billettsteuer

KUONI

WENN REISEN
DANN KUONI
Tel. 01 / 221 34 11

Phil Rimmer's
tickets from
the Marbella
Tournament
semi final and
final in 1982

IV Trofeo Ciudad de Marbella
13 DE AGOSTO DE 1982
10.30 NOCHE
Bayer 04
C. D. Málaga
Fondo S
Nº 01113
estadio municipal de marbella

IV Trofeo Ciudad de Marbella
14 DE AGOSTO DE 19
10.30 NOCHE
Liverpool F
R. Betis
Preferenc
Nº 01435
estadio municipal de marbella

IV Trofeo Ciudad de Marbella
15 DE AGOSTO DE 1982
7.30 TARDE
PARTIDO DE
CONSOLACION
Fondo Sur
Nº 00022
estadio municipal de marbella

IV Trofeo Ciudad de Marbella
15 DE AGOSTO DE 1982
10.30 NOCHE
FINAL
Preferencia
Nº 00043
estadio municipal de marbella

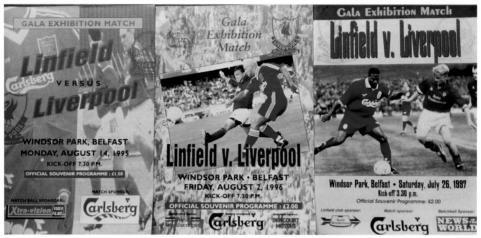

programmes from Liverpool FC's three mid 1990s friendlies against Linfield

A signed player
card presented
to Chris Wood in
Tromso in 1992

Singapore 1991, Liverpool v
Arsenal programme

Programmes from Liverpool's three North American tour games in 2004

Liverpool FC v Toronto, 2012. Photo courtesy Steve Parry

Above and right: Liverpool FC fans in Indonesia. Photos courtesy of Steve Parry

Enthusiastic support in Malaysia, 2011. Photo courtesy of Steve Parry

Martin Skrtel signing autographs in Boston's Fenway Park, 2012. Photo courtesy of Steve Parry

Ticket for Liverpool FC's open training session at the Melbourne Cricket Ground, 23rd July 2013. Courtesy of Mark Platt

Liverpool fans in Thailand, 2013. Photo courtesy of Lye Cs

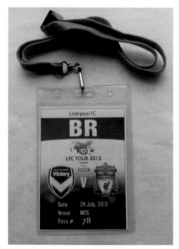

Access all areas stadium pass for Melbourne Victory v Liverpool, 24th July 2013. Courtesy of Mark Platt

Liverpool's next visit to Dundalk was in August 1994 for their eighth and last game of the pre-season campaign, which was not arranged in relation to any specific event. In a fixture that took place just five days before the start of the season and was described by the Reds' boss as an important friendly, goals from Robbie Fowler and Michael Thomas gave the Reds a 2-1 win.

CARLSBERG TROPHY AND BELFAST CHALLENGE 1998 T0 2000

At the end of the 1990s Liverpool's visits to Dublin and Belfast took on a competitive edge as they took part in four-team mini tournaments three years running, all of which were sponsored by club sponsors Carlsberg. They involved one game against a local side and another against another big name from European football.

The Dublin tournament first took place in 1997 with Celtic, Newcastle and PSV Eindhoven joining League of Ireland champions Derry City. In 1998 it was rebranded the Carlsberg Trophy and with the Reds being sponsored by Carlsberg and having a huge following in Ireland it seemed natural that they would be asked to take part.

The big talking point in 1998 as the Reds set off for Dublin to face St Patrick's Athletic on Friday 31st July was the appointment of Gérard Houllier to work as joint manager alongside Roy Evans and in three friendlies so far there had been one win, one draw and one defeat. South African-born German B international Sean Dundee would be the major new signing on show, but a far bigger draw was teenage striker Michael Owen, who had shot to worldwide fame in the World Cup and now Irish fans had a chance to see him close up.

The Reds were given a scare against the part timers as Patrick Berger's 16th minute goal was cancelled out just after the half hour. Karl Heinz Reidle spared the blushes by restoring the lead and Danny Murphy put the Reds in control before half-time. To the delight of fans Owen was introduced in the second half along with Steve McManaman, who with just a year left on his contract was now the subject of much speculation. There were no further goals and St Patrick's got a consolation shortly before the end. The following day Liverpool met Leeds United in the final. They had beaten Sven Goran Eriksson's Lazio on penalties but were no match for the Reds who ran out 2-0 winners with goals in rapid succession from Owen and Berger just before the hour mark. Owen was then given a standing ovation on going off with 15 minutes left to be replaced by Sean Dundee.

In 1999 and 2000 Carlsberg sponsored a tournament in Belfast that was set up on a league basis with the winner being the team that had the most points from two games played. Home clubs Linfield and Glentoran each played against one of the guest sides at their own ground in midweek before a double header at Linfield's Windsor Park on the Saturday. This consisted of a match between Linfield and Glentoran, which in 2000 doubled as the Charity Shield and then the headline act between the Liverpool and the other guest side.

The 1999 trip to Belfast preceded Gérard Houllier's first campaign in sole charge and gave fans an early glimpse of the relatively unknown signings he had made that would hopefully transform the Reds' fortunes. On Thursday 22nd July the Reds strolled to a 4-0 win against Linfield at Windsor Park, but Houllier saved the new signings for the Saturday game with Feyenoord. Only Sander Westerveld and Erik Meijer started against Linfield, with Titi Camara coming on as a second half substitute. Against Feyenoord Vladimir Šmicer and Dietmar Hamman, the two most high profile arrivals played, as well as the unknown Finnish defender Sami Hyypia, who would go on to have an immensely successful career with the Reds. Both Šmicer and Camara were on target as Liverpool won 2-0, an encouraging result against the Dutch champions, who had future Reds keeper Jerzy Dudek playing in goal.

The following year Liverpool again beat the local side, this time Glentoran, 4-0 although the game was marred by a serious injury to Robbie Fowler sustained in a collision with their keeper. Two days later Titi Camara and Michael Owen were on target in a 2-2 draw with Benfica at Windsor Park, a game that saw new signings Markus Babbel, Nick Barmby and Gary McAllister feature.

The games in Belfast in 2000 came two months after Liverpool had played a Republic of Ireland side in Dublin, a game that was arranged as a testimonial for Tony Cascarino and Steve Staunton. It would be 13 years before a Liverpool first team was back in Ireland, when they lost 1-0 to Celtic in an exhibition match at the Aviva Stadium on 10th August 2013. In the years between, the increase of budget air travel significantly increased the potential for Irish fans to come over to Liverpool since 2001 Liverpool's pre-season has taken in a completely new dimension that has not been reversed since.

OMAGH 1999

Liverpool's only visit to Northern Ireland which has seen them play outside Belfast came in 1999 when they played a friendly against Omagh Town, a game organised as a result of a bomb outrage in the town just over a year earlier.

Despite the ongoing peace process, splinter terrorist groups were forming after breaking away from organisations which were observing ceasefires. On 15th August 1998 29 civilians were killed by a Real IRA bomb in the small market town of Omagh in County Tyrone, making it Northern Ireland's largest single terrorist atrocity. The following year local football team Omagh Town, of the First Division of the Irish League, played three high profile matches in aid of the Omagh Memorial Fund, with Liverpool's visit on 18th October coming soon after Chelsea and Manchester United had also visited.

Liverpool's executive vice-chairman Peter Robinson wrote in the match programme how the Reds were more than willing to send a side over, especially in the light of having seen tragedy at first hand:

> 'Liverpool has always enjoyed a close relationship with the many supporters who regularly travel from Ireland to watch games at Anfield and when we first heard of the terrible incident in Omagh immediately offered to play a game to raise funds for those affected by the tragedy. Ten years ago we suffered our own grievous loss and none of us at the club have ever forgotten the huge amount of emotional and financial support that was forthcoming from Ireland for the families and friends of those lost at Hillsborough. Although none of us could have foreseen the awful event that brought about tonight's match, we are grateful for the chance to repay a little of the kindness shown to us then.'

The Reds flew into Belfast International Airport on the morning of the game, where a number of schoolchildren wearing replica shirts were waiting to greet them. When they arrived at Omagh Gérard Houllier, Jamie Redknapp and Michael Owen left a card and flowers at the memorial garden in the town centre.

Omagh's St Julian's Road was a far cry from the facilities Liverpool's players were used to, with portacabins acting as changing rooms. They were then given another shock when Omagh, who had been beaten 8-0 by Chelsea and 9-0 by United, took the lead. However the Reds got over this early scare to win 7-1 in front of 7,000 fans, the pick of the goals being a diving header by Jamie Redknapp. The biggest cheers of the night came when Michael Owen was introduced midway through the second half, while Patrik Berger was by far the best player dictating the play for most of the game.

In addition to the funds raised from the match itself, Omagh were presented with a cheque for £250 from the Liverpool International Supporters' Club. A small group of members travelled from Liverpool for the game as guests of the West Belfast branch and enjoyed a night on the town afterwards before returning home the next day.

DUNMANWAY/DUBLIN 2009

In May 2000 Liverpool provided the opposition for a joint Tony Cascarino/ Steve Staunton testimonial against the Republic of Ireland national side at

Lansdowne Road. With unlimited substitutions being allowed, it meant Gérard Houllier could play all of the big names, but also give some big game experience to youngsters such as Frode Kippe and John Miles. This disruption to the shape of the team though did show eventually as the Reds, who had taken a third minute lead through Emile Heskey, lost 4-2 with all the Irish goals coming in the last 20 minutes.

It was 13 years before the Reds were back in Ireland and two main explanations can be given as to why. First, the club have been seeking new areas to attract and retain fans in the Far East, where the support is fanatical and income possibilities huge. Secondly, the onset of budget air travel has made Anfield far more accessible to Irish fans. In the 1970s and 1980s air travel was only available to the richest of fans, with the majority having to make the trip to and from Anfield by overnight ferry. Nowadays though, day trips are possible for as little as £30.

28-year-old Erik DeLacy is one fan who regularly travels over from Ireland for games. His love affair with Liverpool began after watching Ireland during the 1990 World Cup, in which Reds players Ray Houghton, Steve Staunton and Ronnie Whelan, as well as ex-striker John Aldridge all featured for the side that reached the quarter finals. Erik gets over to Liverpool as many times as he can and since 2004 has made it at least twice a season, on one occasion attending 11 games. Erik says that if the Reds played more often in Ireland, this would not mean he would reduce the number of times he went over to England to see the Reds play, instead it would just be an added bonus. Although the pound has weakened in recent years against the Euro, making the travel and ticket costs for Irish fans much cheaper, Erik himself hasn't been able to take advantage of this and head over more often due to personal circumstances, although he is sure there are plenty who have.

With Liverpool's first team travelling further afield it has meant that when it comes to games against Irish opposition, they have sent reserve and youth sides over. These games have still attracted significant interest despite tickets for the matches sometimes costing amounts that fans in England would baulk at paying for the level of football involved.

Although not a tour as such, with the games played 11 days apart and another friendly in Scotland against Partick Thistle in between, the Reds played two contrasting fixtures in Ireland in 2009. One was against one of the biggest names in the League of Ireland and the other saw the Reds face tiny Dunmanway Town of the West Cork League, one of a number of regional leagues that operate below the two national divisions.

The game against Dunmanway took place on 6th August and came about thanks to a speculative call from David Hall, the Dunmanway captain who came up with the idea of one of the smallest clubs in the world playing one of the biggest. Writing in the match programme, Liam Mackey of the *Irish Examiner* wrote:

'Dunmanway Town said "phone them and they will come". Dunmanway's David Hall was the man who made that fateful call to Anfield and irrespective of the result of today's game, the very fact that the fixture is now taking place is proof positive that who dares wins. But as well as being testament to the West Cork club's sense of adventure, the David versus Goliath nature of the game can't help but stir the romantic sporting soul, evoking memories of those far off days when the European Cup was an open draw and League of Ireland clubs could find themselves pitched into battle against some of the most fabled sides in the world game. Football can be a great leveller, so David v Goliath, yes, but, also, once the whistle blows, 11 against 11 in the proverbial game of two halves. And while it might be pushing the fantasy just a little too far to speculate on an act of outrageous giant-killing, of one thing we can be certain – there will be no losers on what promises to be a memorable occasion.'

Dunmanway spent €100,000 erecting a temporary 6,800 seat stadium for the match at the Mary Immaculata secondary school in the town. Despite match tickets costing €40 there was still a sell-out crowd for a match that the Reds won 1-0, Dani Pacheco scoring the only goal against a side that contained five guest players from the League of Ireland.

On 17th August a Reds XI was back in Ireland to take on Bohemians at Dalymount Park in Dublin. One of Ireland's most successful clubs, Bohs were on their way to their 11th title and had just run Red Bull Salzburg very close in a Champions League qualifier, going down 2-1 on aggregate. The match was again a sell-out, 7,000 being present in a now crumbling ground that was once home to the Irish national side and accommodated 40,000 in the 1980s for an international against Italy. Against a youthful Bohemians side Liverpool left it late to seal their victory, Krisztian Nemeth scoring in the 90th minute and then Pacheco converting an injury-time penalty.

BELFAST AND BRAY 2012

Reds reserve sides were back across the Irish Sea for the next four years after the Dunmanway and Bohemians games, with the difference being that the visits became two game mini-tours rather than isolated friendlies. In 2010 they went down 1-0 to Galway United before moving across the border to face Dungannon Swifts, who they beat 5-1. The following year both matches were played in the Republic, drawing 1-1 at Bray Wanderers then losing 1-0 at Waterford. In 2012, it was back to playing games on both sides of the border, as they took on Crusaders in Belfast and then Bray Wanderers.

Despite it just being a Reds XI taking part, such is the draw of Liverpool FC that to satisfy demand the match with Crusaders was played at Ravenhill, the 14,000 capacity home of the Ulster rugby club rather than Seaview which could hold only 3,000. In front of a full house the Reds ran out 3-1 winners thanks to goals from Suso, Adam Morgan and Nathan Eccleston. From Belfast Rodolfo Borrell's side moved on to County Wicklow where they played Bray Wanderers for the second year running. Whereas they had drawn the previous year there was no mistake this time as the Reds ran out 5-1 winners, Michael Ngoo hitting a hat-trick.

The crowd that had attended the Crusaders game was larger than had seen the Reds' first team squad play in Belfast in 2000, showing how eager the people of the city were to see a Liverpool side play there again. To further emphasise the Reds' popularity in Belfast as compared to other Premiership clubs, when Crusaders had been drawn against Fulham in the Europa League the previous year, they had not switched the home leg to a larger venue.

Liverpool's under-21 side were back in Belfast in 2013 playing friendlies against Glentoran and a full strength Heart of Midlothian side, winning both games 1-0. Given the popularity and loyalty shown by fans in Ireland in terms of crossing the Irish Sea to Anfield and turning out in vast numbers to watch junior sides, it remains to be seen if the club go back to sending full strength sides to play there again on an annual basis.

10

Mini-Tournaments

From the late 1970s, Liverpool's pre-season preparations took on a much more competitive edge when they started to appear in four-team tournaments, which on the whole involved games against other top teams and had a trophy awarded in the end. These tournaments, as well as being lucrative from a financial point of view, also gave a good opportunity to new players to test themselves in a competitive environment before the real action started. It meant that whereas any previous summer journeys to Spain would involve matches against lower division sides they would now involve games against much tougher opposition, while trips to Germany and Holland tended to be for a tournament in one place rather than a series of friendlies in different venues.

AMSTERDAM TOURNAMENT

The Amsterdam Tournament was first held in 1975, inaugurated as part of the city's 700th birthday celebrations. It went on to become an annual event, held either at Ajax's old De Meer Stadium or the Olympic Stadium until 1992. After a break of six years it returned in 1999, being played at the Amsterdam ArenA and during its history Liverpool have been invited to take part on three occasions.

The Reds first competed in 1977 after their first European Cup win. After kicking off their pre-season with a friendly against Hamburg SV Liverpool's players moved on to Amsterdam, where they faced the hosts in the semi-final on Friday 5th August. Ajax won the game 2-1, the Reds' goal being an own goal by René Notten. Two days later, Liverpool beat Barcelona in the third place play-off thanks to a David Johnson strike in the 17th minute. Barcelona, beaten 4-0 by AZ67 Alkmaar in their semi-final, showed such a lack of interest in this game that the crowd slow handclapped them in the second half and Bob Paisley expressed disappointment that it hadn't been as competitive as he'd have liked.

By the time Liverpool next appeared in the Amsterdam Tournament in 2001, Ajax were playing in the Amsterdam ArenA and instead of a knockout tournament, the winner was decided on a league basis although not all of the teams would play each other. As an extra incentive to encourage attacking play, additional points were now being awarded for goals scored.

As in 1977, Liverpool went to Amsterdam as holders of a European trophy, this time the UEFA Cup which had been won with a thrilling 5-4 extra time victory over Alaves in Dortmund the previous May.

The Reds were backed by 1,000 fans and in illustrious company, with five times European champions AC Milan and Valencia, losers of the last two Champions League finals, also in the tournament. On Friday 26th July Jari Litamen delighted his former club Ajax's fans with the only goal in a 1-0 win over Valencia, but two days later the Reds went down 3-1 to the hosts, meaning they finished in third place. With the Reds' first ever Champions League game, a qualifier against Finnish side Haka coming up the following Wednesday, these two games were perfect preparation for their bow in the competition.

Two years later Liverpool were back in Amsterdam competing alongside Ajax, Inter and Galatasaray in the 2003 tournament. On Friday 1st August the Reds drew 0-0 with Ajax but two days later a jaded side, who had returned to Liverpool from the Far East only to jet off straight for Amsterdam, lost 2-1 against Galatasaray to finish last in the tournament. The finishing position was the least of Liverpool's worries though, as they ended the game with nine men after Neil Mellor was sent off for a late challenge and Steven Gerrard for dissent. Luckily for them the referee did not forward a report regarding the sending offs to the Football Association and they were not banned for any league games. The Reds have not been back to Amsterdam since, with Manchester United and Arsenal being the Premiership's regular participants, although Sunderland did appear in 2009.

SCHALKE TOURNAMENT

In 1979 Schalke 04 marked their 75th anniversary with a four-team tournament at the Parkstadion in Gelsenkirchen. Liverpool were invited to take part, giving an opportunity for that summer's two new signings to impress.

Before taking part in the tournament the Reds first had a match against the familiar foes of Borussia Mönchengladbach, who they had beaten in the final and semi-finals of the European Cup in 1977 and 1978. Despite the short time span this still wasn't the first meeting since 1978, as earlier in 1979 Mönchengladbach had provided the opposition at Anfield for Emlyn Hughes's testimonial, beating the Reds 1-0.

There was some disturbing news on 1st August when the *Liverpool Echo* reported how there had been some trouble involving Liverpool fans in Mönchengladbach the night before, with eleven being arrested for causing damage and committing thefts. These included some of the most unsuccessful robbers to have ever followed the Reds abroad, with a group of five being thrown out of a shop by an ex boxer, then finding no money in a sex shop, before they finally thought they had struck lucky in a lottery shop, only to be scared off by a dog. Liverpool's chairman John Smith was quick to disassociate the club from those causing trouble, stressing that no official trips had been organised but also expressing 'regret that they are damaging the reputation of Liverpool.'

In the game Liverpool won 4-2 thanks to goals from Ray Kennedy, Terry McDermott, Graeme Souness and Kenny Dalglish. It was a fine performance by the Reds, with Mönchengladbach's manager Jupp Heynckes saying that his team had only been allowed to play for one minute. Striker Frank McGarvey, a £300,000 signing from St Mirren came off the bench for the last 25 minutes and played a part in the fourth goal. However Bob Paisley chose not to introduce the summer's other arrival, Israeli left back Avi Cohen who had a slight strain which may have been aggravated in the wet conditions. Both signings had generated significant interest, McGarvey due to his goalscoring prowess with a middling Scottish club and Cohen because he was Liverpool's first overseas player since the 1950s. Phil Rimmer was one of the fans who hadn't got caught up in any trouble although he does recall having a problem getting into the ground:

'We decided to go in at the cheapest turnstile as none of us could speak German. I was the last to enter the ground where I was stopped by an official, sort of bouncer, who was questioning the ticket. He kept poking me in the chest and pointing at my beard. I was getting annoyed, but eventually he let us through. On returning home I asked a friend to have a look at the ticket and it was a for a youth! At the time I was 27 with a beard! The other thing I remember about the game was number of drunken squaddies there as Mönchengladbach had a large Army base. They wore scarves from all over the UK, with most having difficulty standing up.'[35]

As they moved on to Gelsenkirchen for the tournament, Paisley stressed that both his new signings would have to serve their apprenticeships at Anfield and learn to play the Liverpool system. He told Michael Charters of the *Echo* on 3rd August:

'Don't expect too much too soon from either of them. They have to learn our style. They've been playing in very different set ups with their previous clubs and it will take them time to settle into the way we want them to play with the emphasis on teamwork. They've been big stars with their other clubs. Now they have to learn quickly that they are part of a team.'

In the opening game against Feyenoord the Reds got exactly the sort of test that they were looking for with the Dutch giants, who would knock Everton out of the UEFA Cup the following month, giving them a much more competitive game than Mönchengladbach had done. Liverpool twice took the lead but were pegged back and the game went to penalties after finishing as a 2-2 draw. The Reds won the shoot out 4-1, with Alan Kennedy demonstrating why he volunteered to take one five years later in Rome when he stepped forward to coolly convert his kick. Due to the hard fought nature of the game, neither McGarvey nor Cohen got any taste of the action with Paisley's only change being forced on him when David Johnson went off with a calf injury to be replaced by David Fairclough, whose position at the club was arguably most under threat by the Scot's arrival.

In the final the Reds faced Benfica, who had beaten hosts Schalke 1-0 in the other semi-final. They were again involved in an extremely competitive game with the score remaining level for over an hour. When Kenny Dalglish was forced off with an ankle strain, Paisley sprung a surprise when he left Frank McGarvey on the bench and sent on Avi Cohen instead. Cohen made an instant impact, setting up Alan Kennedy in the 73rd minute for the opening goal. Then 10minutes from time Benfica got a fortunate equaliser when Ray Clemence saved an Alhino shot but Phil Thompson couldn't get out of the way and the ball bounced off him into the net. Before full time Cohen almost capped a memorable first performance with a goal but his header bounced back off the bar. Extra time couldn't split the sides although Cohen, who didn't look out of place in an unfamiliar striking role, again went close.

Before heading to Germany Liverpool had only been involved in one penalty shoot out, against Leeds in the 1974 Charity Shield. Now they had faced two in three days but they couldn't return home with the trophy, as they went down 4-3 after it went to sudden death. Benfica keeper Bento, who had been so erratic when the sides met at Anfield in the European Cup quarter final of 1977-78, was this time in far better form and saved three of the Reds' kicks.

Phil Rimmer had continued on to Gelsenkirchen for the tournament and recalls there was some level of hostility between the German and Dutch supporters:

> 'Most nights the Dutch fans smashed a bar. On the final night my future wife and I were walking around the inside of the ground when we noticed we were being followed. The further we walked the more people were following. Eventually we came to a large fence and no escape. I said to her that we would have to turn and face them, and that I would see her back at the hotel or in hospital. As we turned the Germans realised we weren't Dutch and they just turned and walked away!'[36]

This 1979 trip to West Germany showed that even in pre-season Bob Paisley would not play new signings just for the sake of it, with McGarvey left on the bench for both games of the tournament and Cohen only given an opportunity as a result of an injury to a team-mate, and even then he was played out of position. This was one of the rare seasons when both new signings didn't really work out. Avi Cohen, who sadly died in a motorbike accident in his native Israel in 2010 aged 54, made just 24 appearances in the next two seasons. However he will forever be remembered by Reds fans for scoring an own goal then one at the right end against Aston Villa as Liverpool clinched the title in 1979-80. McGarvey never made a single competitive appearance for the Reds, but they still recouped his fee when he was sold to Celtic in March 1980. Both players had reasonably successful careers elsewhere, they just couldn't break into a settled Liverpool side that Bob Paisley had shown he wasn't even prepared to disrupt in pre-season.

1982 MARBELLA TOURNAMENT

The Reds spent many a summer week in the Spanish Costas during the 1960s and 1970s playing a low key friendly followed by a holiday but by the time the 1980s came around, any trips there were solely football-related. They played three tournaments in Spain during that decade although the first one very nearly turned out to be the last as the Reds found themselves subject to chaotic organisation leaving the latest new arrival wondering just what he had signed up for.

The Reds were in Switzerland, having just played a friendly against Servette Geneva, when David Hodgson signed on the dotted line on 11th August. Liverpool had paid relegated Middlesbrough £200,000 for him and he flew to the Costa del Sol to meet his new team-mates the following day. Bob Paisley though made it clear that Hodgson would not be going straight into the team and told the *Liverpool Echo* that his arrival was 'to maintain the pressure for places.' Liverpool's first game was supposed to take place on Friday 13th August against Real Betis but it turned out to be an unlucky day for them. The Reds' contract had stated that they would play on Friday and Sunday but when they were advised on the Friday morning that they were to play on the Saturday night Paisley was so enraged that he threatened to take the team home. With posters around the town advertising the game as taking place on Saturday the 14th and Betis not even there, it was quite apparent that the Reds had been taken for granted, leading to crisis meetings to try and save the tournament. It wasn't just what day the first game was to be played that was the problem, as they weren't provided with enough hotel beds, the catering was inadequate and training facilities weren't provided. Facing these problems in extreme heat didn't help the mood and Ian Hargraves, who was in Marbella reporting for the *Liverpool Echo,* wrote that evening:

'The whole situation seemed unreal. When Liverpool arrived last night in Marbella they found an official reception for the tournament was in full swing without representatives from any of the four teams. There was also a shortfall in the number of beds at the hotel, while catering arrangements for the team left a lot to be desired. But these were minor problems compared with what was to come. Liverpool officials discovered this morning that no arrangements had been made to provide the Reds with training facilities. A coach eventually arrived, almost by accident but enquiries to Malaga and a local football ground ended without success. Eventually a representative of the organisers was found but she turned out to be a young woman who had no knowledge of either football or sports grounds. By mid-morning manager Paisley and his coaches were in a state of simmering rage and frustration, not improved by the heat which was tremendous even at breakfast time.'

Although Paisley himself may have been fuming, the players weren't too bothered about being in such an environment with Graeme Souness recalling: 'The arrival of a group of fit, tanned young men caused quite a stir among the topless beauties around the resort and we did not complain either.'[37] If there weren't enough beds for all of the club's party, then there was no chance for the handful of fans who made the trip from Merseyside. Phil Rimmer arrived in Marbella by plane from Geneva but with no accommodation sorted. He recalls spending around five hours going around hotels only to be told they were all full, before a cleaner in one of them eventually offered him and his friend lodgings with her and her family.

Eventually, after much persuading, Liverpool agreed to play Betis on the Saturday night and Paisley did spring a surprise by pitching Hodgson straight into action. The decision was justified when he set up a goal for Kenny Dalglish and then scored himself in a 2-0 win. The final was the following night against Malaga, who had beaten Bayer Leverkusen in the other semi-final. The Reds found themselves involved in a bruising game against a side that had just won promotion to the top flight. Ian Rush and Craig Johnston were both subjected to a series of harsh tackles from the Malaga defenders and in his *Liverpool Echo* report Ian Hargraves described them as playing 'like a bull seeking vengeance on its persecutors in the local ring.' The referee gave the Reds players no protection and an indication of where his loyalties lay could be seen in the fact that Phil Neal, who wasn't booked at all in 1981-82, had his name taken in both games of this tournament.

The Reds fell behind after seven minutes but found an equaliser through Alan Kennedy in the 67th minute and were the better side for the rest of the game, with Hodgson having a shot well saved although they did miss the creativity of Dalglish, who was left out with a sore foot. The last thing they wanted though was 30 minutes of extra time and when this couldn't produce a goal it went to a penalty shootout. By the time the penalties started it was after 1am and many of the fans from a relatively small crowd had already left. Phil Rimmer remembers that the crowd was small anyway and many, himself included had gone onto the pitch to watch the shoot out from the centre circle. Hodgson saw his kick saved and after Howard Gayle blasted his over the bar Ray Clemence failed to save Astrorga's effort, which confirmed a 4-2 win for Malaga and led to triumphant celebrations on the pitch by the home supporters.

The following day the Reds flew home, still seething from the organisation as a whole and with Kenny Dalglish and Alan Hansen both doubtful for the forthcoming weekend's Charity Shield. The *Echo* reported that despite the considerable financial sum of £60,000 they had received for taking part, it was highly unlikely that they would agree to playing in Spain again. The only bright spot was the form of David Hodgson, who was selfless and hard working up front, linking in well with others. Despite this promise though, Hodgson would have a disappointing two years at Anfield and after a bright start that saw him score four goals in six games he was sold to Sunderland in 1984, his final tally being 10 from 49.

1983 LA LINEA

Despite Liverpool's threat not to play again in Spain, they were back again just a year later for a tournament at La Linea, situated on the Spanish side of the border with Gibraltar with the 23,000 capacity Municipal Stadium being just a goal kick away.

With Joe Fagan having taken over from Bob Paisley in the summer, this trip drew to a close his first pre-season preparations and was the second tournament they had taken part in that summer, having competed in the Feyenoord one a week earlier. Once again the Reds found themselves messed around by the organisers, who told them on arrival on Thursday 11th August that they would not be facing Cadiz the following day as initially expected, but a much sterner test against Atlético Madrid.

Just days before this tournament the Reds signed striker Michael Robinson from Brighton for £200,000 and he was flown straight out to join his new team-mates but another new signing, defender Gary Gillespie had to remain at home due to a knee injury. Due to a groin injury to Ian Rush that had caused the Welsh striker to miss all pre-season Robinson had an instant opportunity to impress in a game that kicked off at 10.30pm, an hour later than had originally been anticipated. The Reds again found themselves the victim of some extremely dubious refereeing with four players being booked, including David Hodgson for retaliation on a challenge that went unpunished. The most bizarre booking though was when Graeme Souness lost patience as the wall for a free kick didn't retreat 10 yards and he took it anyway. Liverpool lost 2-1 to a Hugo Sánchez-inspired Atlético side, with the Reds' goal coming 15 minutes from time from David Hodgson, whose place was most under threat by Robinson's arrival.

At least this time the Reds had a day's rest before the third place play-off on Sunday 14th August where they faced Romanians Dinamo Bucharest, who they would go on to face in the European Cup semi-final that season. However during their day off nearly half the side had managed to pick up food poisoning, with Phil Neal being the worst affected and having to leave the field after 36 minutes. In an entertaining game Robinson showed his worth with two goals, one from close range and the other a fierce shot after being set up by Graeme Souness. Dinamo were a good side though and hit back twice and extra time looked inevitable until Kenny Dalglish scored a last minute winner.

It had been a useful tournament from the playing side with Robinson demonstrating enough quality to show that a three pronged strike force of him, Rush and Dalglish would strike fear into opposition defences. The form of Steve Nicol, who had got a chance in midfield instead of Ronnie Whelan who was injured, was another positive and gave Fagan a selection poser ahead of the following week's Charity Shield against Manchester United. A sore point though was that the Reds picked up seven bookings across the two games, which they knew could be carried into the new season. That and the food poisoning outbreak meant that tournaments in Spanish holiday resorts would definitely be off the agenda from then on.

FEYENOORD AND PORT OF ROTTERDAM TOURNAMENT

The tournament hosted by Feyenoord has enjoyed nowhere near as much success as the one staged by their great rivals Ajax, with it lasting for just a few years in the 1980s and then being revived briefly two decades later.

Liverpool took part in 1983 when they finished in fourth place despite not losing a game in normal time. In the semi-final against European champions Hamburg SV on 5th August they drew 0-0 only to lose on penalties. Two days later they took on the hosts, who had been beaten by Standard Liège in their semi-final, in a third place play-off and drew 3-3 with Mark Lawrenson netting twice only to again lose on penalties.

In 2007 the tournament was revived as a one-off event called the Port of Rotterdam tournament to commemorate the 75th anniversary of the local port authority. Teams from port cities were invited and Liverpool were accompanied by Shanghai Shenhua and Porto. Having only returned from Hong Kong a few days earlier, the Reds side that took on Shanghai Shenhua on Friday 3rd August had a junior feel to it, with David Martin playing in goal and other youngsters such as Argentinians Gabriel Paletta and Sebastián Leto being given a run out. However new record signing Fernando Torres did start and he gave the Reds a 13th minute lead, with substitute Steven Gerrard scoring the second goal of the 2-0 win in the 64th minute.

The big game of the tournament was on the Sunday, when the Reds took on Feyenoord. Liverpool had been beaten Champions League finalists the previous May so were a big draw, while the match had added interest for the home fans as it was the first occasion on which Dirk Kuyt had returned to face his old club since leaving there for Anfield a year earlier. The Dutch striker said of facing the club where he had played for three seasons: 'It's going to be a brilliant experience. That game is the big one in the tournament. I hope it'll be a great night and a great feast of football. It would be brilliant if a lot of fans came.' Kuyt was not to be disappointed by the attendance, which neared capacity and he was given a great reception by the fans, although the same could not be said for Liverpool's new signing Ryan Babel, previously of Feyenoord's fierce rivals Ajax.

There was no sentiment from Kuyt and he hit the bar in the first half with a long range effort. However Feyenoord looked to be on course for victory only for a late Steven Gerrard strike to earn the Reds a 1-1 draw, a result which meant Porto were the tournament champions on goal difference. There has only been one Feyenoord tournament since, held to celebrate the centenary of the club in 2008 and in which the three clubs they had played in European finals – Borussia Dortmund, Celtic and Tottenham Hotspur, were invited to compete.

PHILIPS CUP

The Philips Cup was hosted in the 1980s by Swiss side Young Boys Berne, with the home side being joined by another Swiss club as well as two foreign sides. Despite strong competition from the likes of Stuttgart and Napoli, Young Boys won the 1981 and 1982 tournaments, before Brazilians Atlético Mineiro triumphed in 1983. They were back to defend their title in 1984, when Young Boys and Swiss compatriots Grasshoppers were joined by Liverpool.

The Reds trip to Switzerland was demoted to second place in the local press, which was devoting a lot of coverage to the Olympics in Los Angeles as some of the main British medal hopes were competing over those days. Whilst the Reds were preparing for the new season Daley Thompson was winning gold in the decathlon for the second Olympics running and distance runner Zola Budd, running bare footed, caused controversy when she was alleged to have tripped American crowd favourite Mary Decker-Slaney in the 3,000m.

What the press did report of the Reds though was of much interest to Liverpool fans, keen to see how their team could cope without influential captain Graeme Souness who had left for Sampdoria after the Reds' fourth European Cup win in May. This tournament would give an interesting glimpse of what manager Joe Fagan would do, as so far no obvious replacement had been signed. They were into their pre-season stride and had already enjoyed a 1-0 win over Borussia Dortmund and 6-0 hammering of Belgian side Charleroi. In those games John Wark had played in central midfield, partnered by Kenny Dalglish on one occasion and Michael Robinson in the other but Ian Hargraves wrote in the *Liverpool Echo* on 8th August that such a partnership may not stand up too well under pressure.

A tough test in this tournament was predicted by Hargraves as Swiss football had steadily improved in recent years and the previous evening Grasshoppers had beaten Mineiro in the opening game of the tournament. Joe Fagan was forced into a change for the first game against Young Boys when Wark suffered a muscle spasm in training, meaning Steve Nicol came in to the side. The young Scot provided Fagan with further food for thought as he put in a strong display as the Reds won 1-0 thanks to a goal from Alan Kennedy. Liverpool missed a host of chances too and were almost made to pay the price at the end but Bruce Grobbelaar, playing his first game of pre-season after missing the first two to attend the birth of his daughter, dived at the feet of Mongi Ben Brahim. It had been a hard game for the Reds, played on a saturated pitch against a much fitter side who had already started their domestic campaign.

On 10th August, the date of the final against Grasshoppers, the *Liverpool Echo* reported that Wark was still unavailable due to his muscle spasm and that Nicol had another chance to stake his claim in central midfield. Wark though made a late recovery for this game and was able to play, but Fagan surprised everybody by leaving Dalglish out of the side and playing Nicol alongside Wark. They put in an outstanding display that allowed Liverpool to totally dominate the game, which the Reds won 1-0 thanks to a goal from Wark in the 72nd minute.

Hargraves wrote in the *Echo* the next evening that Liverpool 'would take an awful lot of beating in the months ahead', while the paper also reported that the Reds had agreed a deal that day to sign Danish midfielder Jan Mølby for £200,000 from Ajax. He would go on to become a popular figure at Anfield after but he did not feature too much in 1984-85 when the Reds fell below the extremely high standards they normally set, losing out to Everton in the title race. That was followed by the horror of Heysel, something that would have implications on where the Reds would play in pre-season in future.

1988 LA CORUÑA TOURNAMENT

When Liverpool returned to Spain for their first tournament there in five years they did so to a completely different part of the country than previously and without any major new signings. However a few days after returning home they would rock the football world when a new arrival was announced, the fine details of which had been ironed out while the Reds were in Spain.

The tournament in La Coruña, which took place over the weekend of 12th-14th August, involved Atlético Madrid, Real Sociedad, Liverpool and European champions PSV Eindhoven. This meant that potentially Liverpool's highest profile match on the Continent since Heysel was a possibility if they met PSV in the final. Football Association officials were determined to minimise the threat of any disorder that may cause further harm, given all other English teams were still banned as well and violence by England fans at that summer's European Championships had not done them any favours. As such Liverpool's participation was only sanctioned on the basis it was not at a resort popular with British holidaymakers and that they didn't publicise it in the preceding weeks.

After the all-conquering 1978-88 season it was difficult to see where the Reds could strengthen that summer and with the new season just two weeks away, the only new arrival so far was defender Nicky Tanner, who had arrived from Bristol Rovers for £20,000 and was one for the future. John Aldridge, who got 29 goals in 1987-88 but was devastated to miss a penalty as the Reds lost the FA Cup final to Wimbledon, was determined to start banging the goals in to make amends and had got six in three games already in the pre-season games that were played in Norway beforehand. This tournament was a big step up in class though, with semi-final opponents Atlético Madrid seeking to challenge city neighbours Real, having been taken over by the charismatic Jesus Gil the year before.

Liverpool had been out of Europe three years and although they were almost invincible in the English league, Atlético taught them a sharp lesson as to what they could expect when they eventually returned to European competition. Paulo Futre, who had signed for a then massive £2.5 million from Porto a year earlier, scored twice as the Reds were hammered 5-1, the first time they had been beaten by that scoreline since 1976-77. Even more worrying was a twisted knee sustained by Alan Hansen, which was guaranteed to rule him out for the start of the season but would ultimately keep him sidelined for seven months.

In the third place play-off Liverpool showed more of the form they were capable of, convincingly beating Sociedad, managed by ex Reds striker John Toshack, 4-0 in game in which all the goals came after half-time. Midfielder Jan Mølby partnered Gary Gillespie in defence and Nicky Tanner was given a run out at left back, with Steve Nicol moving into midfield so that John Barnes could join Aldridge in attack. Gillespie told Ken Rogers of the *Liverpool Echo* that the players were determined to put on a good show after what he termed as a 'drubbing' by Atlético: 'Hopefully we went out last night and showed what we can really do. It was a little bit like the old Liverpool, obviously things didn't go too well for us in the first game but we had done a lot of travelling after our trip to Norway.' Gillespie also revealed that Hansen was in their thoughts as they awaited news on the seriousness of his injury and that despite their captain's consistency over recent seasons, Mølby was able to come in and do a good job.

The Reds returned home on the Monday to prepare for the following Saturday's Charity Shield with Wimbledon. There was then a sensation on the Thursday 18th August when a press conference was called and the arrival of Ian Rush was announced, which stunned those present as they had been expecting a defender to sign given Hansen's injury. In that night's *Echo* Ken Rogers called it 'the biggest transfer coup in the history of the game', while the following day Ian Hargraves described it as a 'cloak and dagger deal', which chairman John Smith had said was concluded in just a few hours over the telephone.

Rush told the *Echo* that he had become aware that Juventus would be prepared to let him return to Liverpool the previous Saturday, the day the Reds had no game in Spain. Once Rush had received that call, it was inevitable a deal would be concluded and the player most affected by Rush's return was John Aldridge, who later recalled that many of the club's officials were 'drunk and looking happy with life'[38] after the win against Real Sociedad. Kenny Dalglish recalls of the deal:

> 'We were off on a pre-season tournament in La Coruña when the call came through from the Italians. We were actually at lunch with the press lads when the phone rang for Peter. After lunch, Peter told me that we could have Rushie back. The journalists never knew what was going on; the phone was always ringing for Peter wherever he went. The deal was done very quietly.'[39]

Aldridge and Rush remained at Liverpool together for a season but early in 1989-90 Aldridge was ironically off to Real Sociedad, who paid over £1 million to take him over to the Basque country. He was then back at Anfield a year later with his new team-mates as they provided the opposition for Kenny Dalglish's testimonial.

TOURNOI DE PARIS

The Tournoi de Paris (Tournament of Paris) started in 1957 and was played at the Parc de Princes, involving a leading local club as well as three guests. Until 1967 that local club was usually Racing Paris, but from 1973 when the tournament was re-established after a break of five years the hosts became Paris Saint Germain (PSG), formed out of a merger of Stade Saint Germain and Paris FC in 1970.

Liverpool's only invitation to appear came in 1992, when the Reds returned to the Parc de Princes for the first time since their 1981 European Cup triumph. It was held over the weekend of 26th/27th July and the first time the Reds had been in pre-season action that summer, meaning new keeper David James was set to make his debut. The return to European competition meant a change in Liverpool's transfer policy, as UEFA rules at that time only allowed four foreign players in each team. It led to James being an ideal candidate to bring in with Zimbabwean Bruce Grobbelaar nearing the end of his career. Another arrival was imminent too, with the finishing touches being made to complete the signature of Tottenham's English midfielder Paul Stewart as the Reds set off for Paris. On his way out of Anfield was Irish international Ray Houghton who signed that weekend for Aston Villa, one of several players whose leaving of the Reds was down to the UEFA rules.

Liverpool's preparations that summer were different than normal, with Graeme Souness taking the players to Italy for a week's training camp, where every aspect of the players' diet and rest could be monitored. Souness believed it was good for morale too, telling the *Liverpool Echo* on 25th July that 'the togetherness was important, I don't feel that was there last year.'

With two games to play in two days, Souness utilised his squad fully, giving both keepers a chance to impress so Grobbelaar retained his place for the semi-final against Monaco, which was lost 2-1. An unfamiliar back four which saw David Burrows play in central defence and Steve Nicol at left back struggled to cope with the pace of Youri Djorkaeff and Monaco, potential opponents in the forthcoming European Cup Winners Cup campaign, could have won by more.

The following day James made his debut against Borussia Dortmund, who had only lost out on the German title on goal difference the previous season. The Reds again went down, this time 3-2 with James having a mixed debut, making some good saves but also letting a shot from Stéphane Chapuisat through his hands. Grobelaar warned afterwards that he wouldn't be giving up his position as the Reds number one so easily, saying: 'I've just got to play to the best of my ability and then it's up to the management. David is very confident and he is providing a very good challenge for me.'[40] As it was James would begin the new season in goal but Grobbelaar did get his chances again too before leaving the club for Southampton in 2004. Despite the two defeats Souness wasn't too concerned, given that Monaco and Dortmund were more advanced with their training than the Reds were meaning they had an extra yard of pace.

The proceeds from this tournament were donated to the victims of the Bastia stadium disaster that occurred in May that year, when 18 people were killed and over 2,000 injured as a temporary stand collapsed prior to a French Cup semi-final between Bastia and Marseille. This turned out to be the penultimate Tournoi de Paris as after the next year it was dropped due to PSG's financial deficit, although it was held as a one-off in 2010 to celebrate their 40th anniversary.

MÖNCHENGLADBACH TROPHY

In 1995 Borussia Mönchengladbach hosted a four-team tournament that gave Roy Evans' exciting new Liverpool side a chance to pit their wits against the very best in Europe. However things didn't exactly go as hoped from a playing point of view although for fans it was the start of a good friendship.

In Evans' first full season in charge the Reds had won the League Cup and finished fourth in the Premiership, meaning a return to European competition after an absence of two seasons. Liverpool issued a statement of intent in the summer when they broke the British transfer record to sign Stan Collymore from Nottingham Forest for £8.5 million and with Robbie Fowler and Steve McManaman continuing to impress, big things were expected in the forthcoming season.

On Wednesday 26th July Collymore made a low key debut at Birmingham in a game that Liverpool won 1-0, but three days later they faced a much sterner test against European champions Ajax in Mönchengladbach. Evans was forced to make some changes to his side due to injuries to Phil Babb, John Barnes and Rob Jones who had all been ruled out against Birmingham, as well as Ian Rush who also picked up a knock in that game. It meant that Neil Ruddock skippered the side for the tournament, which would be watched by England boss Terry Venables as he considered a number of Reds players in his plans for a series of friendlies in the countdown to Euro 96.

Things could not have got off to a worse start for the Reds, who found themselves a goal down from Patrick Kluivert after just 16 seconds and went on to lose 5-0 with sloppy defending being partly to blame. The only consolation that could be sought was that some of the players who featured, such as Nigel Clough, Jan Mølby, Michael Thomas and Mark Walters were not part of Evans' plans for the future, while Robbie Fowler never gave up and went close on three occasions including hitting the bar with one shot. Afterwards a shellshocked Evans admitted that his players had been to school and that Ajax were a side they needed to aspire to:

'Ajax must be the yardstick for us all. I don't think I've ever seen a team dominate Liverpool the way they did in all my time at the club. Although the scoreline looks bad I wasn't too disappointed by our performance as a whole. This match will have been beneficial providing we all learn from it, including myself. We are capable of being a good team, we are striving to be like Ajax because we have already been at that level. But everyone needs to pull together and work very hard.'

Evans' last sentence was probably a hallmark of the mid to late 1990s at Liverpool, as a talented team on so many occasions went on to fail at the final hurdle. In the forthcoming 1995-96 season they lost a dire FA Cup final 1-0 to Manchester United, the players being remembered for their white suits more than anything. Then in 1996-97 they finished fourth after being in the top two for most of the season. After the Ajax drubbing, the Reds regained some pride the following day when Stan Collymore opened his Reds account with the equalising goal in a 1-1 with Fiorentina. Collymore's goal, which came shortly after a streaker had run onto the pitch to greet him and kick a plastic ball into the crowd, brought a large cheer from both the Reds contingent and the Mönchengladbach fans who had got there early prior to their final with Ajax. In the penalty shootout Liverpool won 3-2 with keeper David James the hero, making two saves and scoring the decisive kick himself. In the *Liverpool Echo* Reds correspondent Ric George wrote that despite the result against Ajax, the tournament had been a useful exercise for the Reds and had taught them more than playing lower division Swedish sides, as they often had before, could have done.

Although the first result had been a shock, the tournament did help seal a long running friendship that now exists between Liverpool and Borussia Mönchengladbach fans. In the aftermath of Hillsborough Mönchengladbach fans had raised around £7,000 for the disaster fund, which was presented to Hillsborough Family Support Group chairman Trevor Hicks and former Reds defender Ron Yeats in 1991. The following year 100 of their fans visited Anfield to attend a match and pay their respects at the Memorial. A further visit followed in 1994 and the tournament gave them the chance to show some hospitality to Liverpool fans in return. Several hundred Reds fans made the trip and since then Mönchengladbach fans have made an annual visit to Anfield, while Liverpool supporters have visited games in Germany every year since 2007. Mönchengladbach's Borussia Park, where they have played since 2004, even has a 'Liverpool suite.'

REAL MADRID CENTENARY TOURNAMENT 2002

By far the most prestigious pre-season tournament Liverpool have played in was in 2002, when they were invited to take part in a four-team event that marked the centenary of the club who had won the European Cup more times than any other.

Despite the remarkable history of Liverpool and Real, they had amazingly only ever met once in European competition at this time, in the 1981 final at Paris. The only other meeting between the two clubs had been in August 1989, when the Reds were invited to be the opposition for Real's annual Trofeo Santiago Bernabéu game, a one-off match played in pre-season. Liverpool lost that game 2-0, but had still fared better than Everton two years earlier, the Blues having been thrashed 6-1.

For this centenary tournament the Reds were invited along with AC Milan and Bayern Munich, meaning the four participants could muster 22 European Cups between them at that time. Despite the glamour of the tournament and some tickets costing as little as €8 (about £5), the stadium was barely a quarter full as Liverpool went down 2-0 in the semi-final on Friday 2nd August. The Reds, who had reached the quarter finals of the Champions League the previous season, in which Real won the competition, rarely threatened and five half-time substitutions didn't help the flow of their game. Both Michael Owen and Steven Gerrard were missing due to injury and afterwards manager Gérard Houllier said tiredness had played a part, with Liverpool having been training hard in the preceding week and also playing two other friendlies.

The Reds received sad news from home that day too, when it was announced that Bill Shankly's widow Nessie had died of a heart attack at the age of 82. Houllier's assistant Phil Thompson said of her: 'Bill Shankly was the person who gave me my big break in football, and I knew Nessie for many years. She was a wonderful woman who stood behind Bill throughout the fantastic period of success he brought to Anfield. It's a sad day for everyone associated with the club.'[41]

Back on the pitch, the Reds faced AC Milan in the third place play-off and restored some pride with a 2-1 victory in a game that also saw a number of substitutions, this time seven in all. With temperatures in the 30s though that can hardly be surprising and there were further boosts in this game due to Steven Gerrard recovering from injury to play and Czech striker Milan Baroš getting a goal. After this Bayern Munich spoilt the party by beating Real 2-1, leaving Liverpool to return home to get ready for the following Sunday's Charity Shield against Arsenal, the Reds having been invited to compete as Premiership runners up as the Gunners had won the Double.

11

Great Sheikhs

In the 1970s and 1980s Liverpool had enormous global appeal, yet the financial state of the British game was not in great shape meaning they were willing to play one-off friendlies around the world for a lucrative fee. With Arab countries keen to develop football and money being no object to them Liverpool played there a number of times, including in mid-season when the extensive travelling involved had to be offset against the amount of money that could be earned.

1978 DUBAI

Liverpool's first visit to the Middle East came in May 1978, when they travelled to play AL Nasr two weeks after they won their second European Cup by beating FC Bruges 1-0 at Wembley.

Al Nasr had just won their first United Arab Emirates league title and were managed by Pat Saward, who had formerly been in charge of Brighton and the Republic of Ireland. The Reds visited Dubai at the request of Sheikh Mana, a Liverpool supporting member of the ruling Al Maktoum family who had been educated in England.

The Liverpool party were accompanied by Michael Charters who covered the trip on behalf of both the *Daily Post* and *Liverpool Echo*. A delay at Heathrow meant it was nearly midnight when they arrived and Sheikh Mana was at the steps of the plane to greet every player personally.

The following morning the players left their air conditioned hotel to find temperatures had already hit the 90s. With the game to be played that evening on a synthetic pitch at the Al Wasl Stadium, Bob Paisley put them through a light training session so they could get used to the bounce of the ball. The Reds boss had readily agreed to Saward's request for the Al Nasr side to make up to eight substitutions, to allow all of his squad to have a chance of facing the Reds. Paisley himself had only taken 13 players with him, but did say he may make rolling substitutions if the heat became too much.

In the *Echo* on the evening of the game Charters quoted Paisley as saying: 'This is an important game for the local team and we as European champions are looking on it to put on an exhibition type of performance.' Charters also made it clear in his report that the players intended taking it seriously:

> 'Although the match is meaningless to them, they are very conscious of
> the fact it means a great deal to the locals to see the famous Liverpool in
> action for the first time in this incredible land of the United Arab Emirates,
> probably the fastest growing country in the world where riches of oil have
> turned desert into a luxury.'

The game was a major event and beforehand the Royal Dubai Rifles
marched around the pitch playing the bagpipes then hundreds of pigeons,
their wings painted red and blue in the colours of the two teams, were
released from sacks by a man riding a camel. The European Cup was also
shown to the crowd but the crowning moment was just before kick off,
when a parachutist jumped out of a helicopter and delivered the match
ball to the centre circle.

The only empty seats in the 12,000 capacity stadium were around the
VIP area, where Dubai's ruler Sheikh Rashid was surrounded by 20 gun-
toting bodyguards. Against a team that Charters felt would struggle in the
English non league, Liverpool dominated and had no problems with the
surface. They cruised to a 5-0 victory, with Ray Kennedy and Colin Irwin
both scoring twice and Alan Hansen netting the other. By the end of the
game the players had perspired so much that their red strips were virtually
all black, with the temperature still around 80 degrees even after the sun
had gone down. Despite the unfamiliar surroundings, the Reds were made
to feel at home as much as possible by 200 ex-pats, who sang a number of
Kop songs. The only downside was an ankle injury to David Fairclough,
which prevented him from joining up with an England B party that was
touring Malaysia and New Zealand.

Liverpool were given an open invitation to return to Dubai and they did
two years later at the end of the 1979-80 season, again playing Al Nasr
although it was given nowhere near as much coverage as the first trip. This
time the temperatures were even higher, the *Liverpool Echo* reporting that
they had been around 110 degrees. The Reds still strolled to an 8-0 win,
David Fairclough getting a hat-trick. The game was the second of a two
game mini-tour, the other of which had taken place three days earlier in
Bahrain, where the Reds had beaten a national XI 2-1.

1978 SAUDI ARABIA

Liverpool's only visit to Saudi Arabia was in October 1978 when they
faced a national side in Jeddah, a match arranged as part of the ongoing
development of football in the desert kingdom.

Former player and television pundit Jimmy Hill, who had been appointed
the country's London based Football Supremo in 1976, organised the

match. This was a job which saw him advise Prince Faisal, who had devoted £25 million over five years for the development of the game, on coaching appointments and administration.

After playing Bolton at Anfield on 30th September the Reds flew from London to Jeddah the next day, in readiness for the match that was to take place on the evening of Monday 2nd October. With no journalists accompanying them, the game was given very little coverage in the Merseyside press. The *Echo* and *Daily Post* each gave only four short paragraphs to the report on the game, which ended in a 1-1 draw. Kenny Dalglish opened the scoring for the Reds in the 56th minute with a fortunate goal that came after the keeper's clearance struck him in the back and he turned quickly to hammer the ball into the net. Midway through the second half Yusuf Handan equalised with a splendid solo effort that saw him skip through the Liverpool defence and chip the ball over the advancing Ray Clemence. It was the first time that Saudia Arabia had failed to win one of the prestige friendlies that Hill had set up, as they had previously beaten Arsenal, Benfica and Coventry.

The Reds spent the whole of the next day travelling back to Liverpool then had to prepare for the long trek to Norwich the following Saturday. With the riches that the Premiership has now brought to English football, it's hard to see them or any other club ever again undertaking a midweek inter-continental venture sandwiched between two weekend games.

MOROCCO 1983

The only time Liverpool have been to one of the Arab countries of North Africa was in the pre-season of 1983, when they played a friendly against WAC Casablanca in a game staged to mark completion of renovations to the national stadium.

The Stade Mohamed V, renamed from the Stade D'Honneur, was refurbished for that year's Mediterranean Games, with its seating capacity more than doubled to 80,000. The Moroccan government had wanted a high profile side to play in the inaugural game there and arranged for the ambassador in Britain to approach the Reds, telling them that they could play the game at any date that suited. With the Reds due to begin a pre-season tournament a short plane hop away in southern Spain on 12th August, it was arranged for them to play in Morocco two days earlier.

WAC, short for Wydad Athletic Club, were one of the strongest sides in the country but would be without their keeper Zaidi, who was being held back on FA orders due to Morocco having a crucial African Nations Cup qualifier a few days later. The match also gave an opportunity for Labri Abadane, who had played for the club for 15 years, to say a final farewell to the crowd after announcing his retirement at the end of the previous season.

Michael Robinson made his first appearance for the Reds in what was a one-sided game, WAC having failed to finalise arrangements to have some high profile guest players. Steve Nicol gave the Reds a first half lead and Robinson then got a debut goal in the 56th minute. The only surprise was that they only added one more, through Graeme Souness with 15 minutes to go.

Due to the excessive heat the match kicked off after 10pm, which may have limited the crowd to 30,000 instead of the anticipated 50-60,000. Those that turned out though applauded the Reds on many occasions and were provided with some bizarre incidents, with a youngster circling the touchline performing ball juggling skills during the game, and Abadane insisting all his team-mates join him on a lap of honour before he was substituted.

During this trip Moroccan football officials took the opportunity to offer Bob Paisley, who had retired at the end of the previous season but was accompanying the side as a director, a role as an advisor to the national team. This was one of several he was offered and in the *Liverpool Echo* Ian Hargraves speculated that he may be interested as it was not a full time commitment, but in the end he turned it down.

DUBAI SUPER CUP 1986 AND 1989

As part of the ongoing development of football in the United Arab Emirates in the 1980s and to showcase itself to the western world, the Dubai Super Cup was devised to be played for as a one-off match between the champions of England and Scotland. The lack of European competition due to the Heysel ban meant that the extra income was welcome to the English entrants, with Liverpool taking part twice.

When it came to these games, the question of how much prize money should be made available to the players was sure to come up. In 1983 Liverpool had played in Hong Kong at the end of the season and the sponsors gave the money to the team, whereas club officials had expected to receive it themselves. By now though there were clear measures being put in place so everybody knew where they stood, but also so the incentives were there to take the game seriously, as Alan Hansen explained:

'Liverpool were always looking for ways to maintain and strengthen this camaraderie. Even the board appreciated its importance. One of my responsibilities as captain under Kenny Dalglish was to negotiate with the chairman and secretary over the team bonuses for exhibition matches or competitions such as the British Championship game – involving the winners of the English and Scottish titles in Dubai. I would always use the line "there is a great spirit in the camp and you don't want to undermine it by causing players to feel they have been short changed financially." While the chairman and secretary did not allow this to cloud their financial judgement, they were possibly more sympathetic to the argument than some of their counterparts at other clubs.'[42]

The first Dubai Super Cup was played on 9th December 1986 between Liverpool and Celtic in the Al Wasl Stadium before a crowd of 15,000 who were cheering for both sides. Owen Archdeacon gave Celtic the lead early in the second half but Alan Hansen equalised two minutes from the end, leading to a penalty shootout. The Reds won this 4-2, Bruce Grobbelaar saving from Archdeacon and Maurice Johnston hitting the post.

The following year Everton and Rangers had won the respective titles and their match ended in a 2-2 draw, Rangers winning 8-7 on penalties. That match drew a crowd of just 8,000, demonstrating the appeal of Liverpool and Celtic, who were back again on 4th April 1989 and watched by 12,000 fans. The Liverpool and Celtic squads had flown out together from Gatwick Airport on Sunday 2nd April but although it was seen as a welcome diversion from the chase for honours, Dalglish still put the players through a hard training session in the heat the following morning. The competition had now been rebranded the Dubai Champions Cup and for the third year running it went to penalties after John Aldridge had cancelled out Mark McGhee's first half strike in the 76th minute. This time Celtic were 4-2 winners, Steve Staunton hitting the post and Steve McMahon having his kick saved.

The meeting of the 1988 champions was the last time the Dubai competition was played and the trophy is still on display at the Celtic museum.

12

Building Bridges and Confidence

The Heysel Stadium disaster of 1985 changed Liverpool FC's standing in football. After 21 years of unbroken European competition and excellent fan behaviour, the club's reputation was destroyed. Some 39 people were killed following a charge by Liverpool fans at the stadium in Brussels prior to the European Cup final between the Reds and Juventus. UEFA had deemed the crumbling venue fit for such a prestigious game despite serious misgivings by Reds secretary Peter Robinson.

The Government and Football Association immediately withdrew all English teams from European competition, while FIFA imposed a worldwide ban on all English teams playing friendlies abroad, including within other countries of the British Isles. This was later formalised into an indefinite ban on English teams competing in UEFA competitions, with Liverpool to serve an extra three years whenever it was to be lifted. The ban meant that prior to the 1985-86 season all of Liverpool's pre-season games were played against lower division opposition, but within a year things had relaxed and friendlies abroad were allowed, subject to FA approval and strict conditions regarding ticket sales and minimal publicity. This meant Liverpool's pre-season approach changed from before the ban, as tours were arranged in places that were difficult to access for fans.

Under the management of Kenny Dalglish games were arranged against low key opposition that should be quite easy to beat and give the players a chance to build confidence going into the new season. This approach saw the Reds tour Scandinavia eight years running, with Graeme Souness continuing with Dalglish's methods even after the they were readmitted back into Europe for the 1991-92 season. Liverpool didn't restrict themselves to Scandinavia though in their preparations. As they slowly got accepted back into the European fold, their domestic dominance meant that they remained attractive opposition and they were invited to play a number of big name teams in friendlies and take part in tournaments, although the FA at times did disrupt the Reds in this.

SCANDINAVIA 1986

Liverpool's first venture on foreign soil since Heysel saw them undertake a four-game tour of Denmark and Sweden before moving on to West

Germany for a friendly against Hamburg SV. It was a tour that saw them make a number of friends on the way and also come up against an old foe.

The Reds had won the Double in 1985-86 and made just one signing during the close season, 21-year-old defender Barry Venison arriving from Sunderland for a £200,000 fee. There was also a new member of the backroom team as Dalglish continued to stamp his own authority on the club. Phil Thompson, who had left the club for Sheffield United the previous year but failed to settle there, was now back at Anfield where he replaced Chris Lawler as reserve team manager.

When it came to players leaving, the Reds had been unable to resist a £3.2 million bid from Juventus for Ian Rush, who was offered a contract that dwarfed what he earned at Anfield and also gave him the opportunity to play European football again. However due to foreign player quotas in Italy, the Welsh striker was to be loaned back to the Reds for the 1986-87 season so Dalglish had time on his side when it came to lining up the right replacement. The publication of the club's annual report on 28th July emphasised just how damaging the European ban was to the Reds. Despite their most successful domestic season ever, they had made an operating loss of £202,567 during 1985-86 as gross revenue fell by 10%.

After a civic dinner at the Town Hall on the evening of 28th July, the Reds' 16-man squad flew to Copenhagen the following day. A surprise inclusion was reserve forward John Durnin, who began the previous season playing for Waterloo Dock in the Liverpool County Combination and after joining the Reds in March scored eight goals from 11 Central League appearances. He got his chance due to Paul Walsh suffering ankle ligament damage and another striker looking to prove himself was John Wark, who had been leading scorer in 1984-85 but missed most of the Double season through injury. Under the headline THE NIGHTMARE ENDS the *Daily Post* wrote on 30th July that Liverpool's 'worldwide reputation for sportsmanship had been unceremoniously dragged through the mud' by 'mindess morons'. They also said that this tour was 'distinctly low key' and that the 'fever pitch atmosphere that they had become accustomed to' would be missing.

The first game back was to be played 33 miles from Copenhagen at Holbæk and was arranged as part of the town's 750th anniversary. The Reds' opponents would be a select side made up of players from the Brøndby and Lyngby clubs, who had won the Danish league and cup respectively the previous season. The Denmark national side had come on leaps and bounds in recent years and surprised everybody during that summer's World Cup, winning all three of their group games against West Germany, Uruguay and Scotland before losing to Spain in the knockout stage. Only seven of their 22-man squad played at home, but Liverpool's Danish midfielder Jan Mølby believed that the game would still be tough for the Reds, warning beforehand: 'These sides are halfway through their domestic season whereas we are only just warming up. Little is known of their club football. That doesn't mean to say there isn't talent because there is and I am sure they will prove that against us.'

On arrival at the ground Liverpool did all they could to endear themselves to the locals, nothing being too much trouble as players signed autographs and posed for photographs while plenty of souvenirs were handed out. The Reds suffered an injury blow though when John Wark was forced to pull out of the game with a knee problem that occurred in training beforehand. The far fitter home side opened the scoring after just four minutes and when the Reds got going they came up against a stubborn defence. Eventually in the 77th minute Kevin MacDonald equalised after accepting an Ian Rush pass.

The following day a frustrated Wark flew home for further treatment at Anfield as his team-mates moved on to Sweden. Their first game there was on 1st August against Third Division IS Halmia at the Örjans Vall ground, which they shared with Halmstad BK. Allan Simonsen, who had scored against the Reds for Borussia Mönchengladbach in the 1977 European Cup final guested for Halmia but he was unable to prevent a 3-0 defeat for the home side. Kenny Dalglish showed no sign of age as he inspired the Reds side, having an involvement in just about every attacking move they undertook but he couldn't find the net himself, the goals instead coming from Craig Johnston, Ronnie Whelan and Kevin MacDonald.

After the Halmia match the players attended a VIP function organised by the local branch of Pilkington Glass, who had sponsored the game. The £350-a-head event attracted leading local industrialists and national celebrities and ended with the players on stage singing their FA Cup final song followed by *You'll Never Walk Alone*. It was a great way of letting the players unwind, with the tour now fulfilling its dual aims of getting the players fit and building links with the Europeans again.

The Liverpool party then ventured north to Örebro for a game against a Swedish Select XI on 4th August, which was billed as the biggest game in the town since France had played Scotland there in the 1958 World Cup. The Reds players were individually announced on to the pitch, with Kenny Dalglish and Ian Rush getting the biggest cheers from the 10,000 crowd. Rush didn't disappoint by getting his first goal of the tour and Jan Mølby struck two penalties as the Reds won 3-1. There were some arguments with officials in the second half though when the home side made six substitutions, but Dalglish's protests were ignored by the referee. Back at home, none of the games were being shown on television or had radio commentary, as was the norm for friendlies at the time. The local press were giving the tour plenty of coverage although by now the big story from

Channel 4's Merseyside based soap *Brookside* was filling the pages too, as on 5th August it was to be finally revealed who had raped Sheila Grant.

It was then back to Denmark for the last game in Scandinavia, against Jan Mølby's home town club Kolding on 6th August. Mølby had joined them aged just six but left for Ajax in Holland when he was 18. Despite having left at such a young age there was great pride in Mølby from both the club and town's inhabitants and earlier that summer he had been granted civic recognition when he was named Citizen of the Year. Kolding were a First Division club when Mølby joined Ajax in 1982 but they were now struggling at the bottom of the Second Division and gates had dropped to 400 at their Mosevej Sportsplads ground.

The fixture against the Reds meant they were financially secure for another season and Mølby was extremely proud to be returning for a game where he would face his cousin Johnny. The *Daily Post* reported on the morning of the game that he had said: 'This is a very special occasion for me, I have always kept in touch with the team. It's lovely to come back and it was emotional just to drive through the town yesterday with the Liverpool team.'

There was one slip up by the Danish organisers of the game when Liverpool were booked into a blue and white painted hotel. It looked like the Reds would seek vengeance when Steve McMahon gave them a third minute lead, but the rest of the game was played at a relatively low pace and it ended up as a 1-1 draw. After patiently awaiting his chance during the tour and then helping carrying the kit skip from the team coach, John Durnin was finally given an opportunity and didn't look out of place in the hour that he was on the pitch before being replaced by Dalglish. The Reds were again up against Allan Simonsen in this game, while Kent Neilsen and confusingly Allan Hansen (who scored the equalising goal) also made guest appearances for the home side.

There was good news from home as it was discovered that John Wark's knee injury was not as bad as feared and he would be ready for the start of the season. It had been a good tour for the Reds as they built up fitness and made good progress on the restoration of their reputation. It wasn't quite over though as it was now on to Hamburg for a match on 8th August that would prove a stern test.

Given the FA's insistence of vetting every foreign friendly that was arranged by English clubs, it was somewhat odd that they sanctioned matches in Holland and West Germany for Liverpool, Everton, Manchester United and West Ham at the same time. The consequence of this was fighting on an overnight North Sea ferry from Harwich to Hook of Holland between West Ham and Manchester United fans, causing the vessel to turn back halfway through its journey. A total of 80 police officers met it at Harwich where 14 arrests were made. All of those arrested were from Manchester or London and the *Liverpool Echo* reported that Liverpool and Everton fans on board were not involved.

The turning back of the ferry meant that any Liverpool fans on board didn't make the match, but those that had got there by other means were reported to have behaved 'impeccably.' They didn't witness a Reds win though, as they went down 1-0 to a goal from Heinz Gründel in a fiercely contested game that saw three bookings and Kevin MacDonald injured after being caught by Manny Kaltz. Liverpool though had given a good account of themselves against a side who were European champions just three years earlier and had been preparing for the new season two weeks longer.

SCANDINAVIA 1987

The success of the 1986 tour meant that Liverpool were back in Scandinavia for their preparations the following year, with another round of games against low key opposition where they met old foes, tagged on to a friendly against a big name West German side.

1986-87 had ended in disappointment by Liverpool's high standards as they finished second to Everton in the league and lost to Arsenal in the League Cup final. With Ian Rush departing for Italy there were real fears that the balance of power was shifting on Merseyside, but Kenny Dalglish made two summer signings that excited the fans. Winger John Barnes arrived quite early in the summer from Watford for £900,000, with Peter Beardsley joining from Newcastle for £1.9 million on 14th July.

Pre-season training had already begun when Beardsley signed, the negotiations having been complicated by payments he believed were owed to him by Newcastle. When he did finally arrive, Liverpool chairman John Smith told the press conference: 'Patience is a virtue so Peter was worth waiting for. Not only is he one of the best players in the country, in my book he is the leading player in Europe and the world. Liverpool Football Club can count themselves very fortunate in signing him.' Barnes and Beardsley were bought to provide the ammunition for striker John Aldridge, who had arrived from Oxford the previous January, but whose opportunities had been limited so far due to Rush's presence.

As Liverpool negotiated Beardsley's transfer, they were also in discussion with the Football Association who again showed their inconsistencies when it came to sanctioning friendlies. At the beginning of July the FA refused to agree to the Reds playing a friendly against Celtic in Glasgow, even though they had allowed a visit there by Arsenal to go ahead. Secretary Peter Robinson wrote to the FA asking them to reconsider, and on 13th July the *Liverpool Echo* reported that the FA had made a U-turn. It was anticipated that the Celtic game would be the last pre-season friendly, but plans for the league fixtures were thrown into chaos on 15th July when it was announced that a collapsed sewer underneath the Kop would mean the postponement of the first two home games. Robinson dismissed suggestions that they could be switched to Goodison Park, saying that they would look to rearrange them for later in the season, maintaining fitness by arranging away friendlies instead.[43]

Whereas a year earlier the hardest game came after playing in Scandinavia, this year it was the other way around in a tour that took the Reds away for nearly three weeks. It would start with a game against Bayern Munich, beaten in the European Cup final by Porto that year, in a testimonial game for Dieter Hoeneβ. Although Liverpool would have preferred to play this game much later, no suitable date could be found so they had to make do as best they could. The Reds flew to Munich on 22nd July without Jan Mølby who suffered a blow when he broke a bone in his foot the day before, while long term injured players Jim Beglin, Mark Lawrenson and Kevin MacDonald were also missing. John Wark and Paul Walsh, two players whose Anfield careers were under serious threat due to the arrival of Barnes and Beardsley, were included in the 17-man squad, as was Northern Irish youngster Jim Magilton who got his chance as a direct result of Mølby's injury.

The following night Kenny Dalglish named Aldridge, Barnes and Beardsley in the starting line up for the game, telling reporters beforehand that although the timing wasn't ideal, 'if the game helps our build-up to the new season and improves our sharpness we will feel that it has been well worthwhile.' Liverpool's 3-2 defeat, in which both Aldridge and Barnes scored, did not unduly concern Dalglish who told Philip McNulty of the *Daily Post* afterwards: 'These games are designed to iron out our faults, improve our sharpness and get to know each other again. There was a bit of each of these in this game.'

From Munich the Reds flew to Denmark on 25th July, where their first game would be the next night against Aalborg Chang, who played in the regional Third Division. The match was part of the Danish club's 75th anniversary celebrations and attracted a crowd of 4,100, who saw Barnes get on the scoresheet again in a 4-0 win for the Reds. Jim Magilton also got a run out as substitute, while Paul Walsh showed he had no intention of giving up his place easily as he had a hand in three of the goals including winning a penalty which was converted by Aldridge. Ian Hargraves, covering the tour for the *Liverpool Echo* described the Reds' style as exciting to watch, but did wonder if Dalglish would look to play the same way against stronger opposition.

The Reds had again received a warm reception in Denmark, and Jan

Mølby had flown out to help with the public relations aspect of the tour. This was a relief to the big Dane and he recalls:

'I was living in a house by myself at the time and it wasn't much fun being laid up. In fact I was having real problems getting around. But then, at the start of the next week the phone went. It was Kenny, ringing from Germany. "We're flying from here today," he said, "but we're not going to Denmark, Norway and Sweden without you. I want you to come out here now – we need someone to speak the lingo." So I made it on to the tour after all. It was a bit awkward with my crutches but Peter Beardsley was my minder, carrying my bag and generally looking after me. I really enjoyed my fortnight away.[44]

The next game was on 28th July against Brønshøj BK and their officials said they would be pleased to see Liverpool back in European competition[45]. Although Brønshøj are based in a northern suburb of Copenhagen the match was played at Ringsted, 35 miles away. They are one of the less glamorous Danish clubs but despite modest budgets had managed a sixth place finish in the First Division and would give the Reds a bigger test than Aalborg Chang had done. However the 1-1 draw was still a major surprise, even considering Aldridge and Beardsley were rested allowing Dalglish to give himself a run out. The game was played on a perfect pitch that should have suited Liverpool's style but they couldn't even take advantage in the second half when the Danes were forced to field a reserve keeper due to injury. The Reds were so sluggish that apart from Steve Nicol's goal, when he headed in a John Barnes cross, the most entertaining element of the second half was when a rabbit ran on to the pitch.

The next match on 1st August was again at a semi neutral venue, as the Reds took on First Division Vejle at the tiny Spjald Stadion in Ringkøbing, some 50 miles from where the Danish team were based. As part of the ongoing public relations exercise, an open training session the day before the game was well attended by locals. In the game itself the Reds would again be up against former Borussia Mönchengladbach player Allan Simonsen, who was now playing for Vejle as well as being a director of the club. Another familiar opponent was Jan Mølby's cousin Johnny, who had now moved there from Kolding.

Aldridge, Barnes and Beardsley all played as the Reds found their form again, cruising to a 3-0 win with Beardsley netting his first goal for the club just before the half hour mark when he was set up by Barnes. The match was played in a carnival atmosphere before a crowd of 3,000 who crammed into the tiny ground which had one wooden stand and is home to Spjald IF, a team so small they don't even have a Wikipedia page. At half-time many fans were allowed on to the pitch to join in the kickabout with the substitutes as Jan Mølby gave a commentary over the public address system. Such was the friendly nature of the game that the one policeman at the ground even enjoyed a beer during the second half.

The Vejle game was the last in Denmark but there were still two more countries to go and Sunday 2nd August involved a plane and coach journey to central Sweden in readiness for the following day's game against Karlstad BK. Despite the length of time the players were away from home John Aldridge had no doubts that this was the right way to be getting ready for the season ahead, with Roger Kent writing in the *Daily Post* that he had said:

> 'After all the uncertainty last season it is great to feel part of things and to be involved right from the start. I know a long tour like this can pose a lot of problems and you seem to be living out of a suitcase, but that is only a minor inconvenience. The beauty of it is that we are all away together, settling down as a unit and getting to know each other.'

The need for Liverpool to get back in Europe was again emphasised by the publication of the club's annual report that week. The Reds made a net loss of £285,000 during 1986-87, with chairman John Smith concluding: 'The football industry is still paying a high price for the appalling behaviour of certain sections of society.' A further financial blow was dealt with the news that the *Today* newspaper was pulling out of its sponsorship of the Football League with immediate effect, leaving the league in the embarrassing situation of going into its centenary season without a sponsor.

Against Karlstad Dalglish again named an attacking team with Aldridge, Barnes, Beardsley and Walsh all starring against the Swedish Second Division leaders. The crowd tried to make the Reds feel at home by playing the British National Anthem at the start, then only the heroics of the home keeper kept the score down to 3-0. Beardsley found the net for the second game running as well as hitting the bar, as he showed that he was now beginning to settle down after being a little rusty in the early games having started training later. But it was Barnes who continued to excite the most, with Roger Kent's report in the *Daily Post* describing him as 'having the crowd in raptures' and Ian Hargraves writing in the *Echo* that he was 'a joy to watch.'

Whilst in Sweden speculation began to mount that the Reds may make a move for 21-year-old Anders Limpar, who played in midfield for Örgryte and had recently forced his way into the national side. Dalglish watched him in action whilst there, but nothing would come of this and it would be three more years before he ended up in England at Arsenal, via Switzerland and Italy. The Karlstad game was the only one that the Reds would play in Sweden, as from there it was on to Oslo for a match with Vålerenga at the Bislett Stadium, which was attracting huge interest in Norway.

Fans were travelling from as far as the Arctic Circle for the game on 6th August, the *Liverpool Echo* reporting that Jan Mølby was president of the 1,500-member Norwegian supporters' club, which published a 60-page magazine. That magazine, *The Kopite*, is still being published today and is edited by Torbjørn Flatin, who spends as much as half the season in Liverpool. He has been following the Reds since the early 1970s and the first time he saw them play was in the European Cup Winners Cup tie against Strømsgodset in Oslo in 1974-75. He remembers how this and other games in Norway involving Liverpool in the 1980s were a great social occasion:

> 'There was always a get together the night before and then after the game, and we would always invite the fans who had travelled from Merseyside too, often they would then be leading the singing. Sometimes the supporters' club managed to get players to come along too, as in the 1980s they were really keen to develop relations after what had happened at Heysel.'[46]

With regard to Liverpool's following in Norway, Torbjørn says that it goes back to the early 1970s when the club was regularly featured when live matches from England began to be shown on television there. It wasn't just the successful clubs though that got a following, he remembers that the company that produced the games was from the Midlands so there was an imbalance of teams from that region shown, meaning sides such as Coventry and Leicester attracted support too.

One of the Liverpool supporters from England following this tour was Chris Wood. He stayed in Oslo and had attended the Karlstad match, travelling there by train and receiving a lift back to Oslo from a Norwegian fan. Chris remembers how the signings of Barnes and Beardsley were exciting the fans but by now Dalglish seemed to be tiring of the questions regarding them. He recalls:

> 'Kenny was quite surly and was clearly already bored by being asked so many questions about his most recent signings. One of the newspapers sent to cover this press-conference had a picture of Kenny in the next day's edition looking really miserable and above the picture was their headline "TRØTT AV SPØRSMÅL" ("Tired of Questions").'

Those following the Reds in the 7,275 crowd, which included the country's Foreign Minister Thorvald Stoltenberg, would not be disappointed as they saw John Aldridge get a hat-trick in a 4-1 win. It was another attacking line up from Dalglish with just three at the back, although the home side did exploit this and took the lead after 16 minutes. However after John Wark was moved into defence to help plug the gaps, the Reds took control with Barnes again outstanding. There was some concern though over Peter

Beardsley, who had a quiet game and was substituted midway through the second half. In the Daily Post Roger Kent speculated that he was likely to start the season on the bench, with Aldridge and Walsh being the preferred front two.

The tour had again been a success from a playing and public relations point of view and on 9th August the Reds beat Celtic 1-0 to show they could get results against the top sides. When it came to the 1987-88 season, the seeds laid down in Scandinavia were an unqualified success as the Reds romped to the title, going the first 29 games unbeaten.

There was one disappointing element though in Liverpool's attempts to convince the authorities that they could be trusted to play abroad. As they tried to arrange some extra games to compensate for Anfield being unusable at the start of the season, the FA again stepped in to disrupt plans. A friendly in Spain against Atlético Madrid had been scheduled for 26th August but under pressure from Sports Minister Colin Moynihan the FA told the Reds they could not sanction the game, as Everton were playing Real Madrid at the Bernabéu the previous day. The decision was blasted by supporters from both clubs, with Bob Gill, secretary of the Liverpool Supporters' Club telling the *Liverpool Echo*:

> 'If these games had gone ahead then fans of Liverpool and Everton would have travelled together. Families – half supporting Liverpool, half supporting Everton – would have made it a family holiday. Who can forget the sights on the M1 last year with red scarves out of one side of the car and blue out of the other? This decision will do more harm to football. Merseyside fans are the best in the world.'

Despite the protests the FA and government refused a change of heart and Liverpool had to re-arrange their game for 23rd August, satisfying the authorities as it was 48 hours before the Everton game.

SCANDINAVIA 1991

Liverpool continued to undertake pre-season tours to Scandinavia for the rest of the decade, playing three games in 1988, four in 1989 and 1990. The latter two tours both involved visits to Sweden, meaning a return home for 1989 signing Glenn Hysén and also included friendlies in Finland against HJK Helsinki, who the Reds had played in the European Cup in 1982-83.

For striker John Aldridge a game against Vasalunds IF on 3rd August 1989 marked what he recalls as the time when 'I finally gave Liverpool an excuse to dispense with my services.' In his autobiography *John Aldridge – My Story*, published by Hodder & Stoughton in 1999 he wrote how he had been getting a particularly hard time from one of the Swedish defenders and elbowed him in the face whilst the referee wasn't looking. Having avoided being sent off Aldridge was substituted at half- time and dropped for the next game against Halmstad. When the new season began, he made just two substitute appearances in six games before being sold to Real Sociedad.

After the resignation of Kenny Dalglish Graeme Souness continued to take the team to Scandinavia, doing so in each of the three pre-seasons he was in charge. The first of these was in 1991 when the Reds toured for the best part of a fortnight, playing one game in Germany followed by four in Scandinavia as they prepared for a return to European competition.

When the 16-strong Reds party prepared to fly to Germany on 25th July for the following day's game against Bayer Leverkusen, the new UEFA ruling looked to have influenced the decision of who to leave behind. Glenn Hysén, Jan Mølby and Ronny Rosenthal were all omitted from the squad as Souness explained to the *Daily Post:* 'The European rules are causing us a hell of a headache and Gary Ablett and David Burrows are two players I'm looking to really mature.' Other English youngsters included were Mike Marsh, Steve McManaman and Nick Tanner.

Souness had spent £5.1 million in the summer on Mark Wright and Dean Saunders, who both arrived from Derby County. Unfortunately Saunders' Welsh striking partner Ian Rush had to be left behind due to an Achilles tendon injury. The *Liverpool Echo* had reported on 22nd July that he was in plaster and likely to be out until October. Rush was joined on the treatment table by winger Jimmy Carter who had a similar injury, something that would become a recurring theme of much of Souness' time as manager, with changes to training methods being blamed by many. The omission of Rush gave Peter Beardsley a chance to impress Souness. With the boss looking to recoup some money and also trim the squad, he was one of those players on the wrong side of 30 who were vulnerable as he looked to the future. Souness though did slam any speculation linking keeper Bruce Grobbelaar with a move to Real Sociedad, telling the *Echo* on the day of the Leverkusen game: 'I played with Brucie a number of years and know what he is capable of,' while Grobelaar himself said that any move from Anfield would be going downhill and he didn't want that.[47] One player who did become an early casualty of the UEFA rules though was Irish left back Steve Staunton, who stayed behind to discuss personal terms with Aston Villa who had tabled a £1 million bid, meaning a late call up to the squad for Jan Mølby.

The match against Bayer Leverkusen, UEFA Cup winners in 1988, was arranged to commemorate the 100th anniversary of the Bayer pharmaceutical company moving to the town and was subject to maximum security. The near capacity 26,500 crowd, who had been let in free and which included 2,000 German Reds fans as well as a large number from England, witnessed a 0-0 draw. This was Liverpool's second pre-season game having also ended up goalless against Dundalk a few days earlier. The Reds were on the back foot for most of the game, but it had to be taken into account that Leverkusen were far more advanced in their preparations, with the beginning of the Bundesliga season being just a week away. Although he hadn't found the net so far Dean Saunders was still lively in attack while Mark Wright put in a solid defensive display.

From Leverkusen the Reds party headed to Sweden where their first match was on the afternoon of Sunday 28th July against Second Division strugglers IK Sirius in Uppsala, 45 miles north of Stockholm. The Reds again drew 0-0 and this time the lack of firepower did give cause for alarm for fans. Although Souness acknowledged they should have beaten a side whose players were paid expenses only, he remained defiant saying:

'Our sharpness will come. It was disappointing that we did not win. I think the boys were extremely tired and that the game in Germany on Friday took a lot out of them. Yesterday was hot and Sirius must have used 18 players, so we were up against fresh legs and made to work hard. I think, as anyone will tell you, the sharpness required to score goals is the last thing that comes. We've been back in training for two weeks now and I'm hoping after three weeks we will have that sharpness.'[48]

Injuries were also becoming a worry, with Steve Nicol and Ronnie Whelan being ruled out of the Sirius game with groin and hamstring trouble respectively, while John Barnes continued to struggle with an Achilles tendon problem that had been sustained in Dundalk. After training on the morning of 29th July the Reds undertook a three-hour coach journey to Ludvika where they were to face Third Division Ludvika FK on the next evening.

On the morning of the game there was a sensational development when Peter Beardsley left the Reds camp to fly to Heathrow Airport for talks with Everton manager Howard Kendall, after he had agreed a £1 million fee with Graeme Souness for his transfer. Although a sizeable fee was being received, that Everton should be his destination was a shock to fans, with the *Daily Post* reporting that the Reds had alerted Leeds and Newcastle to his availability, but they weren't interested.

Against Ludvika the Reds and Dean Saunders finally got off the mark, but the performance was again far from convincing as they held out for a 3-2 victory. The Reds coasted into a 2-0 lead in the first 10 minutes thanks to goals from Ronnie Whelan and Steve McManaman, but they went on to miss a host of chances and after the break they inexplicably let the home side back into it, with Kent Sjöberg scoring midway through the second half. Although Saunders scored with 15 minutes remaining, slotting home a Ray Houghton cross to restore the two-goal advantage teacher Magnus Barkstog pulled another back for the amateurs.

Souness was again defensive about the result, saying afterwards: 'It's easy to criticise us for not beating these teams more easily but we are not preparing to play these teams, we are here to get fit and there are signs we are sharpening up.'[49] For 19-year-old McManaman, a product of the Reds youth system it was his first goal for the first team and he told Ric George of the *Liverpool Echo* that he was 'made up' and that 'everyone one counts' even though it was against a Third Division side. George wrote though that it was unlikely he would be a regular in the coming season, with Souness believing that he and Mike Marsh still lacked experience to cope with the rigours of First Division football.

Liverpool's next game was the hardest of the four they would face in Scandinavia, as they travelled to Oslo to take on Norwegian champions Rosenborg Trondheim at the Ullevaal Stadium. Only a handful of fans from Merseyside had followed the team on this tour due to a combination of factors, not least the difficulty in finding out information about games in pre-internet days. Chris Wood, a veteran of pre-season games going back to the early 1970s remembers going to the ticket office that summer to enquire about the Swedish friendlies, having had details of the one in Oslo confirmed to him by friends in Norway:

'I went to the ticket office and asked for confirmation that there would be games in Sweden. I was immediately asked how I knew about the Oslo game and replied that I had been in Norway recently and read about it in newspapers there. The response I got was that I should read some Swedish newspapers which annoyed me so much I wrote to club secretary Peter Robinson. He took the trouble to ring me while I was in work and apologised for the ticket office worker's attitude but told me that even in 1991, when we were being readmitted to European competition, the question of our supporters travelling abroad was still a very tricky one. As such, staff had been instructed not to divulge any concrete information about matches the team would be playing abroad. I can also recall seeing chairman Noel White in Uppsala looking closely at some souvenirs on offer from hastily erected stalls manned by English sellers who had loaded a van up and followed the team around. One quite repulsive T-shirt on sale had a picture of a snarling British bulldog, the word "Liverpool" somewhere on the front and a slogan reading "Our Colours Don't Run", a double-meaning that the young Swedes I saw wearing this shirt could not possibly have understood. They just wanted something with Liverpool on it. I could see that Noel White was visibly shaken by what he saw on sale in Uppsala. I think the hierarchy at the club has always found it hard to stop unofficial stuff being sold but I was ashamed of what was being sold in both Sweden and Norway in the early-to-mid 1990s. Post-Heysel we all had to be so careful what we said, how we behaved ... and what we wore on matchdays. Seeing so much stuff like this being sold so openly was really, really horrible to witness at a time when the club was trying to repair the damage and boost its image.'[50]

Rosenborg had won a four-team tournament for the right to face Liverpool and stood to win £10,000 if they could beat the Reds. Liverpool's presence in Oslo was a big event and the match was preceded by a legends game in which Kevin Keegan and Graeme Souness took part. Liverpool responded to the stronger opposition as well as the much more atmospheric setting, with the 21,000 crowd being more than four times who had watched the two other games.

Souness didn't use any of his substitutes during the game and also experimented with the fit-again John Barnes in a central role. Despite Liverpool's need to recoup some of the money spent on Wright and Saunders it had also been made clear Barnes was going nowhere, with a £4 million bid from European Cup finalists Marseille being rejected. The Reds players passed the ball around well and took the lead through Dean Saunders in the 25th minute and although Rosenborg equalised, a Jan Mølby penalty restored the advantage before half-time. Some 10 minutes after the break Bjørn Tore Kvarme, who would sign for the Reds later that decade, made it 2-2 but in the last minute Saunders scored to give the Reds a deserved win. Chris Wood remembers how this game made him aware just how much Liverpool meant to the people of Norway, as three sides of the ground were supporting the Reds and they 'exploded' when Saunders got the winning goal: 'It was a wonderful moment being so far away from home but seeing just how much this Liverpool team meant to the vast majority of that crowd.'[51]

The Reds party then returned to Sweden for the last game of the tour, against Second Division Elfsborg in Borås on 4th August. The weather continued to be hot even by Swedish standards but there was no let up in the training for the players as Souness strived to get them towards full fitness. The session was watched by Chris Wood and his friends and they were pleased to receive complimentary match tickets from the Reds boss, who handed them over through a gap in the fence. Wood also recalls seeing another side to Souness in a park in Sweden as he relaxed amongst his own thoughts while Ronnie Moran looked after his son Fraser, who had also been taken on the tour. There were 8,021 fans in Borås and they saw Elfsborg, who had beaten Liverpool 5-2 in 1939 look like they could be on their way to a shock result again when they took the lead in the 37th minute. The Reds' blushes were then spared when John Barnes equalised in first half injury time then set up Dean Saunders for the winner in the second half. It was another solid performance by the Reds in a physical game played in humid conditions. Souness again kept a settled side on the pitch and made just one change out of necessity, Gary Gillespie coming on for the injured David Burrows. There was a setback though with Gary Ablett being sent off for dissent leaving the Reds sweating as to whether the referee would report it to the FA.

Liverpool's players then returned to Merseyside to round off their preparations for the season with a friendly against Tranmere, with Souness expressing his satisfaction that the Scandinavian tour had gone well. He told Chris James of the *Daily Post* after the Elfsborg game: 'Liverpool is still the scalp that everyone wants to get and that's shown in the matches we've had. Results have been good even though they weren't important. Fitness was the main thing and now we've got that.' When it came to the new season though, a series of injuries hindered Liverpool's progress in the league and they had to settle for an eventual sixth place finish, their lowest since 1965, although there was the bonus of FA Cup glory as the Reds beat Sunderland 2-0 in the final.

This trip in 1991, the last year the Reds had been exiled from European competition was also the last time they went on extended tours of Scandinavia, although that wasn't just down to the end of the ban. Graeme Souness changed the pre-season schedule to include training camps in Italy where fitness was developed but no games played. This meant less time was available to tour extensively, but they did go on mini tours in 1992 and 1993 playing two games each time. After Roy Evans took over, the team tended to play more difficult warm up games although visits to Scandinavia continued to take place, including two game visits in 1997 and 1998. What did change though was the quality of opposition, with games against more familiar sides such as IFK Gothenburg and Brøndby, rather than lower division teams. One-off friendlies in Norway have taken place as recently as 2008, 2009, 2011 and 2013, with the vast majority of the crowds on each occasion supporting the Reds. It has always been a common sight in Scandinavia to see this but in the 1990s Rosenborg manager Nils Eggen was critical, Torbjørn Flatin remembering that he hated the idea of a match involving a Norwegian team having so many fans against them. Liverpool's visits, Torbjørn recalls, were only ever upstaged by cup finals and international tournament qualifiers against the top teams.

Liverpool's failure to win a league title since 1990 hasn't seen their support in Norway dwindle, with Torbjørn suggesting that they and Manchester United have the lion's share of support in the country. The recent emergence of Chelsea and Manchester City as major forces has seen them attract some support but, while Arsenal have always been relatively popular, nowhere near as much as the Reds. One new phenomenon Torbjørn believes has begun to occur in recent years though is that many fans will now follow a player rather than a club, therefore switching allegiances as that player is transferred.

Torbjørn also doesn't believe that the increase in low cost flights, meaning it is far easier for Norwegians to visit Anfield has been a factor as to why the Reds haven't toured there, instead it is purely down to money:

'When Peter Robinson was at Liverpool he didn't see the pre-season as the way of making money that it is today. Now it's very different and when the Reds come to Norway the prices are very high for a friendly game due to the stadiums being so small. Prices of tickets are £50-70, more than double what you pay for a Norwegian league game but it's the only way that Liverpool's fee can be paid. Of the Scandinavian countries, I think Norway is unique in that Liverpool can visit and everybody can profit, with only the Norwegian clubs being prepared to pay the match fees beforehand. I doubt that a Liverpool visit to Sweden could generate enough interest at the price required to generate profits, but Copenhagen in Denmark is possible. It is just the reality of the modern game that Liverpool are looking to tour further afield and see greater riches to be made in the Far East than in Norway.'[52]

INTO THE ARCTIC CIRCLE 1988 AND 1992

Liverpool's visits to Norway in 1988 and 1992 saw them play in Tromsø, 200 miles north of the Arctic Circle, making the games by far the furthermost north the club has ever played. Both matches there were against Norwegian Premier League side Tromsø IL, the northernmost top flight club in the world.

In 1988 the Reds first played in Bryne and Sunnmøre, situated in the south west and west of Norway respectively, before heading to the far north of the country. They then drew 2-2 with Tromsø IL, John Aldridge and Ronnie Whelan scoring for the Reds. This was the first match that Liverpool had played in the Arctic Circle, the nearest they had been there previously being in the 1971 visit to Scandinavia when they played at Luleå in Sweden, 62 miles to its south.

In 1992 the match at Tromsø came two days after the Reds had been beaten 1-0 by Rosenborg in Oslo, with new signing Paul Stewart scoring an unfortunate own goal when a cross struck his leg and went in after the striker had failed to connect with the ball. He made amends in this game though, scoring the opening goal in a 2-1 victory for the Reds. David James, playing just his second game for Liverpool, had a good performance but he could do nothing about Mark Wright's misplaced header that sailed past him into the net. Sadly torrential rain, which put the fixture in doubt at one stage during the day meant an extremely disappointing crowd of 2,049 turned out, only a third of the attendance for the 1988 fixture.

Chris Wood was one of the handful of fans who went to Tromsø for this game, having flown there from Oslo on 30th July on the same scheduled flight as the team, which was seen off by a large number of Norwegian supporters. On the morning of the game he went to watch the Reds train along with his travelling companion 'Little Jim' from Belfast, and one of Liverpool's most travelled fans, 'Big Jim' Gardiner. However due to rain the pitch had to be protected for the evening so they went to the clubhouse for a drink, where they were told it was free due to the distance they had travelled and were presented with signed photographs of Tromsø players by the daughter of one of the club officials. This was the start of a long acquaintance for Chris and the girl who handed out the cards visited Anfield with him in April 2012 when the Reds played Aston Villa.

After the match had finished a reception was laid on in a hotel for the Liverpool players, which many fans also managed to get in to. All food and drinks for the visitors were free, but Chris recalls how the locals soon found out that anyone who ordered in English wasn't charged, so they started to order their drinks that way and that it must have cost the bar a fortune.

The team flew home the following day to continue their pre-season preparations, which included a friendly at Tranmere and Jim Beglin's testimonial against Leeds at Elland Road. Chris though stayed on in Tromsø for a few extra days, which allowed him to see the midnight sun. He recalls: 'The midnight sun thing was a bit weird to someone who had not experienced it before. The sun itself disappeared briefly below the horizon before popping up again soon afterwards. But it never got properly dark and I could sit outside at one in the morning and read without any difficulty.' Summing up, Chris recalls watching Liverpool inside the Arctic Circle: 'I'll probably never go back but it remains one of my favourite-ever trips watching Liverpool because it was so different.'[53]

13

Holidays in the Holy Land

Liverpool nearly played in what is now Israel before the state was even created. In 1947 the Reds were invited by Egon Pollack, manager of the 'Land of Israel' team and later first manager of the national team after the state was formed the following year. However Reds manager George Kay declined the request due to the extended league season which had been caused by the severe winter and the fact that after a lengthy tour of the USA the previous year, he felt the players were in need of a long break.

The Reds would eventually make it to Israel 32 years later for what would be the first of four visits that were made at the end of the season. The visits allowed the players a chance to unwind while the expense of this could be recouped by playing a game. However the trip of 1984 was an essential part of the club's preparations for their fourth European Cup triumph, even though it contained plenty of laddish behaviour.

1979 ISRAEL

The first trip to Israel wasn't just arranged as an end of season break for the players, but also to conclude the transfer of the first non-English speaking player to play for Liverpool FC, as Israeli defender Avi Cohen completed his move to the Reds.

Liverpool won the league at a canter in 1978-79, collecting a total of 68 points (a record under the two points for a win system), scoring 85 goals and conceding a meagre 16. Their last game was a 3-0 win at Leeds on 17th May, but the British Championship meant that they couldn't head off for the trip to Israel just yet. On 26th May six Liverpool players were involved at Wembley as England beat Scotland 3-1 and the following day the Reds party that included 14 players flew out to Tel Aviv.

The Reds had promised to send their strongest side to Israel for the friendly and the *Liverpool Echo* reported that they expected to complete the signing of Avi Cohen whilst there. The Israeli international, who at just 22 was his country's most capped player, had impressed during a trial at Melwood the previous February after Reds scout Tom Saunders had described him as 'a man among boys' when he saw him playing in Tel Aviv. At just £200,000 it looked like a bargain price for a versatile player although the deal had been delayed due to Israel's participation in the Olympics qualifying tournament, which at that time was strictly for amateur players only.

Cohen formally signed for the Reds on the day of the game, 28th May, becoming the first Israeli player to turn professional. That night in front of 50,000 fans at the Ramat Gan Stadium he turned out for Israel in the first half, which saw the Reds take a 32nd minute lead thanks to a Jimmy Case penalty. After the break Cohen was in the Reds line-up, taking the place of Alan Hansen and goals in quick succession from David Fairclough and Ray Kennedy gave them a 3-0 lead. The home side hit back however and scored three times, the equalising goal coming with a minute to go from Beitar Jerusalem's Danny Neuman, who is now a leading sports commentator in the country.

The Liverpool party then remained in Israel for two days of rest and relaxation before flying home on Thursday 31st May as many of the players were required to join up with their international squads for European Championship qualifiers. Their latest recruit stayed behind however, as Cohen was to get married that summer and would be joining up with his new team-mates for pre-season training in July. Also remaining in Israel were Paisley and Saunders, as they were contracted to carry out some coaching sessions until the following week.

ISRAEL 1984

Liverpool's visit to Israel in 1984 was unique in that it didn't come after their last competitive match of the season. Although the English league season had finished, there was still the European Cup final to play but the visit was seen as a good bonding exercise and went a long way to helping the Reds triumph in Rome.

The Reds had also been there a year earlier, losing 4-3 to the Israeli national side just two days after their last match of the First Division season away to Watford. They had won the league title for the second year running in what was Bob Paisley's last season as manager and at half-time during the match against Israel the Reds' boss went on to the pitch to be presented with a commemorative plaque. The players then stayed in Israel for a well earned break which generally involved drinking in the city's main square, having played 59 competitive games over the season. Bruce Grobbelaar recalls how one night a drinking game called 'buzz' got out of hand and half a dozen of the players ended up brawling, but it was soon forgotten about and they were laughing by the time they got back to the hotel as 'a tangled mass of arms, legs and bodies' where David Hodgson told director Sidney Moss in his North East accent: 'Yer old bugger you, you and me are just the same you know.'[54]

In 1984 it may have been thought that the club's impending fourth

European Cup final in eight seasons would mean a sunshine break was the last thing the players needed. However there was a gap of two weeks between the last league game of the season and the final against AS Roma in their own home stadium, so this friendly allowed for some match practice but also gave the players a chance to unwind and calm any nerves.

Joe Fagan's first season in charge had seen the Reds clinch a third successive league title as well as a fourth consecutive League Cup. They clinched the title on 12th May with a 0-0 draw at Notts County and were then presented with the trophy at the final home game of the season at home to Norwich on 15th May. Already though the club were planning for the next season and two days later they strengthened the squad with the signing of 21-year-old Paul Walsh from Luton for £750,000. On the same day the Reds played a friendly away at Newcastle, arranged to commemorate Kevin Keegan's retirement from playing. A capacity crowd of over 36,000 witnessed a 2-2 draw, with Keegan being airlifted from the pitch before the end of the game by helicopter.

On 18th May Liverpool's departure to Tel Aviv was virtually unnoticed by the Merseyside media, who were preoccupied with Everton's FA Cup final appearance against Watford the following day. Liverpool's approach to the final cannot have been in starker contrast to that of their opponents AS Roma, who were staying in the hills above Rome and training every evening on the pitch at the Olympic Stadium. The Reds though would train in the morning and spend their evenings sat in the sun with a few beers, to the disbelief of Italian journalists who had gone out to spy on them and reported back to their papers of the unprofessional approach. If the attention of the journalists got too much, they simply went back to the Sheraton Hotel and drank there.

It gave the players the opportunity to strengthen their bonds and relax and they watched Everton beat Watford 2-0 in the FA Cup final at the Glasgow Bar, where Grobbelaar decided to stay on and play cribbage afterwards. Not fancying a walk back to the hotel he borrowed a bike, but the person he paid to return it to the bar must have seen the Reds' keeper coming and went missing with it, leading to him having to fork out £150 to replace it. Grobbelaar's embarrassment was not as bad as Steve Nicol's though. So often the victim of wind ups, he fell for perhaps his worst yet when Alan Hansen convinced him the reason Kenny Dalglish had stayed in the hotel rather than go out drinking one night was because he was dying of an incurable disease. As Nicol went to have a private word with his fellow Scot, Hansen rang the room to make sure Dalglish was in on the joke and when Nicol arrived, he put his foot in it somewhat by saying he had wondered why Dalglish had been playing so badly.

But of course there was a European Cup final to be played and to keep the players match fit a game was arranged against the Israeli national side on Tuesday 22nd May, eight days before the final. There was no question of the players treating this game lightly as they responded with total professionalism to having been given some leeway by Joe Fagan. Souness recalled: 'That is the Liverpool style and how well it worked after a long hard season. Joe Fagan and his backroom boys treated us like adults and we responded, whipping the Israeli national team 4-1.'[55] The game was played at the Bloomfield Stadium, the shared home of Tel Aviv's major clubs Hapoel and Maccabi. Michael Robinson, playing instead of Ian Rush who had stayed behind to play for Wales in the British Championship against Northern Ireland, scored the opening goal with the others coming from Graeme Souness and a brace by Ronnie Whelan.

The Reds then came back to Merseyside to make the final preparations for the European Cup final, with Joe Fagan making a whistlestop trip to Glasgow to attend a lunch where he collected the Manager of the Year Award. The following week in Rome Liverpool defied the odds to win the European Cup in their opponents' backyard, triumphing 4-2 in the penalty shootout after a 1-1 draw. It was one of the club's finest hours and although it was the culmination of a 10-month season, the previous week's trip to Israel had gone a long way to helping complete a historic treble. The *Daily Post* reported that the players had returned to Merseyside refreshed from their longest break of the season, while Ronnie Whelan said it was 'a great idea because it got us away from the pressure that was building back home.'[56] It meant that when it came to the game itself, they were not nervous as Joe Fagan had timed the preparation to perfection and his players delivered.

ISRAEL 1987

Liverpool's next, and to date, most recent game in Israel was at the end of 1986-87 when Ian Rush made his last appearance for the club prior to joining Juventus in a game that didn't do the Reds many favours.

Rush made an emotional farewell to Anfield on 4th May when he scored the only goal in the Reds' 1-0 win over Watford. The only dampener on that day was that Everton won 1-0 at Norwich to clinch their second title in three seasons, then the following Saturday the league season drew to a close as Rush scored the opening goal as the Reds drew 3-3 at Chelsea. They then headed straight to Heathrow Airport for an overnight flight to Tel Aviv, arriving at 6am local time the following morning.

Ken Rogers accompanied the Reds to cover the game, in which Juventus had no objection to Rush taking part, for both the *Daily Post* and *Liverpool Echo*. On the day of the game he wrote a thank-you message from Rush for all Reds fans, which said: 'I've had countless letters and cards from supporters all over Merseyside. Obviously I can't reply in person to them all but I would like to take this opportunity to thank all those people who encouraged me throughout my Liverpool career.'

Liverpool were invited to Israel to play this friendly which was arranged to close the Hapoel Games, a week long multi-sports event hosted by the Hapoel Sports Association. The Reds match started at 7pm and was preceded at 5pm by a game between the Israel Olympic side and Rangers, who were managed by Graeme Souness. That game was a bad tempered affair in which Rangers defender Graham Roberts and an opponent were sent off for brawling and the Israelis won 3-2.

Before the match between the full national side (for whom Avi Cohen lined up) and the Reds, Rush was presented with a silver trophy and Juventus shirt. The home side then romped to a 3-0 lead before half-time and despite a rollicking from Ronnie Moran Liverpool couldn't claw back the deficit in the second half, although Rush did force two outstanding saves from the home goalkeeper. The following day's *Liverpool Echo* report suggested that the players were feeling the effects of a long hard campaign, but John Aldridge later shed some light on the real reasons for the lacklustre display, recalling:

'We got to Tel Aviv at six o'clock on a Sunday morning and decided against going to bed. Instead we went straight for breakfast, washing down our food with large amounts of lager. In fact we spent most of the day drinking and ended up in a square in the city centre. Drunk and tired due to lack of sleep, we could not have felt worse, which is why we didn't welcome the attentions of a photographer who insisted on taking pictures of us. The following day, the morning of the match, we boarded a coach which would take us for a light training session. We all felt rough but the sight of Steve McMahon vomiting on the back seat lightened the atmosphere. He'd been drinking a local brew and it had obviously assaulted his digestive system. Ironically in our 3-0 defeat Steve was one of the best players. The same could not be said for me. I played up front with Kenny for the first time and did not impress. We paid for our unprofessionalism. In the local newspaper on the Tuesday, the day we left the country, there was a picture of us looking worse for wear in that Tel Aviv square. The headline summed it up: "Israel does not beat Liverpool 3-0 but it does beat eleven beer barrels 3-0." John Smith and Peter Robinson, Liverpool's top officials, were less than happy. So was Kenny. He had spent most of the match moaning, probably because he felt we'd let him down by allowing our behaviour to be photographed.'[57]

Although there are various reasons why Liverpool have not been back to Israel, the political situation and more lucrative opportunities existing elsewhere being amongst them, this incident hadn't helped the club's situation and more than likely played a part in them not going there in the years immediately afterwards. Such was the draw of Liverpool that the friendly games attracted far bigger crowds than competitive internationals would get yet the fans had wanted to see a proper show put on and there had seemed to be genuine disappointment in Israel at the way the Reds players had approached the game. In 1988 Aston Villa were invited and the following year saw Dynamo Kiev play there. Even the presence of Israeli international Ronny Rosenthal in the Reds squad from 1990 to 1993 didn't lead to them returning, although the first two years of his time at Anfield coincided with tensions in the area caused by Saddam Hussein's invasion of Kuwait.

14

Into Africa

Liverpool have now visited five of the six permanently inhabited continents, the 2013 trip to Australia being the most recent addition leaving South America as the only one they have not been to. Prior to Australia, the most recent one they added to the list of destinations was Africa, where they visited for friendlies three successive years in the 1980s before returning in 1994 to tour South Africa after the country was welcomed back into the sporting fold.

SUDAN 1982

In December 1982 Liverpool made a one-off visit to Sudan to play a Khartoum XI, in what remains one of their most unusual destinations ever visited.

The match was arranged following a visit to Merseyside two years earlier by President Gaafar Nimeiry whose wife was receiving specialist medical care. After visiting Anfield he became a Reds' supporter and invited them on an all-expenses paid VIP trip and after two years of trying a suitable date was finally arranged, with a special envoy visiting Merseyside in the week before to ensure all arrangements went smoothly.

An official from the Sudanese Embassy in London told the *Liverpool Echo* that English matches were shown on television in Sudan every Friday and that news of Liverpool's visit had captured the imagination of the locals: 'They know all the names of the Liverpool team and will be delighted to see the players in person. The players will get a great welcome in Khartoum.' Despite the fact it was an 8,000 mile round trip, secretary Peter Robinson did not see it posing any problems, telling the *Liverpool Echo*: 'It's not the most difficult trip we have taken on, but it's probably the most unusual. This trip should be straightforward. It is a long journey but the VIP charter flight should make it a pleasant one.'

The Reds flew to Khartoum on Sunday 19th December, a day after beating Aston Villa 4-2 at Villa Park. Ken Rogers was accompanying the party and described their arrival for the next evening's *Liverpool Echo*:

'Graeme Souness led his team-mates from the aircraft to be greeted by the president. It was an exciting moment for the soccer mad Sudan leader who has been trying to arrange this friendly for two years. He introduced his team-mates to the VIP gathering on the runway. Goalkeeper Grobbelaar delighted the crowd by lifting a little boy high above his head as he stepped forward. Three more youngsters approached Phil Neal clutching a piece of paper with a list of questions and holding a tape recorder. The full back patiently answered them as the Sudanese fans looked around for more well known faces. The party moved on by a fleet of Mercedes and coaches to the impressive People's Palace Hotel which stands on the banks of the Nile. Here they met the opposition, an amalgamation of two local sides who will form a Khartoum select side for tonight's sell-out game.'

The game itself took place against a side made up of players from two local clubs, Hilal and Marika, on a rock hard pitch at the 60,000 capacity Khartoum Stadium with a 1.30pm kick off, with some fans taking their places five hours beforehand. The crowd wore a mixture of t-shirts and robes and Ken Rogers was impressed with their knowledge, with one fan giving his opinions of Trevor Brooking and West Ham United, while another enquired about how Craig Johnston had fared since arriving from Middlesbrough. Amongst them were 82 British expatriates, who had paid £5 for the most exclusive seats in the stadium.

With the Sudanese players eager to impress their president and a live television audience, Rogers reported how they treated it like a European Cup final and very nearly pulled off a sensational win as Soksok gave them the lead just after half-time. However Kenny Dalglish equalised four minutes before the end when he lobbed the keeper in temperatures which soared into the 90s instead of the usual 60 degrees for this time of year. Phil Neal said afterwards he wasn't surprised by the quality of the local side given Cameroon's performance at the World Cup six months earlier. He told Rogers: 'They surprised a few people with their skill and showed plenty of confidence and I expected the Sudan team to show this kind of style.'

In a nice gesture after the game Bruce Grobbelaar presented his gloves to the opposition keeper Hamid and crowds lined the streets to cheer the Reds team back to the hotel. The only complaint from manager Bob Paisley had been that the referee hadn't allowed rolling substitutions given the heat even though he had agreed it with the Sudanese beforehand.

Liverpool returned home the following day, six days before their next scheduled game and having been away only 48 hours. Paisley had seen it as a useful trip, telling the *Daily Post*: 'We wouldn't have taken the Khartoum trip if we had been playing on Saturday, but the lads had a few days away with the sun on their backs.' Liverpool may well have finally given President Nimeiry his wish of seeing them play in Khartoum but there would never be any return visit. The following year Sudan descended into civil war following Nimeiry's imposition of Sharia law, which led to him eventually being ousted and seeking exile in Egypt in 1985.

SWAZILAND 1984

On 1st June 1984, just two days after winning the European Cup in Rome to complete a historic treble, Liverpool's players were jetting off to Swaziland (via Heathrow and Johannesburg) for their first extended stay in Africa. They did so though without the scorer of the winning penalty kick Alan Kennedy, who along with Sammy Lee had been called up for an England tour of South America.

This was the third successive year the Reds had been to Africa, having played a one-off pre-season friendly in Casablanca against WAC in August 1983. This visit to Swaziland was recreational in the first instance, with the players being invited by 16-year-old Crown Prince Mswati to relax for 10 days at the Royal Swazi Sun Hotel in the capital Mbabane, playing two exhibition games against fellow tourists Tottenham Hotspur. In what was dubbed the 'sporting spectacle of the year in southern Africa'[58] the aggregate winners of the two-legged affair would be awarded with the Royal Swazi Sun Challenge Trophy and Reds players were also paid £1,000 each for the trip.

On the day the Reds left most of the sports pages were filled with the mounting speculation regarding the future of Graeme Souness. The inspirational captain insisted before leaving England that he would be with Liverpool the following season, telling the *Liverpool Echo*: 'I'll still be playing here next season, I know the stories have been circulating, but I don't know what's behind them'. Manager Joe Fagan was dismissive of the rumours, saying: 'As far as I am concerned it is all paper talk and Graeme is staying'. However chief executive Peter Robinson appeared to leave the door open, saying candidly: 'All I can say is we still have not received an official approach from any club for any of our players'. One player who didn't make the trip was Phil Thompson, who was one of 17 who had travelled to Rome but been the odd man out and not been named as one of the substitutes. Devastated that he was then made to sit in the stands with the wives and girlfriends rather than on the bench, he had told Joe Fagan: 'You can shove your trip to Swaziland. You have to understand me. I don't want to go.'[59]

The journey to Swaziland involved a flight from Speke to Heathrow, then another much longer flight to Johannesburg, from where they took a turbo-prop plane to Swaziland. Although the small country bordered by Mozambique and South Africa may have seemed an unusual destination the Reds had no need to be cautious as Spurs were in a position to recommend it having been there the previous year along with Manchester

United, who they had beaten 3-2 on penalties to win the trophy. Striker Ian Rush was excited by the trip, telling the *Daily Post*: 'We are looking forward to the trip even though it is only 48 hours after Rome. Hopefully we can mix business with pleasure'.

In his book *My Liverpool Home*, published by Hodder & Stoughton in 2010, Kenny Dalglish remembers how Spurs, who had won the UEFA Cup, were far more businesslike. Both sides were staying at the Royal Swazi Sun Hotel and the Reds players arrived just as Spurs were returning from a training session. This moment was captured on video by Danish musician Jan Schnell, who at that time was a child living in Swaziland as his father worked at the hotel. He posted the video on YouTube in April 2012 and it shows the Reds players arriving at the hotel carrying bags and documents, with the Spurs players walking in after them in full kit and with boots.

The night before the first match was due to take place on 3rd June a pianist played in the hotel restaurant whilst the players were having dinner and then moved into the bar. Dalglish says of the subsequent events:

'Alan Brazil, a friend from Scotland, sneaked in to join us. "I can't stay long, the gaffer wants us in bed for nine thirty," Alan said. Hansen, Souey and I burst out laughing. "Nine thirty in the morning?" I asked. "No, night time." Brazil was serious. Spurs were treating this competition very professionally, certainly more than Liverpool were. Their manager Keith Burkinshaw marched across. "Time for bed, Brazil," he barked. "Big game tomorrow". Charlie knew Burkinshaw from Spurs, so he thought he'd intervene. "Behave yourself, you're not sending the boys to bed at half nine are you? Let them have a drink, man. We're just having a wee singsong". "Bed," insisted Burkinshaw. "Come on Keith, let them relax," said Graeme. Brazil shifted uneasily on his barstool. "Bed," Burkinshaw declared. "I'll need to go," said Brazil sadly. He sloped away, casting a final, doleful look at the bottles of wine lined up on the bar ready for inspection. "Have a good night." Alan can rest assured we didn't let him down. By the end of the night, we'd been through the wine list and the pianist almost had steam coming out of his fingers.'

Schnell can confirm that the players had a good night, remembering his father telling him the next day that 'a few of the Reds and Spurs players had something to drink that night and that furniture had been messed about with.' Dalglish went on to describe how Graeme Souness's hangover was so bad he was unable to play in the match against Spurs, with Joe Fagan believing he had eaten too many prawns. Dalglish dropped back into midfield to cover for him and despite their totally unorthodox match preparations the Reds still ran out 5-2 winners in the sweltering heat at the Somhlolo stadium. Paul Walsh, who had signed only a fortnight earlier from Luton Town, scored his first for the club with three minutes left with the others coming from Ian Rush and Craig Johnston who netted two each.

Meanwhile, things were moving quickly on the Souness transfer front, as Italian side Sampdoria made an approach to Liverpool and a £700,000 fee was agreed. The skipper was instructed to fly back to discuss personal terms but despite the offer of a lucrative pay package that dwarfed what he was earning at Liverpool he insisted that he hadn't made up his mind to leave. He told the *Liverpool Echo* at Heathrow after arriving back from Swaziland on 9th June: 'If it's not what I want and they don't interest me I wont sign, after all I am not going to go from playing for the best team in Europe to just any other club.' Two nights later the *Echo* delivered the bombshell that Reds fans feared. The paper reported that it had taken Souness just an hour to make up his mind after speaking with Paulo Mantovani, the Sampdoria president, who offered him a £150,000 package and also the prospect of playing in a country that Souness himself described as the focal point of world football.

On the day Souness arrived back in England the Reds, fresh from a few days sightseeing away from the capital, faced Spurs for the second time, Ian Rush scoring a last minute equaliser in a 1-1 draw. With the news of Souness' departure and this game taking place on a Saturday, the story carried only minimal coverage in the following Monday's *Daily Post*, its report consisting of just 33 words and describing Rush as 'Liverpool's goal hero in the bush'. The *Echo* didn't mention the match at all with the players' return being given just one line within a wider article regarding Souness, whose transfer had pushed the game's newsworthiness into the background.

SOUTH AFRICA 1994

Liverpool's one and only visit to South Africa came 45 years after they had first been considering a visit there. In 1949 the South African FA contacted four English clubs regarding a tour and the Reds expressed an interest, although nothing ever materialised. The country's ban from FIFA from the early 1960s due to Apartheid meant that the country was then out of bounds for tours for nearly three decades.

Ten years after visiting Swaziland Liverpool were back in southern Africa, visiting a South Africa nation now free from sporting sanctions due to the ending of Apartheid. The Reds were invited to take part in a soccer festival at the end of May organised by the United Bank, playing matches against Aston Villa and Kaizer Chiefs in Johannesburg, and Cape Town Spurs in Cape Town.

Bruce Grobbelaar and Steve Nicol were the only survivors from the Swaziland trip 10 years earlier, with the club now entering the infamous 'Spice Boys' era when players seemed to be getting more headlines for what was going on off the pitch than on it. Injuries and international call-ups forced manager Roy Evans to include three youngsters who had yet to, and never would, feature for the first team in a competitive game – Ian Brunskill, Andy Harris and Ashley Neal.

The players flew on an overnight South African Airways flight from Heathrow on 18th May, a non-stop 16-hour journey. But they were soon on the receiving end of complaints from fellow passengers who telephoned radio station Channel 702 to say that Reds players were drunk, rude and that one had even attempted to urinate on a fellow passenger. The *Daily Post* reported on 21st May that chat show host Mike Mills had told them: 'This is the talk of Johannesburg, the team was invited over here to play in our country. They are supposed to be your ambassadors but this is not the kind of behaviour you expect.' By that evening though the claims had been dismissed by chief executive Peter Robinson who had remained on Merseyside. He was quoted in the *Liverpool Echo* as saying: 'From what I am hearing from Roy Evans I feel the matter has been totally exaggerated. It appears that a couple of elderly passengers could not sleep and had to be moved'. By then one of Mills' superiors, Channel 702's acting sports editor Janet White had also spoken out on the Reds behalf, saying:

> 'From what I have heard certainly the lads had a few drinks, got a bit boisterous and started chatting up the air hostesses – a bit like young men do when they are enjoying themselves. Perhaps more conservative members of the community took exception to that. But the players are really being welcomed over here and everyone loves them for their easygoing friendly behaviour.'

The flight rumpus over, the Reds could now get on with playing their first game at Ellis Park on 22nd May against Aston Villa. Although the day before the players exuded an air of relaxation as they sunbathed by the hotel pool, Roy Evans promised there would be no slacking on the pitch, telling the *Liverpool Echo*: 'We know we have a large local following in this country and we are looking forward to a good hard tour'. The players were a huge draw, a get together with members of the South African International Supporters' Club going on longer than planned as over 500 fans asked questions and sought autographs. John Barnes was attracting the most attention so far, being approached by autograph hunters everywhere he went as he assisted with the making of a documentary for Granada TV. Having been an outspoken critic of Apartheid, he also expressed a desire to meet ex political prisoner Nelson Mandela, who had recently become the country's first fully democratically-elected president.

Against Villa the Reds didn't disappoint their followers, showing great commitment for a friendly in which they came from behind and deservedly won 2-1 thanks to goals from Robbie Fowler and Michael Thomas. The match had been televised back in England live on ITV, something almost unheard of for a foreign friendly at the time and those watching saw how John Barnes, playing in a midfield holding role, was a big favourite with the local crowd. There was also a good reception for South Africa born Bruce Grobbelaar, who replaced David James in goal with 20 minutes remaining.

As well as the local following, a small number of supporters headed out to South Africa from Merseyside. They included one of Liverpool's most recognisable fans 'Big Jim' Gardiner, who would rate this trip one of the most memorable he had been on and he had plenty to choose from. One of the highlights for him was visiting the original Spion Kop along with three friends Phil Antrobus, Ian Fyfe and Ian Davies. The hill was at the site of a crucial battle in the Boer War that took place on 24th January 1900, when British troops led by Lieutenant Colonel Thorneycroft captured the vantage points from the Boers. Gardiner wrote of the experience of visiting it in the programme for the game between Liverpool and West Ham United on 10th September 1994:

'It seemed particularly apt to be visiting the Kop in South Africa when the Anfield version was in the process of being demolished. The "Spioenkop" battlefield site is situated near Ladysmith and about a three-hour drive south of Johannesburg. The last five miles of the journey were along a single lane dirt track.'

The players themselves didn't make the trek to Spion Kop, heading on a safari to Sun City for two days after the Villa game before moving on Cape Town where they were joined by Rob Jones, who had been on England duty. Given the fact it was the end of the season Roy Evans allowed the players time one night to have what Robbie Fowler described as 'a bit of a blast' providing they got down to the serious business of training the next day. Steve Nicol went to extremes however as Robbie Fowler recalls in his autobiography *Fowler* published by MacMillan in 2005:

'The next morning Roy Evans came down to breakfast and saw Steve Nicol there with about eight massive beers all around his table as he tucked into his bacon and eggs. The boss went ballistic and started shouting that he'd told everyone they could have a drink the night before but in the morning the serious stuff has to start. So Steve turns around, fairly cabbaged, looks the boss in the eye and says "But gaffer this is still from the night before." Even Roy saw the funny side.'

Liverpool were first English team to play in Cape Town for 20 years and they were warmly received by the crowd which included Nelson Mandela, who made an impromptu visit to the dressing room before the game which was played at the Newlands cricket ground. Although Robbie Fowler put the Reds ahead Cape Town Spurs showed their ability in the first half, forcing some fine saves from Bruce Grobbelaar, who was making his last appearance for the club. The second half was played in a tropical storm that filled the pitch with puddles but it didn't stop Phil Charnock from scoring a fine solo goal and Neil Ruddock heading in a John Barnes cross to complete a 3-0 win.

Fowler said that meeting Mandela was a 'real thrill' for a 19-year-old not long off the streets of Toxteth even though the man himself 'must be bloody sick of lining up having his picture taken with every two-bit celebrity from just about every country around the world'. For John Barnes it wasn't to be his last meeting with Mandela as the president agreed to an interview for the documentary which took place after returning to Johannesburg. Barnes recalls of that meeting in his autobiography, published by Headline in 1999:

> 'We pulled up outside Mandela's house and the man himself let us in. He made coffee and we did the interview. We talked only briefly about football. I don't know if Mandela is a football fan. He is a people fan. When you have been on Robben Island for 20 odd years you get out of touch with football. I think Mandela is more into boxing. Of his many qualities that became apparent during the two hours I spent with him, the most shining was his humility. When Mandela reflected on the ANC movement he was so self-effacing, talking of his sadness that greater men than him had not survived the struggle against Apartheid. I have never been in awe of anyone. I love Pele but could not understand why anyone would want to collect his autograph. Pele is flesh and blood like the rest of us. But I was in awe of Mandela because of his unbelievable humility.'

The meeting with Mandela was much more informal than that with the former president, F.W. de Klerk, with whom Barnes was only allowed 10 minutes. Barnes described the making of the documentary as a 'fascinating time' and Roy Evans could not speak highly enough of his work visiting townships whilst in South Africa. He said of the player who had been appointed captain for the tour:

> 'John Barnes has been doing an absolutely magnificent job in the name of the club. I'm proud of him and all the players. John is a hero out here, the fans and kids love him. He has been working a lot in his own time, visiting the townships and proving a real diplomat. The way John has handled himself has surpassed all my expectations.'

As well as carrying out a new role as a television presenter, Barnes was also being deployed in a new role in the team as a holding midfielder, a position he would go on to play in his last three seasons with the Reds. Evans had in many ways been forced to use Barnes there on this trip due to a limited number of players being available and wouldn't be drawn on at that stage whether this would be his future position in the team, but did concede:

> 'Many people still expect to see the old Barnes powering past defenders with pace and skill as he did earlier in his career. The reality is we won't see that as often but he can still go past people. And he is always going to give us good possession with his ability.'[60]

The final game of the trip was back in Johannesburg at Ellis Park on 29th May against Kaizer Chiefs, winners of the National Soccer League in 1991 and 1992. Such was the interest in this game that the crowd of 40,000 was 10,000 more than the attendance for the Reds game against Aston Villa. However they saw the most lacklustre performance of the tour in a 0-0 draw. Johannesburg is 6,000 feet higher in altitude than Cape Town and the Reds players were visibly struggling for breath in the second half compared to the local players who were accustomed to such conditions.

The game rounded off what on the whole had been a successful tour though with the Reds flying home the next day. They had been one of the first teams to play in the new South Africa and made a lot of friends there, the players being fine ambassadors for the club.

15

Going Global

After nearly two decades of spending pre-seasons in Ireland and Scandinavia things changed fairly abruptly in the new millennium when Liverpool started to tap into the massive potential that markets in the Far East offered.

As England's most successful club they had a lot of followers there that had grown up supporting them in the successful years of the 1970s and 1980s when matches were shown in highlights packages. Now with the advent of satellite television matches were being shown live, and those that were early kick offs in England were prime viewing times in the Far East. The commercial prospects were and remain huge and Liverpool couldn't stand still as other clubs benefited. They too had to travel there to ensure they could retain the fans they had and win more.

HONG KONG AND THAILAND 1983

The first time Liverpool visited the Far East was in 1983 when they were invited to play two lucrative games in June, which would be Bob Paisley's last in charge before officially retiring and handing over to Joe Fagan on 1st July. It was a totally different tour to those that would take place 20 years later, in that it was more of a holiday with a couple of games thrown in rather than part of a pre-season programme.

Before flying out to Hong Kong Paisley collected the Manager of the Year award at a function attended by 40 other managers. He also gave them a warning for the future, declaring that his successor Joe Fagan was 'even hungrier.'[61] The Reds were without Kenny Dalglish, Ian Rush and Ronnie Whelan for this tour as they were recovering from strains sustained towards the end of the season. There was very little coverage in the local press, with only the very briefest of match reports being printed and no information in between.

The first match was on 5th June against Hong Kong league champions Bulova, a team that had only been formed in 1977 and made it to the First Division with two successive promotions. Liverpool were one of a number of teams that they faced in exhibition games (Manchester United would play there a year later) and Arsenal stars Pat Jennings and Alan Sunderland guested for them against the Reds. The game watched by 28,000 at the Government Stadium, with the local crowds cheering Sammy Lee's name more than any other of the Reds team. It ended in a 2-0 win for Liverpool, the goals coming from Mark Lawrenson and a screamer that flew into the top corner from reserve Robby Savage, who had spent part of the previous season on loan at Wrexham. Liverpool's victory earned them an additional US$21,000 in prize money with Singapore-based English language broadsheet *The Straits Times* reporting that: 'The Reds were rarely troubled by an energetic, if ineffective, home side'. The prize money on offer was certainly something that motivated the Reds players, although Phil Thompson recalls that it did pose some problems and confusion afterwards as the cheque had been presented by the sponsors to Graeme Souness:

> 'Graeme got changed quickly, found a bank and cashed the cheque immediately, giving every player an equal share. The two younger lads were thrilled. Then Bob Paisley came on to the scene and said: "Where's the cheque? That's the club's money." Graeme wasn't going to be pressured. He went to the representative and asked who the cash was for. The answer was "the team." That was all he wanted to hear. It meant everybody had a few bob to get the presents for going home. It was an incredible thing and something I've never witnessed before or since. Bob was not happy. In fact he went berserk because he would normally control these things.'[62]

From Hong Kong it was on to Bangkok where they took on the Thai national team on 11th June, winning 3-0 with Sammy Lee, Graeme Souness and Alan Kennedy scoring. The *Daily Post* carried no report at all of this match, while the *Liverpool Echo* allowed it just on 50 words, dedicating much more space to reports of Australia v England and Wales v Brazil friendlies. Most of the party then flew home, but Lee and Phil Neal headed to Australia to link up with England and Souness went to Canada to join a Scotland touring party.

SINGAPORE 1991

Liverpool's first visit to Singapore was in May 1991, when they were invited to play Arsenal for the Caltex Cup, a trophy presented by the Asian petrol company Caltex.

Arsenal had won the first Caltex Cup a year earlier, when they beat the South Korea national side who were preparing for the World Cup in Italy. They were an obvious choice to be invited back, but organisers deliberated on who they should play against. After speaking to AC Milan, Bayern Munich and Sampdoria as well as Liverpool, Caltex settled on the Reds, who were also being sounded out about playing prestige matches in Indonesia and Malaysia.

Between them Arsenal and Liverpool had won the last four First Division Championships, the Gunners having beaten the Reds to the title less than a fortnight before this game took place. With both sides promising to field full strength sides it was billed as 'battle of the giants', 'soccer event of the year' and 'clash of the titans' in Singapore, while Hsu Tse-Kwang, president of the Singapore FA wrote in the match programme:

> 'Fans have glued their eyes to television whenever either team is featured. Now this football extravaganza is brought "live". Our fans will be delighted, just as we will be. Our fans will enjoy and our footballers will learn. And we all thank Caltex (Asia).'

With $75,000 prize money at stake the game was being treated extremely seriously by both sides, with Liverpool chief executive Peter Robinson writing to J.M. Valentine, managing director of Caltex (Asia):

> 'Despite our unequalled success and worldwide travel we have not previously played in Singapore where from the fan mail we receive, we know we have many supporters. We are keenly looking forward to this new experience. The game gives us the early opportunity to play a competitive game against Arsenal, with whom we have been in fierce competition all season for the English First Division Championship. We enjoy an excellent relationship with Arsenal "off the field" but are great footballing rivals "on the field". The match is being taken very seriously with the reputation of two famous and long established clubs at stake. Although our domestic season has ended the pride in winning is still enormous and the prize money involved should add a further incentive for the top professionals on view.'

Liverpool kept their word about sending a full strength side. Of the starting line-up, only Mike Marsh had not been involved in the league match at Anfield between the two sides 11 weeks earlier. A crowd of 45,000 saw Ian Rush give the Reds a 52nd minute lead only for Nigel Winterburn to equalise and force a penalty shootout. Arsenal triumphed 4-2 with Ray Houghton and Ian Rush both having kicks saved by David Seaman.

CHINA 1999 (Under-19s)

As part of the twinning of the cities of Liverpool and Shanghai in 1999, the Reds under-19 side spent a week in China in October 1999 where they played two matches. This exercise was part of a wider mission to develop links between the two cities but the reception the players received was no doubt instrumental in the decision to concentrate on playing in that part of the world more regularly in the coming years.

The party flew out of Heathrow Airport on 18th October, the same day the first team were travelling to Northern Ireland to play Omagh. The 17 players were accompanied by coaches Hughie McAuley and Steve Heighway, as well as chief executive Rick Parry. Also on the trip were a trade delegation and city council officials including the Lord Mayor of Liverpool Joseph Devaney, as well as pop group Space who were to play a concert there. After a 10-hour flight they arrived on the Tuesday morning and Liverpool's players spent the rest of the day in bed to try and get jetlag out of their system, before holding a light training session in the evening.

As city council officials inspected the building of the Chinese arch which was soon to be shipped in piecemeal fashion to Liverpool to be used as a ceremonial gateway to the city's Chinatown, on the Wednesday the players were treated to a sightseeing tour. Heighway and Parry met the Chinese FA to discuss youth coaching, explaining to them how youth development worked at Liverpool now the Academy had been open for a year. The following day they played their first game against Shenwai and lost 1-0, but given the fact they were a senior side it was no disgrace and it was only the lack of clinical finishing that prevented the Reds getting a draw.

The players were given a day off on the Friday but for Heighway, McAuley and Parry there were further meetings with the FA. The next morning children from a local orphanage were invited to train with the players in a light session that was being held prior to the side having a second game that evening. Such was the interest in Liverpool's visit that the match against Shanghai was played in the 65,000 capacity Shanghai Stadium and broadcast live on television. An entertaining match finished in a 1-1 draw, with the Reds losing 6-5 on penalties which were hastily arranged given a trophy was up for grabs.

Summing up the trip, McAuley said: 'I think the lads really enjoyed themselves and it really was a once in a lifetime experience for them. There was more to the trip than just the football and I am sure everyone who travelled thoroughly enjoyed it.'[63]

SINGAPORE AND THAILAND 2001

Liverpool 's first visit to the Far East in the Premiership era came in 2001 and was huge event as it came on the back of the cup treble success and they found out just how fanatical their following over there was.

Planning for the tour started quite a few months in advance, with chief executive Rick Parry and assistant manager Phil Thompson flying to Bangkok in March 2001 to promote the game there. Guarantees were also made that all available players would make the trip, with no big names left behind. Michael Owen was one of the biggest names in world football at the time and in terms of ticket sales for the matches, his presence was a must.

Prior to taking the tour the Reds went on a training camp in Austria, where they played a friendly with Bayer Leverkusen on 10th July. They then set off for the Far East, arriving at Singapore's Changi Airport at 6am on the morning of 14th July. Despite such an early hour they were greeted by 1,000 fans in the arrivals hall, many of whom sang *You'll Never Walk Alone*. Some also tried to jump over the barriers to touch their idols but were stopped by security staff and many then followed the team bus as it made its way to the five star, 575-room, Marina Mandarin Hotel where some of the backroom staff signed autographs.

After some rest the players had a brief private workout later that day on a field next to the Westin Hotel, which was then the tallest in the world. Due to the intense heat it consisted of no more than a few runs and stretches and around 100 fans still managed to infiltrate it to see their idols. The official Liverpool website was now up and running and was providing much more updated news as to what was going on during the tour, as well as the reactions of the army of Reds fans in the Far East. One of them Colin Tan, told the official website of this session:

'I was alerted by a friend of the private workout session of the entire team at this field and thought he was joking. When I arrived I knew that he was spot-on as there were already a few guys and gals from the newspaper as well as from the TV stations. As this was a private session, there were no more than 100 people there. When the bus arrived a sense of excitement filled the air. As one by one of the players came down from the bus, the small crowd immediately moved forward for autographs, journalists and all included. The fans were just calling out the different players' names as they limbered up by running round the field with the fans just on the edge of the field. An English friend who was with me couldn't believe what he was seeing as he said that in all his life in England he has never been so close to the players all at one place.

On the evening of the 14th the players went for another session at the Choa Chu Kang Stadium and despite their tiredness still made sure they found time for a smile and wave to fans who had gathered outside to see them leave and board the bus, a gesture which was warmly appreciated by those there.

The club had taken the three cups to Singapore and fans had the opportunity to have their pictures taken with them at the hotel on the 15th July, with queues stretching outside the foyer into the scorching sun with many waiting more than two hours. That evening a one-hour open training session was held, attended by 4,000 fans at the Choa Chu Kang Stadium who cheered every time Robbie Fowler scored or Michael Owen came first in one of the sprints.

The actual match in Singapore was on 16th July against an S League Select XI and watched by 43,880 fans in the 55,000 seat National Stadium in Kallang. The Reds played well within themselves, which is hardly surprising given the heat and humidity and the fact it was only their second pre-season game, but were still able to win 2-0 quite comfortably. Manager Gérard Houllier made 11 second half substitutions but that didn't detract from the crowd's enjoyment, with the team being mixed in such a way that there were big names on the pitch for all 90 minutes.

The following day the Reds flew to Bangkok where a screaming crowd of 1,000 was waiting for them at the Merchant Court Hotel. A press conference was immediately held, attended by Rick Parry and Gérard Houllier as well as players Robbie Fowler, Sami Hyypia and Jamie Redknapp. Houllier promised that all of the Reds stars would be involved in the game and that having seen the reaction of those who had welcomed them, the players were determined to put on a good show.

Several thousand fans attended a training session at the Rajamangala National Stadium that evening, where a toddler managed to run on to the pitch to begreeted by a smiling Michael Owen. The following day the players again engaged with the locals, holding a football clinic for 100 Thai children at the Suphachalasai Stadium, which had been the national stadium prior to the opening of the Rajamangala in 1998. After a brief round of functions with tour sponsors the players were back in the Suphachalasai to train before spending the next day, the 19th July, at rest prior to the match in the evening.

Although most of the crowd at the match against the Thai national side were decked out in red, they were still cheering both teams equally and were delighted at Michael Owen's eighth minute opener as well as Thailand's 17th minute equaliser. Thailand, coached by ex Nottingham Forest striker Peter Withe, made a good game of it but the Reds had enough quality to go on and score twice more, through Owen and Nick Barmby, to win the game comfortably without exerting themselves too much. As in Singapore the Reds made multiple second half substitutions and the only disappointment for the Thai fans was that although he went close on a couple of occasions towards the end, Robbie Fowler was unable to get on the scoresheet. Afterwards Gérard Houllier said that he was surprised at how quick the Thai players were but that Liverpool's experience saw them through. Withe believed his side had done as well as they could given the circumstances, as they were unable to call upon seven regulars who were based in Singapore. Jamie Redknapp particularly enjoyed the atmosphere, telling the *Bangkok Post*: 'It is amazing for me to see the Thai fans cheering on both sides. Most places cheer only for their own country. I think it's good to cheer both sides.'

Exiled Scouser Dez Corkhill who was living in Singapore at the time attended the game, felt the trip was a great public relations exercise for the Reds and one that was essential for the club. He told the official website:

'Truly amazing scenes and one that should remind the players that they really do have passionate support all over the world. Never mind that no-one knew the words to *Scouser Tommy*, or that the atmosphere was muted. These fans were in the presence of true idols. Heskey and Owen scored the goals but the real success of the tour was the PR. It's weird as a Liverpool-born fan to be arguing the merits of such and such a player with a Singaporean or Thai who has never seen them play in the flesh, but such is the profile of the Premier League in this part of the world, the club should heed the presence of a massive army of fans.'

A postscript to the Singapore leg of this tour took place 12 years later when a couple, Mr and Mrs Han, who had met at the game there, finally got married after 11 years together. Much of this had been spent watching Reds' matches on television and their wedding was a Liverpool themed one, with both wearing club shirts and a video being posted on YouTube for fans worldwide to watch.

THAILAND AND HONG KONG 2003

Liverpool indicated towards the end of 2002 that they would be back in the Far East the following summer, although when the *Liverpool Echo* published the story on 11th December it was hinted that Shanghai and Hong Kong would be the destinations. However, with the club being unable to come to any agreements over playing in Shanghai it was decided to visit Thailand again before moving on to Hong Kong.

It meant the Reds were replicating the tour of 20 years earlier although now on a far bigger and more public scale. Whereas that tour had not been accompanied by any local journalists, this time both local newspapers were represented whilst up to the minute updates were available on the official website, which was also televising the games.

The tour didn't get off to the best of starts when a technical problem delayed the flight from Heathrow for five hours, meaning that they arrived at 10.15am local time on 22nd July rather than at the crack of dawn. It meant the reception wasn't as great as the last time, with many fans having tired of the wait. After some sleep to try and get over the jetlag the pleasantries began that evening with a press conference, light training session and gala dinner laid on for them at their hotel by the hosts and sponsors.

Liverpool's arrival had been eagerly anticipated, with the country's English language broadsheet *The Nation* describing that 'Liverpoolmania' was sweeping Bangkok and including an interview with Boonchai Mongkolratanakorn, the president of the Liverpool Supporters' Club in Thailand that had been founded in 1995. He explained how the club met every Sunday and did charitable work locally, including blood donations. Tulshatat Taphim wrote that watching Emlyn Hughes in tears after the 1977

FA Cup final defeat to Manchester United had made him a Liverpool fan. Of being a Red, he wrote: 'It chose my circle of friends, gave me ecstatic joy, sleepless nights and something to look forward to day in and day out.' Another fan, Amnart Kosolrod, explained how souvenirs were far easier to get hold of now than 30 years earlier when the only way was by expensive mail order. He admitted that despite having a wife and two daughters, the walls of his home were adorned by posters but he did say that some fans did switch allegiance too easily if things weren't going so well, saying: 'Some of my friends switched to cheer Man United, who are producing better results. But for me I have always been the same loyal fan. Through good and bad times, Liverpool is the only one.'

Amnart's words emphasised just how important these trips to the Far East were to retain fans, with Liverpool having beaten United in the League Cup final the previous season but having disappointed in the Premiership, missing out on Champions League qualification. If the Reds were liable to lose fans so easily if rivals were seen winning on television, it was essential they went over there to retain them. Liverpool's chief executive Rick Parry knew though that a balance had to be struck between endearing themselves to the Thai people, the needs of preparing the squad for the coming season and those of the tour sponsors. In an interview with the official website he said:

> 'This club is clearly held in such esteem out here and it makes you realise what a responsibility you have. In a perfect world I suppose in pre-season you wouldn't travel this far but I think everybody recognises it's about striking a balance. We don't want to overdo it and that's why we're only playing two games. Also we make sure we don't overdo the sponsor activity. We have a good working relationship with the tour organisers IMG. They understand what we need and it's gone like clockwork.'

Liverpool's players didn't indulge too much at the gala dinner at the hotel, going to bed early ahead of a hectic schedule the next day which began with a visit to the Grand Palace, the residence of the Kings of Siam from 1782 until 1925. They then undertook a coaching clinic at the Huamark, an indoor athletics stadium. The whole squad was involved with players playing head tennis with local children and Rick Parry told the official website: 'It was a truly humbling experience. Thai people are unique and it's brilliant for us to see how we can make so many people so happy just by being here. It was a great session for the players and also for the fans. Everyone really enjoyed themselves and it was a pleasure to be there.' One boy who attended, 16-year-old Wilawan Kadaeng told Chris Bascombe from the Liverpool Echo of the experience:

> 'I had no idea the player who would teach me how to head the ball

would be Michael Owen. I lost my mind and thought about nothing but Owen. I'm also crazy about Gerrard, but I forgot him after spending time with Owen. Although I had less than 10 minutes with him, I can never forget it. He was so nice. He didn't get upset at all when the girl in front of him couldn't play the ball properly.'

After some rest at the hotel the players held an open training session at the Rajamangala National Stadium, attended by 9,000 fans who cheered every tackle and shot. Michael Owen got the most cheers but John Arne Riise also had his fair share of admirers. There was no glimpse of the major new signing of the summer though, Harry Kewell having remained in England to receive treatment on an injury sustained in a friendly at Crewe the week before. Steven Gerrard, who had missed the 2001 visit due to an injury, was shocked at the level of local support. He told the official website:

'The reaction towards us has been unbelievable. It was a bit of a shock to me really because I wasn't here two years ago, but the lads told me what the fans over here were like. Even I didn't think they would be this crazy about Liverpool, but it's great to see so many smiling faces wherever we go. It's a trip we've all been looking forward to and now we're here we glad to have the chance to play football in front of those fans. It opens your eyes a bit when you see how much Liverpool means to them.'

The match itself was played on 24th July and mirrored that of two years earlier, with Liverpool winning 3-1 after Thailand had cancelled out an opening Reds goal. Emile Heskey got the first goal with a number of substitutions again being made in the second half, in which Vladimir Šmicer scored twice. It was a mild and wet evening that allowed the Reds to play at a higher tempo and there were occasional flashes of top form. Fans had packed the stadium for hours before the game and the excitement reached a crescendo when the players lined up to bow to the crowd before kick off. There was one element of confusion in the game when the referee added 10 minutes of stoppage time at the end of the first half. Gérard Houllier believed this was a misunderstanding as he had told him beforehand he wanted to make several substitutions after an hour and the referee took this to mean he had wanted an hour's unbroken play. Houllier didn't mind this though, telling the official website: 'I don›t blame the referee as he was probably enjoying the game and the fans probably enjoyed it too'.

The Thai fans were again supporting both teams, even though they were all decked out in red and although they didn't see Michael Owen score this time, they did put together a song for him, which Andy Hunter reported in the *Daily Post* as going: 'Michael Owen, you're a staaaaar, when you shine like the sun, show them who you really are, he's my boy wonder (repeat countless times), Michael Owen, you're my dream, When you run with the ball, You're the cat who's got the cream.' When the new season began though, it didn't quite catch on back on the Kop who stuck to the 'Michael Owen scores a goal *Hallelujah'* song.

The following morning the Reds party left Bangkok for the four-and-a-half hour flight to Hong Kong. Rick Parry had believed that it would be more restrained than Thailand there but that wasn't the case, with hundreds of fans waiting for them at the airport. One factor in the enthusiastic reception was that the visit had been in doubt due to the SARS respiratory virus, which had killed over 900 people worldwide and began in Hong Kong the previous November. Parry was reassuring over concerns, telling the official, website:

> 'As a club, the safety of our players is of paramount importance, if we did not think it was safe we would not be here, we kept the players informed and consulted them every step of the way. We received lots of information from the Hong Kong government and our medical staff were given the best available information before we made a decision.'

The players were taken to the six-star Grand Hyatt Regency Hotel overlooking the harbour where a press conference was held. Gérard Houllier told of his pride at being only the second Reds manager to take a side to Hong Kong, emphasising: 'We are not here reluctantly and we are here for the fans who gave us a tremendous welcome when we arrived at the airport and hotel.' He also promised that as many of the stars as possible would be given a run out for the fans and joked: 'Can you imagine what would happen if I didn't play Michael Owen tomorrow? I probably wouldn't be allowed to go back to England.'

The following morning the players had a 10am training session at the national stadium which was open to the public and attended by thousands. Fans wearing red shirts also lined the route from the hotel to the stadium, with the euphoria surrounding the visit being just as great as it had been in Thailand. Afterwards the players were introduced to the Chief Executive of Hong Kong, the special administrative region's most important politician. In the afternoon the players were taken on an organised sightseeing tour prior to resting in the evening with the match taking place the next afternoon, Sunday 27th July.

The game kicked off at 3pm and took place in temperatures of 100 degrees, but Liverpool were still able to beat the Hong Kong Select XI at a canter, winning 6-0 with Milan Baroš and Emile Heskey both netting twice. It was a confidence boost for Heskey who had come under fire from fans the previous season, whilst Houllier was also delighted at the performances of his 'French gems' Anthony Le Tallec and Florent Sinama-Pongolle, who he believed were now ready for the first team having spent two years loaned back at their previous club Le Havre since being signed in 2001.

As the Reds returned home for a few days before moving on to Amsterdam to play in the Ajax Tournament, Gérard Houllier revealed he was delighted at the way the tour had gone not just in terms of performances but in the way the players were received by the fans and had responded to this. He told the official website:

'I think most of the players were stunned by the overwhelming support they had over there, both during the open training sessions and at the games. I was told that many fans had been queuing for two days just to get tickets for the matches and we came across a lot of fans who were unable to get tickets to see the boys in action. We played two games in the Far East in front of 90,000 people and it really felt like we were playing home games at times because of the number of people in the crowd wearing Liverpool shirts. This club has a great reputation around the world because of the success it has enjoyed in the past and in the Far East they are able to watch a lot of our games on television. I was surprised that the fans knew a lot about the less high profile players in our squad, for example one fan was talking to me about Vignal coming back this season after being on loan last year. We were very pleased with the attitude of the players over there as well. They were very professional in their work and also in the way they went about the other side of things, such as signing autographs and having lots of pictures taken. The boys were surprised by the support out there and also surprised by the passion. It has really touched their hearts. I enjoyed this tour even more than the last one two years ago. I thought Hong Kong was fantastic. We all knew about Thailand before but Hong Kong was a bit of a surprise to me. It's a great city with great people. I'd like to thank all the fans from both Thailand and Hong Kong for the support they have given us over the past week. You were all absolutely superb and I hope we can give you a season to enjoy over the coming months.'

2011 MALAYSIA, CHINA AND SINGAPORE

During the 'noughties' a pattern developed whereby Liverpool visited the Far East every year when there wasn't a major international tournament. The only time this didn't happen was in 2005 when a planned trip to Japan had to be called off due to the Reds being forced by UEFA to begin their defence of the Champions League at the first qualifying round stage in July.

Liverpool were back in Hong Kong in 2007 when they played in the Barclays Asia Trophy, a four- team tournament also including South China, Fulham and Portsmouth. After beating South China 3-0 the Reds then lost 4-2 on penalties to Portsmouth after a 0-0 draw. In 2009 the Reds had a re-run of the 2001 tour, visiting Thailand and Singapore where they were once again given a huge reception with both games being watched by 50,000 fans. After drawing 1-1 with Thailand they beat a Singapore Select XI 5-0 and in both venues they were followed wherever they went, although in Singapore tight security meant fans were kept away from the hotel. With Steven Gerrard absent Fernando Torres was the main attraction and there were also plenty of posters and flags in support of Xabi Alonso, who was at the centre of speculation surrounding a move away from the club.

In 2011, new ground was broken when the Reds visited China and Malaysia for the first time. This was to be the club's biggest tour by far to that part of the world, with three countries being visited. The news process had moved forward even more and in addition to the updates in the local newspapers and the official website, the club's official television channel was now available on satellite and cable to show matches and daily news round ups. Players Charlie Adam and John Flanagan were also providing regular video updates for the club's official media outlets, as were Ian Rush and Phil Thompson who had travelled in an ambassadorial role, while the community coaches were also reporting on what they were up to. In addition to their official duties, many players were now updating on what was happening via their own personal Twitter and Facebook accounts.

The sheer numbers travelling –the club were even taking their own chefs – meant it was feasible and economical to charter a jet, meaning no more delays at Heathrow as in 2003. The party took off from Liverpool John Lennon Airport on the afternoon of Sunday 10th July, stopping to refuel in Kazakhstan before landing in Guangzhou on the Monday morning. There was little time to rest as that afternoon there was a meet and greet session for fans in the Chateau Star River hotel and then a training workout in hot and humid conditions at the Tianhe Stadium that evening.

The first full day in China saw the players train in the air-conditioned gym and pool in the morning before carrying out activities lined up by sponsors Standard Chartered in the afternoon. They then had another training session in the stadium in the evening before attending another hotel where a cocktail reception was arranged by Standard Chartered. The club's community coaches had a busy time too, spending the day travelling around the city for sessions with local disabled children which involved passing their skills on to local coaches. With the game against Sunray Cave just a day away fans began to arrive, having flown in from all over China or undertaken train journeys lasting as long as 24 hours.

Liverpool's community coaches were again out on 13th July joined by Ian Rush and Phil Thompson. As well as the coaching clinics, they also attended a cancer hospital where a 16-year-old fan suffering with leukemia was presented with a shirt signed by all of the first team squad. The hospital visits included a display of head tennis as well as a very brief singing of

You'll Never Walk Alone at the children's request.

The players rested in preparation for the game against Sunray Cave which was to take place in the evening. All of them were popular with the fans, but youth team player Conor Coady seemed to be getting the most attention from the female followers. There were 35,000 fans in the 60,000 capacity Tianhe Stadium, with blocks 18 and 19 being filled with hardcore Chinese followers who sang almost non stop from well before kick off and displayed several banners including one that said 'Mongolian Kopites Heart LFC'. LFC TV's head of content Paul Rogers and cameraman Mark Volante tried to stand with them in the first half, only to cause confusion amongst police who thought they wanted protection and formed a ring around them.

The fans were delighted to see the Reds run out 4-3 winners in a game that was more comfortable than the scoreline suggests and which saw the whole team changed at half-time. Christian Poulsen and David N'Gog got the first half goals with Conor Coady and Andy Carroll finding the net in the second. Little more than two hours after the game ended, the Liverpool party was leaving China on a midnight flight bound for Kuala Lumpur while back at home (where it was only late afternoon) the signing of winger Stewart Downing from Aston Villa for a £20 million fee had been confirmed.

The Reds landed in Malaysia at around 4am on Thursday 14th July and despite the arrival time there were still plenty of fans camped outside the hotel waiting for them when they arrived there a couple of hours later. Kenny Dalglish and Phil Thompson showed no signs of tiredness when they held a question and answer session at the hotel in the afternoon, before Dalglish left for home to welcome Downing to the club, leaving the team duties to assistant Steve Clarke. The reception in Malaysia was far less reserved than in China, with some fans who had travelled from Singapore having managed to secure rooms in the hotel itself. That night the squad held an open training session in the Bukit Jalil National Stadium attended by 38,000 fans, four times as many as had seen Arsenal train there a few nights earlier and emphasising just how popular Liverpool FC are in the region. The session ended with the squad doing a full lap of honour and the reception amazed even the likes of Thompson and Rush who had seen it all before.

The following day the community coaches were out running clinics again where John Barnes was a surprised spectator, being in Malaysia to cover the Copa America and Liverpool match for local television. Although there were heavy downpours this didn't dampen the enthusiasm of those involved, with Phil Thompson happily posing for photographs and signing autographs after he had passed on some of his skills to local children.

That afternoon 1,000 fans turned out at a shopping centre to see some of the players in a Standard Chartered sponsored event where there was complete pandemonium and police were needed to clear crowds to allow them through. A photograph of the scenes appeared on the front page of the *Malaysia Star* the next day, alongside a story about errant private colleges.

On Saturday 16th July, the day of the match a barbeque was held at the Double Tree Hilton hotel attended by Phil Thompson who went on to answer a series of questions put to him by fans. Then in the evening there were 85,000 fans in the Bukit Jalil Stadium where the Reds won 6-3, Maxi Rodriguez and David N'Gog both scoring twice and Charlie Adam getting his first goal for the club from the penalty spot. Afterwards the crowd greeted the players on a lap of honour as if they had just won the Champions League. The game had kicked off at 5.45pm making the conditions much more difficult than in China but again all the players were changed over at half-time.

After the game the Malaysia team coach, a Manchester United fan, criticised the fact that most of those in the stadium were wearing red and not the blue of the national side. This led to an angry response from many Malaysians. One of them was Sheldon Xavier, who was writing a blog for the official website. He wrote of the manager's comments:

'Gobsmacked Liverpool fans today flooded the forum boards and all social media sites to convey their dismay at his ignorance let alone arrogance. Fans have been starved all these years to see their beloved Reds play on our shores as not many can afford to travel 7,000 miles to watch a game in Anfield. And when they finally turn up, Rajagopal expresses his wish to see the Liverpool fans turn up in blue? Sacrilegious or what? What he failed to realise was that this was a once-in-a lifetime opportunity for Malaysian Reds who paid quite an exorbitant premium amount for ticket prices to watch this historical match featuring their beloved team in Liverpool FC. Ticket prices ranged from RM388 (approx. 75 quid) for top end seats and RM58 (approx. 12 quid) for seats located high up in the sky. Imagine now, a family of four turning up after paying for top end seats? Now that would almost come up to RM1500 (approx. 300 quid)! And Mr.Rajagopal's expectation was that they turned up to watch Liverpool in Everton colours? That alone calls for a red card, Mr.Gaffa! Please just do your job as a coach and let the fans be fans and come as fans in their club colours that they love!'

Of the Reds time in Malaysia on the whole Xavier was more than satisfied, writing:

'My reflection of the week that went by brought me with a smile of satisfaction. Liverpool FC turning up in KL was alone a testament. It brought one big happy red family coming together from near and far in unison, in support and in one voice. And the entire squad right from the players, the kit man, the TV boys and everybody that was connected with this team one way or the other gave the fans here in Malaysia meaningful time! One that will forever live in their memories to tell their grandkids one day that they spotted and spoke with Jamie Carragher's dad, that they chatted up Mr. Agger, that they were asking Mr Carroll on the maintenance and the length of his beard.'

As with the match in China, the Reds were again heading straight off to the airport from the stadium, flying that night to Singapore where they would be holding a training session. It had initially been intended to visit South Korea that year but due to problems obtaining insurance for the trip that leg had to be cancelled. The Singapore stop off gave the Reds a chance to connect with fans there again but no game was possible due to reconstruction work at the only suitable venue.

Despite the Reds being in Singapore for only 24 hours and no actual match being played, Mayur Bhanji wrote on the club's official website of the excitement ahead of the visit:

'It may only be a training session but it's a chance for the many thousands of Liverpool fans to see their heroes up close in the flesh. Many had already made plans to go to Kuala Lumpur for the game on Saturday but it's been a nice surprise to many to hear that the team are coming here for a training session.'

The Reds stayed at the Marina Bay Sands hotel, a resort in itself with three towers, 2,500 rooms, shopping mall and casino. On arrival they were allowed to unwind and attend a drinks reception at the 57th floor Skypark bar which went on into the early hours. The following day the community coaches had coaching clinics to do, organised by Adidas and Standard Chartered. One of them involved an elite group of 16-year-olds at the Singapore Sports School, while the coaches then moved on to groups from the Disability Sports Council and Children's Society. To the delight of those present Daniel Alaya, Andy Carroll and Brad Jones arrived and joined in the sessions, with Carroll putting on a display of ball juggling.

Whilst Alaya, Carroll and Jones were with the community coaches, Dirk Kuyt and Martin Kelly attended a question and answer session at the Adidas store in the city centre. Kuyt told those who attended: 'Pre-season is the right time to come to Asia and give something back to the fans over here. Even though we know it is hard work it's part of the job and we can see the people over here with a smile on their faces'. Kelly said: 'It's a great experience for all the players coming a long way like this, we love training in front of so many fans.'

Before the training session which had been scheduled for the evening there was still time to unwind in the world's highest swimming pool, a 150-metre long creation that linked the three towers of the hotel. The session was attended by 3,000 Standard Chartered invitees at the Bishan Stadium, home of S-League side Home United. It wasn't just the players that were getting the attention though, with the club television channel's Claire Rourke finding it impossible to record any pieces from the running track due to the crowd cheering her, with one fan even shouting out for her to marry him. After the session the Reds took off on their private jet for the 15-hour flight to Liverpool, which included a brief stop in Abu Dhabi. They finally arrived at Liverpool John Lennon Airport at 9am on Monday 18th July.

Paul Eaton of the club's official website believed that this tour demonstrated the power of Liverpool FC across the world. He wrote on the tour blog on returning home:

'Last week was a stark reminder that distance is no barrier when it comes to following your heroes. From country to country we were greeted by a sea of red as fans gathered at all times of day and night just for the chance to sneak a glimpse of their idols. For me, there are so many memories: the unexpectedly (in my head, anyway) rapturous reception when we landed in China; Guangzhou locals turning out in their thousands to welcome players at a Standard Chartered sponsored event; arriving at our KL hotel at 5am to see the lobby packed out with Reds after we'd been chased down the motorway by eager fans taking pictures out of their car windows; hearing stories of supporters camping out in the hotel and others from fans who followed the Reds every step of the way on the tour; open training in front of nearly 40,000 fans and then a friendly match in front of over 80,000 fanatical Reds. For someone who takes for granted watching Liverpool week after week and seeing the players day after day, this was almost impossible to take in. It was also impossible to take more than a few steps throughout the hotels in China and Malaysia without being stopped by fans just wanting to shake hands with anyone who represented LFC. Even for those of us who have worked for Liverpool for many years, it was an incredible experience to live long in the memory.'

The tour had been a great success, with Reds managing director Ian Ayre telling the official website on returning that it had exceeded expectations from a commercial point of view and showed to sponsors the appeal Liverpool FC held, despite a few trophyless seasons. He also praised the work of the players in acting as ambassadors doing more than they were expected to do, while the community coaches had showed that the club wanted to put something back into the areas they were visiting and not just make money.

2013 INDONESIA

In July 2013 Liverpool FC visited Indonesia, which at 242 million is the fourth most populous country in the world, for the first time. The visit came about as part of the club's partnership deal with Garuda Airlines and involved a four day stay in the capital Jakarta, playing a match against an Indonesia XI.

The Liverpool party flew from John Lennon Airport on a Garuda jet decorated with the Liverpool badge on the afternoon of 16th July. After a refuelling stop in Abu Dhabi, they arrived in Jakarta at 2pm the following day, where they were met by hundreds of fanatical fans. As the coaches carrying the players and officials edged their way through the crowds singing 'We Love You Liverpool We Do,' many of the players were capturing the moment themselves on their own mobile phones.

In addition to the players and coaching staff, there were also members of the community department on board, legendary players Ian Rush and Robbie Fowler, as well journalists from the club website and television channel. This time it was Joe Allen and Fabio Borini keeping fans updated with video updates, with Borini describing the reception they had received as 'amazing' and the 'warmest welcome I had ever received from the fans.'

On Thursday 18th July the players had their first training session at the Gelora Bung Karno Stadium. The conditions were hot and humid but Brazilian midfielder Lucas didn't believe this would go against them, telling the website that the conditions tested the players to the limit and increased their fitness levels. As the players got to work, the community work was beginning with coaches from the Liverpool FC Foundation and former Reds midfielder Dietmar Hamman helped with eye tests for some local children before undertaking a coaching session on an indoor futsal pitch. Even the club mascot Might Red was there, handing out the awards afterwards. The club's managing director Ian Ayre made it clear this community work wasn't just a one off , but was laying the foundations for the future. He told the website:

> 'We are committed to delivering a busy programme of activity off the pitch in Jakarta to provide positive change to local people through community football coaching. It is important to us, however, that we don't just provide this support for a day or two – which is why we have created a legacy programme where we can continue to promote our charity partners' campaigns through our global fan base via our extensive communications channels.'

In the evening there was a second training session, attended by 500 fans who had been invited by sponsors Standard Chartered and some were lucky enough to have their pictures taken with players afterwards. The following day, Luis Alberto and Philippe Coutinho met fans at the hotel as part of the launch of the new online store in the country. There were also frenzied scenes at the FX shopping mall as Fowler and Hamman were joined on stage by Martin Kelly, Jordan Henderson, Martin Skrtel and Daniel Agger. Back at the hotel, 15-year-old Sarah Hapsari waited for hours at the hotel and couldn't hold back the tears after Steven Gerrard stopped to sign her shirt. The players again trained at the stadium that night, this time with the session being an open one and thousands of fans sang an amazing *You'll Never Walk Alone*.

The following night the scenes were even more amazing as 82,143 packed into the stadium, many of whom got there five hours before the game started. As well as the replica shirts and scarves, there were also red flares and plenty of banners, including huge ones that read 'Not English We Are Scouse' and 'Justice for the 96.' The most touching one though was a flag that carried an image of Hillsborough mum Anne Williams, who had recently lost her courageous fight against cancer, with the slogan 'The Iron Lady.' This flag was later presented to Reds fans who had made the trip over from Merseyside to be displayed on the Kop.

Brendan Rodgers selected what was arguably his strongest available side to start the match, in which Coutinho gave the Reds a tenth minute lead. At half time only one change was made, with Gerrard who wasn't quite as fit as the other players due to a shoulder operation earlier in the summer coming off to be replaced by Joe Allen. The rest of the team was then changed after 65 minutes and Raheem Sterling made an immediate impression, skipping past a defender with ease before unleashing a 30 yard drive that went just past the post. With two minutes to go the Reds got the second goal their possession and chances had deserved when Sterling, who had also hit the bar, scored with ease after being set up by Oussama Assaidi.

After the game Edhie Baskoro Yudhoyono, who was the son of Indonesia's president, met Gerrard, Fowler and Rush saying 'I've been a really big fan of the club since I was a little boy. I grew up idolising Rush, Fowler, Barnes and McManaman and now my favourite player is Gerrard. To meet three of my heroes tonight made it even more special, I will never forget it.'

The Liverpool party left Jakarta that night for Melbourne, the next leg of the 2013 tour which would also include a friendly in Bangkok against Thailand. Indonesia had certainly left an impression on everybody that was there, Rodgers telling the website as they left Jakarta:

'It is very humbling, I've got to say. You hear about how Liverpool is in Asia; but it's only when you come here that you recognise the sheer passion and love for the football club. The history of the club speaks for itself, but there are lots of modern supporters as well – young kids and families here. It has been great to see. They have obviously bought into the culture and the football family that is Liverpool. We have been treated remarkably well, the kindness that has been offered everywhere we have been has been absolutely first-class. It is sad to leave because they are so passionate and this is the first time the club has ever come here. I'm sure in the future we'll come out again. It's a wonderful occasion and a great experience for our players, staff, management and supporters to come here.'

With the club going into partnership with one of the country's biggest retail groups to develop a 'shop in shop' concept selling Reds merchandise, it is likely the club they will be back in the near future.

16

Alpine Retreats

Under Rafael Benitez, the Continental model of high altitude training camps was a key part of pre-season preparation. It was not necessarily anything new for the club, as Graeme Souness had been a proponent of them in the early 1990s, taking the squad to Italy for a week before embarking on a tour elsewhere. Roy Evans wasn't a fan of the idea but when Gérard Houllier took sole control, he organised Swiss training camps which were usually rounded off by playing one friendly. When Rafael Benitez took control in 2004 he continued the theme, but incorporating more games into them.

2005 SWITZERLAND/AUSTRIA/LIECHTENSTEIN

After the epic Champions League win of 2005 Liverpool began the following season earlier than they had ever done, playing their first competitive game before they had even gone to the training camp. The farcical situation of UEFA not allowing the Champions of Europe to defend their trophy because they hadn't finished in the top four of their league (Liverpool had finished fifth) meant the rules had to be hastily redrawn and a compromise reached. The Reds would be allowed to compete in the Champions League in 2005-06, but only by entering in the first qualifying round, meaning their season would start on 13th July, little over a week after the players returned to Melwood.

The draw could have seriously disrupted the Reds' plans, as one of their potential opponents was from Kazakhstan, more than six hours away by air, but they ended up being paired with Welsh champions Total Network Solutions. This meant a journey of just 40 miles to the away leg which was played at Wrexham's Racecourse Ground. Coincidentally, that was also the venue of the first pre- season friendly on 9th July, where the European Cup was paraded prior to a 4-3 win for the Reds, a game in which Pepe Reina made his first appearance in goal for the club. The Reds then beat TNS 3-0 at Anfield on 13th July in the first leg of the Champions League tie, before flying to Switzerland the next day for the training camp at Bad Ragaz.

Benitez's first summer in charge a year earlier, which wasn't helped by the late return of many players after the European Championships, had seen him assess the players he had inherited at Melwood before going on the tour of America that had been arranged before his appointment. This time he was far more in control of preparations but the Reds' entry to the Champions League in mid-July then gave him a serious headache, as they were only informed by UEFA about this a month beforehand. Benitez opted to go ahead with the training camp, even though it meant flying back to play the second leg against TNS, played in between friendlies against opposition that the Reds had knocked out of the previous season's Champions League. With the Reds holding a comfortable 3-0 lead over the part-timers, Benitez knew that he would be able to rest some players for the second leg.

In addition to Reina Bolo, Zenden had joined Liverpool that summer on a free transfer from Middlesbrough and played against TNS. Midfielder Momo Sissoko though had signed too late to play in that game but was in the squad for the training camp. On his way out of Anfield was cult figure Igor Biscan, an unused substitute in the Champions League final who joined Panathinaikos. Sissoko would make his debut for the Reds against Bayer Leverkusen on the evening of Saturday 16th July. The Reds crossed the border into Austria for the match, which was televised by Channel Five and played at the Reichshofstadion in Lustenau, situated on the banks of the River Rhine which forms the border between Austria and Switzerland. It was the second time the Reds had faced Leverkusen at this venue, having played here whilst away in Bad Ragaz with Gérard Houllier in 2001, Liverpool winning that game 3-2. This time they won 3-0, with Djibril Cissé scoring twice in the first half and Milan Baroš adding another after the break. Sissoko was one of nine second half substitutes as Benitez sought to give as many players as possible a run out. A capacity crowd of 9,400 watched the match, with the visit of the European champions being a big attraction in a town best known for its history in the embroidery industry and being the birthplace of another five times champion. This was skier Marc Girardelli who won five Alpine World Cups and also a silver medal at the 1992 Olympics. Tickets for the game cost just €15, with season ticket holders of Austria Lustenau being given a €5 discount. A handful of fans from Merseyside made the trip, with one poster on the *Redandwhitekop* internet forum describing the ground as a bit like Wimbledon's old Plough Lane. A number of British holidaymakers in the area also took in the game and Liverpool shirts were predominant in the crowd. Most of these were worn by German speakers, with next to no neutrals following Leverkusen.

Benitez was satisfied afterwards, telling the official club website: 'It was a good game for us. We used a different team in each half and I am pleased with the performance. My idea was to see all the players and I now have to analyse the squad before selecting who will fly back to face TNS on Tuesday. That is most important for us now.' Despite holding the 3-0 lead,

Benitez named a strong 18-man party for the match against TNS, with Gerrard, Sami Hyypia and Xabi Alonso all included. The part-timers held their own against the Reds for long periods, with the 3-0 scoreline not being a true reflection as two of the goals, both from Gerrard who came on as a substitute, were scored in the last five minutes.

On 20th July there was another new arrival as Peter Crouch underwent a medical and signed for the Reds. Benitez told the official club website that he was a player that could hold the ball up well and help the Reds keep possession, which he felt was important given they had lost 11 away games the previous season. Crouch flew out to Switzerland to join his new team-mates and as he had been training with Southampton, it was reported that he should be ready to face Olympiacos in Liechtenstein on the evening of Saturday 23rd July. Crouch was the sixth player to sign for the club that summer with competition for places being high in all positions. A big squad was essential given the number of games coming up, with the Reds now facing a trip to Lithuania on 26th July, where they would face FBK Kaunas in the second qualifying round of the Champions League. The Reds boss didn't see this as a bad thing, especially in light of the desire to improve in the league and told the website two days before the Olympiacos game:

'We are playing a lot of games at the moment and so the players are getting chances to improve their match fitness. We've had two good games against TNS and they should stand us in good stead for the start of the season. We're not at our best yet but the more games we play and the more training we do then the better the physical condition of the players will become.'

Vice-captain Jamie Carragher was another who had no complaints about the amount of games, as he always preferred to play than undergo extra training. He also had high regard for the facilities at Bad Ragaz, saying: 'We've been to this training camp a few times in recent years, going back to when Gérard Houllier was the manager. It›s a great place to come and train. It›s quiet and the facilities are impressive. It›s good for helping the new lads settle in and everyone is getting along fine.'

A crowd of just 2,500 were at the tiny Rheinpark Stadium in the Liechtenstein capital of Vaduz to see Crouch making an impressive start, twice going close before setting up Luis Garcia for the opening goal after half an hour. Rivaldo levelled before half-time then after the break Milan Baroš, determined to prove he could still make a contribution at Anfield, scored twice as the Reds went on to win 4-3. Benitez told the official club website afterwards that he was satisfied with Crouch's performance and also the levels of fitness displayed by the players in a game that again saw nine substitutions in the second half, keeper Scott Carson and young defender Carl Medjani being the only players to complete 90 minutes.

The following Tuesday the Reds won 3-1 in Lithuania against Kaunas and although they had a long season, the training camp played a part helping them fight on a number of fronts. The league position improved as they finished third and although they went out of the Champions League in the last 16 there was glory at the end as they beat West Ham on penalties in Cardiff to lift the FA Cup.

2007 SWITZERLAND

Liverpool again trained at Bad Ragaz in 2006, playing another friendly in Liechtenstein where a full house at the tiny 2,800 capacity Sportplatz in Eschen-Mauren saw them lose 4-3 against Kaiserslautern. They then went on to play friendlies against Grasshoppers and Mainz at the stadiums of those clubs. In 2007, prior to moving on to the Far East, Rafa Benitez again took the squad to Switzerland where they had a week's training coupled with friendlies played in local stadiums, introducing new attacking players that would go on to have contrasting fortunes at Anfield.

The Reds had reached a second Champions League final in three years, but this time were beaten 2-1 by AC Milan. Before the Reds had even left their Athens base for home, Benitez made it clear that if they were to continue with the progress made in recent years and replicate their European success in the Premiership, then more signings needed to be made. Co-owners George Gillett and Tom Hicks responded by breaking the club's transfer record to sign Fernando Torres from Atlético Madrid for £20 million and Dutch winger Ryan Babel arrived from Ajax for £11.5 million. The Reds also paid West Ham £5 million for attacking midfielder Yossi Benayoun and Ukraine international forward Andrey Voronin came in on a free transfer from Bayer Leverkusen. Prior to the final the Reds had also recruited young Brazilian Lucas Leiva from Gremio, while the signings of Sebastián Leto and Mikel Dominguez meant the total outlay over the summer had been over £40 million. £20 million of this was recouped from the fees received for Craig Bellamy, Djibril Cissé, Luis Garcia and Mark Gonzalez, with the wage bill also being reduced further as Jerzy Dudek, Robbie Fowler and Bolo Zenden left on free transfers.

The Reds began their pre-season campaign on 7th July when a youthful side won 3-2 at Wrexham, then a week later a stronger team won 3-0 at Crewe. Only Voronin of the new signings was in the side for either of these games, but all the new faces were in the party that flew out to Switzerland on 15th July. A change from previous years though was that rather than hold the training camp in Bad Ragaz, they instead went to Interlaken in the west of the country. Benitez was pleased with the team building he had done and told the official website he was confident that the players he had signed were better than those they were replacing and would suit the style of play he was looking to create.

One notable absentee on this training camp was Javier Mascherano, who was on Copa America duty with Argentina, while Harry Kewell, whose Anfield future was very much in the balance due to both poor form and injuries, was in the Australia squad that was competing in the Asia Cup. The first game was played at the Stadion Bruehl in the watchmaking town of Grenchen on 17th July against Werder Bremen and televised by Setanta Sports for fans back home. Voronin scored twice for the Reds before being replaced just past the hour mark by Torres, who was being eased in gently following an ankle injury. Babel came on with a quarter of an hour remaining for Nabil El Zhar and Benayoun played the whole of the second half in a game in which Liverpool ran out 3-2 winners in front of a crowd of 10,180, many of whom were wearing Reds shirts and able to drink beer whilst stood on the terraces.

Benitez was pleased with the impact of the new players, with Voronin's second goal being a brilliant lob after being set up by Alonso. The Reds boss said: 'You can see the different options we have now in attack. It was good for the supporters to see us attacking and playing some good football.' [64] Benitez also told the club's official website that he had made some minor adjustments to previous training camps, in that there would be less sessions – previous training camps had seen the players train two or three times a day – but with more intensity. Xabi Alonso confirmed that although it was good to have a change of scenery and be away from Melwood, the sessions were still hard, saying: 'It's always good to get away like this because you usually just train in the same place every day. But we are trying hard to get fit for the new season and Pako is always working us very hard – not just in pre-season.'

The second match whilst the Reds were away took place on the afternoon of 20th July against Auxerre in Fribourg. Before taking a coach there the players first underwent a light training session, as they had done before the Werder Bremen game. The game was again shown on Setanta and fans back home saw a new face in goal, with 19-year-old Bulgarian keeper Nikolay Mihaylov being given a run out. Due to work permit issues though, he would make no other appearances for the Reds and spent the three years of his contract on loan at Dutch side Twente. Torres again started on the bench, coming on for the whole of the second half of a game that the Reds won 2-0 in hot conditions thanks to goals from Steven Gerrard and Daniel Agger. From Switzerland the Reds moved on to fulfil the commercial obligations of their pre season as they headed to the Far East. Benitez was satisfied the training camp had done its job however, telling the website: 'We have enjoyed our training camp in Switzerland and the players have worked very hard.' The new season saw an improvement in results but still not enough to finish as champions. The Reds were eight points better off than in 2006-07 and 11 off the top compared to 21, but they also dropped a place to fourth. The form of the strikers was varied though with Torres being a sensation, Voronin a huge disappointment and Babel inconsistent.

Liverpool's 2008 Swiss training camp replicated that of the previous year, with the players staying in Interlaken and matches being played in Grenchen and Fribourg against Lucerne and Wisla Krakow respectively, the Reds winning 2-1 and then drawing 1-1. Whereas in 2007 Benitez had more or less completed his transfer dealings by the time the training camp started, this close season had seen striker Peter Crouch leave the club before any replacement was found. The new signings to date that did travel, defenders Philipp Degen and Andrea Dossena, would go on to totally underwhelm the Liverpool supporters, while that summer's big arrival Robbie Keane, who signed at the end of July, lasted only half a season before being sold back to Tottenham. Nevertheless the Reds pushed Manchester United all the way in the title race and picked up 86 points, at the time the highest total for a team that finished as runners up.

In 2009 the Reds went back to Bad Ragaz for what would turn out to be Benitez's last pre-season. There was a change to the previous routines in that rather than play other Continental sides in small local neutral stadiums, this time the Reds played two games in at the homes of their opposition. On 15th July they drew 0-0 against St Gallen and then four days later went down 1-0 to Rapid Vienna in a game that was played in front of 50,000 at the Ernst Happel Staion, venue for the previous year's European Championship final. Things were now vastly different however and with the American owners having loaded debt on to the club to pay for their initial purchase, money available for transfers was diminishing every year. The summer of 2009 saw no money made available for players and Benitez used the funds from the sales of Xabi Alonso and Alvaro Arbeloa to buy Glen Johnson and Alberto Aquilani. Italian midfielder Aquilani was carrying an injury when he signed and even when he regained fitness he was off the pace and the Reds finished a disappointing seventh, leading to Benitez leaving the club by mutual consent.

2010 SWITZERLAND

Liverpool's new manager, who continued the Swiss training camp tradition was not a universally popular appointment. Roy Hodgson had over 30 years of coaching experience in several countries but his two biggest jobs, at Blackburn Rovers and Inter Milan, had ended in failure. He also did little to endear himself to fans when he said the atmosphere at Anfield was comparable to Old Trafford. Hodgson's pre-season schedule didn't go to plan either, which just about summed up the way things would go when the season proper started.

The Reds party of 22 players flew out on 15th July and were again at Bad Ragaz, although with this being a World Cup year many of the more experienced squad members were missing having been given an extended summer break. A much increased in-house media presence meant that as well as news on the website, television updates were available too on the club's channel LFC TV, which was also showing the matches live. Internet users could also watch iPhone blogs from presenter Claire Rourke.

Prior to training on the 16th July the players posed for pictures with members of the Swiss branch of the Official Liverpool Supporters' Club, who presented each of the players with a box of chocolates. The session was then carried out in intense heat and was broken up every 10 minutes so drinks could be taken, but the official club website reported that it had gone well and the players were responding to Hodgson's methods.

Afterwards a press conference was held, which attracted a lot of interest from the Swiss media with Hodgson having managed their national side in the early 1990s, guiding them to their first World Cup finals since 1966. Hodgson answered questions in both English and German, but most of the attention from the British media was to do with transfer speculation regarding striker Fernando Torres, who was still on holiday having been part of Spain's World Cup winning squad. Hodgson told reporters that he had met Torres and that he was not for sale, although with the Reds facing their first season out of the Champions League since 2003-04 he faced a tough job holding on to the striker if big bids came in. Another player whose future was uncertain was Argentine midfielder Javier Mascherano who was also on holiday after the World Cup, with Hodgson admitting that he hadn't even been able to speak to the player as no reply had been received to phone messages and texts.

The following day the majority of the players had a stroll around the hotel grounds and then took it easy in readiness for the match that night against Saudi Arabian side Al-Hilal across the border in Altach, Austria. They had been chosen as the opposition as they were believed to be at the same level as the young Liverpool side that was being put out due to the number of players who were still unavailable. There was no rest for Sotorios Kyrgiakos and Milan Jovanović though, who weren't quite ready for the game having had more time off than the others due to the World Cup. They were put through their paces in the morning sunshine but later in the day the weather took a turn for the worse and turned to torrential rain, causing the late cancellation of the match. The players had already arrived at the stadium and went out to salute those fans who were already inside, with Hodgson saying he was disappointed for those who had made the long journey but there was no choice but to call the game off:

> 'The referee had no choice. Everyone tried very hard to get the game on but it wasn't possible. We wanted to play, Al-Hilal wanted to play, but to play a football match you need the ball to be rolling properly around the pitch. It wasn't doing that and so it was impossible. We tried everything but you can't fight the weather and even if we had started the game it would have been played at the limit, and I'm not sure we would have finished it.'

The cancellation of the game meant that the players had to forfeit a planned day off on the Sunday and held a full training session in the morning instead, which took place in blazing sunshine. Brazilian midfielder Lucas told Rourke how disappointed he was at the game being called off as he had been asked by Hodgson to captain the side. Following the training session, which involved the players riding on bikes from the hotel to and from the pitches, they were given an afternoon off to play golf or tennis, then attended a barbecue laid on by their hosts in the evening.

On 19th July a new face arrived in Bad Ragaz as Joe Cole, released by Chelsea, joined his new team-mates after he had been persuaded by managing director Christian Purslow to sign for the Reds rather than Arsenal or Tottenham. Cole was the third arrival of the summer, following on from Serb striker Milan Jovanović and 18-year-old midfielder Jonjo Shelvey, although both those deals had been done by Benitez. Two former Liverpool greats – Ian Rush and Phil Thompson – both predicted that Cole, who had his medical in Switzerland, would be a massive success for the Reds.

The fragmented nature of the preparations meant that while the bulk of the squad were in Switzerland, Daniel Agger, Jamie Carragher, Steven Gerrard and Glen Johnson were returning to Melwood for their first day of pre-season training on 20th July. However Torres and Mascherano were still yet to return as were Ryan Babel, Dirk Kuyt and Pepe Reina, whose World Cup campaign had seen them involved all the way to the final. Captain Gerrard welcomed the signing of Cole and made it clear he had no plans to leave the Reds, having spoken privately to Hodgson regarding the coming season. Over in Switzerland, Lucas told the official website that Jovanović was looking dangerous in training and that Cole was a great addition who would help the squad a lot.

On 21st July the weather thankfully remained dry as Liverpool made final preparations for a match against Swiss side Grasshoppers Zurich in Zug. Hodgson admitted beforehand that many of the players who took part wouldn't be featuring in league games and that the real pre-season build-up would be at Melwood. He told the club's official website:

'Realistically, a lot of these players won't take part when we come to the league games because they are players who have come from the reserves and the Academy. They are working extremely well and I couldn't be happier with what we're doing, but we're about to play two really tough games with a team which, in my opinion, isn't ready to play against that level of opponent. It's a great opportunity for them but my real work in preparing Liverpool Football Club to play next season will begin when I get back to Melwood and find the 13 players who went to the World Cup. If you're a young player you're waiting for that chance to get into the first team and show what you can do. These lads are being given a chance earlier than expected and unfortunately they are being given a chance all together. What you hope for when you get your chance is that all the big-hitters are around you and they make it a bit easier for you. Here we are throwing them all in together.'

With the club now up for sale and very little money available for new players, Hodgson also acknowledged that a sense of perspective had to viewed about Liverpool's prospects for the coming season. He told the website before the Grasshoppers game that the arrival of Cole and Gerrard's reaffirmed commitment to the club was a boost, but it would only be when new investment came that supporters could expect to be back at what they saw as their rightful place. This wasn't the words fans wanted to hear as although they craved new owners, there was also a feeling that Hodgson was bringing expectations down to the mid-table level that he was most familiar working at.

Cole, Jovanović and Kyrgiakos were all missing from the Reds line-up on the advice of sports scientists so it was a youthful looking team that took on Grasshoppers, a club Hodgson had managed in 1999-00. Only Alberto Aquilani, Lucas and David N'gog had regularly appeared for the first team and in the second half when Lucas came off after an hour, he passed the captain's armband to 21- year- old Jay Spearing, who had played only seven games for the Reds so far. The match ended 0-0, with N'gog going close on a couple of occasions in a lively first half, but in the second the game lost its flow owing to a number of substitutions by both sides. The average age of the team that finished the game was 19.6 and Hodgson was delighted with the performance of his youngsters, telling the official club website afterwards:

'The boys did very well. This is a group of boys, many of whom have never kicked a ball for the first team or even been around the first team. Players like Tom Ince, Jack Robinson and Victor Palsson are very young players. So, to take on a team like Grasshoppers, who are towards the top of the Swiss League and who've been able to use their full squad, and get a 0-0 is a remarkable achievement with some players who've never kicked a ball outside of the Academy. They've done the club proud. I had no doubts they'd do that in terms of their determination, desire and work rate but the bottom line is that at the moment there are gaps in their play because of their age. That takes time.'

Jay Spearing, who had come through the youth ranks, said it was a 'dream' to captain the side and that their hard work in the preceding week had been a factor in the good performance, telling the website: 'There have been a lot of hard sessions every day and I think it showed in the game with the effort the whole team put in. Right from the goalkeepers to the forwards, everybody worked very hard and it showed in the things we did.' There was an injury blow for the Reds in the game, with Aquilani picking up a knock and the following day he returned to Melwood for treatment. The rest of the players remained in Bad Ragaz until Saturday 24th July, then headed into Germany for a friendly against Kaiserslautern at the Bundesliga side's Fritz Walter Stadion. Jovanović made his Reds debut, playing the whole of the first half but the young Reds side lost 1-0 in a game that again saw Lucas hand the captain's armband over to Jay Spearing when he was substituted.

The Reds party then returned home for Hodgson to begin working with some of the more senior players on 26th July, although the Spanish and Dutch players still had another week off. There wasn't much time to work out though as just three days later they were playing their first competitive match in the Europa League, against Rabotnički in Macedonia. It could be argued that the World Cup of 2010, which seriously limited the number of players Hodgson had available to him for the pre-season training camp was a factor in his disastrous spell in charge of Liverpool. Europa League qualifiers effectively became warm up matches and he ended up being sacked in January 2011 with the club 12th in the table and just four points above the relegation zone. However there were plenty of other factors too, such as an extremely poor return in the transfer market, with players such as Paul Konchesky and Christian Poulsen failing to deliver, while Cole also didn't live up to promise. There have been no training camps since, with Kenny Dalglish and Brendan Rodgers instead starting off preparations at Melwood before undertaking a tour on another continent.

17

Soccer Tours

As Liverpool have such a large following in the Far East it is perhaps not surprising that they have concentrated their long distance tour efforts in making sure that they retain it given the competition from other clubs and the ease with which some fans change allegiances. However there are other continents to conquer and since the 1994 World Cup there has been an increase in popularity of football, or soccer as the Americans like to call it, in the United States. Other sports remain the top draw but with such a huge market to tap, clubs, Liverpool included, have started to make inroads to a place where more interest was shown than on previous visits, but nowhere near the hysterical level of the Far East.

NORTH AMERICA 2004

Liverpool's first tour of North America for 40 years came in 2004 when they were involved in the Champions World Series, a programme of 11 friendlies involving nine top European sides over an 11-day period across the United States and Canada.

Whereas the Reds had always played local sides on Far Eastern tours, in the USA it was felt matches between top sides were better as they were likely to generate more interest and income than those involving American sides. Rick Parry explained to the club's official website that as it was a European Championship year a Far Eastern trip wasn't really feasible. He believed jetlag was far less of an issue on the east coast of America, while it was also felt necessary to visit there due to the Reds kit now being manufactured by Reebok.

The series organisers claimed to have accumulated the 'greatest collection of soccer talent this side of the World Cup' and that it was their goal to 'bring the very best teams in the soccer world to North America to showcase their incredible technical ability, passion and skill against other quality teams to create exciting games in stadia with unforgettable atmosphere.'[65]

It had been a summer of upheaval at Anfield with the departure of Gérard Houllier and appointment of Rafa Benitez. Speculation had also been rife over the future of Steven Gerrard, who was strongly linked with a move to Chelsea before deciding to stay and Michael Owen, who had just one year left on his contract and had still not concluded negotiations over a new one. It meant that as with the trip to Swaziland in 1984, the future of one of the club's key players was very much in the balance as the Reds jetted off.

The players' journey was far simpler and more luxurious than that encountered by their predecessors in 1964, with a charter jet usually used by the Miami Heat basketball team flying them from Liverpool to Newark on 25th July, stopping to refuel in Iceland and Newfoundland on the way. Unlike some of the other teams involved, the Reds would be staying in the same time zone so once in America, travelling would not be too gruelling with no coast to coast flights. There would also be no waiting for news of games or the comings and goings of players this time. All matches were being televised live and journalists from the club's official website provided daily updates of what was happening on the days between games.

The Reds set up base at a New Jersey high school that had been used by Italy in the 1994 World Cup, from where Rafael Benitez conducted his press conferences from behind a school desk. Unlike with recent inter-continental visits to the Far East there was no media frenzy, with training sessions being of no interest to the American media and the players being able to go quietly about their business. In fact when they left the hotel for a stroll around the grounds the biggest danger was the raccoons, which they had been warned were liable to attack humans. The closest to sightseeing that the players got to do early on was when they saw a stunning view of the Manhattan skyline during the short flight to Connecticut on the morning of 27th July where the Reds would play their first game against Celtic. It was there at the Crowne Plaza Hotel in East Hartford that the first sign of excitement from any locals was shown. Even then autograph hunters were unsure of who all the players were with one of the website team, Steve Hunter, having a pen and paper thrust in front of him.

Benitez made it clear that nobody was a first choice starter and it was a clean slate for all the players to stake a place in the side but defender Djimi Traoré suffered a blow when a thigh strain sustained in training forced him to return home before the Celtic match, which was played at Rentschler Field. The 40,000 seat stadium, completed the previous year for the Connecticut Huskies American football team was not much more than half full but those that did attend were well entertained. Benitez said beforehand that there was no such thing as a friendly and the Reds ran riot winning 5-1 with new signing Djibril Cissé netting twice, the play not being disrupted despite seven substitutions being made at half-time.

The continued lack of understanding of post match customs was also emphasised after the match when Danny Murphy, who had swapped shirts with Celtic's Neil Lennon, was ordered by a steward to head for the Celtic changing room. He was only allowed to join his team-mates when he pointed out his red shorts and socks. The following day there was a rare mention in the American press of Liverpool's presence, with the *Hartford Courier* printing a comprehensive match report, which described John Arne Riise's opening goal as 'a rocket through traffic.'

The Reds then returned to their New Jersey base for a few days, where a promotional event took place in which four Reds players – Jerzy Dudek, Sami Hyypia, Stephen Warnock and Zak Whitbread- donned shoulder pads and went through some American football moves with some gridiron stars form the New York Jets and Giants. A rare foray into the training venue by an American journalist also led to an odd question for striker Milan Baroš, who was asked what he ate for breakfast to enable him to score so many goals. He replied 'cornflakes.'

The Reds flew to Toronto on 30th July, where they found that rapper Eminem and his entourage were also staying at the Westin Harbour Hotel. Their welcome was much more passionate than in the USA, with many of the 600-strong Toronto Supporters' Club being at the hotel and they also hosted a welcome night for travelling fans at their Yonge Street headquarters. Things were moving too on the transfer front, with new defender Josemi joining the Reds in Toronto after passing a medical at Melwood the previous day. Despite Vladimir Šmicer suffering a serious knee injury and flying to Colorado for an operation Benitez made it clear that El Hadji Diouf still had no future at the club, the Senegal striker having been left behind and told to line up for the reserves in a friendly at Vauxhall. One player he was keen to have at the club was Michael Owen and the feeling seemed mutual. He told reporters how happy he was to be working with Benitez and that he was hoping to have a new contract sorted out before the start of the season.

On 31st July the Reds faced European champions Porto at the Sky Dome, home of the Toronto Blue Jays baseball side and where grass had been laid especially for the game. They had been scheduled to take a trip to Niagara Falls beforehand but this was cancelled as it was felt a three-hour round trip was too much for a match day, so instead they had to make do with a walk around the harbour. For the game there was a much more encouraging attendance of 40,078, making the stadium 80% full but the Reds were unable to repeat the form they had shown four days earlier. Porto, now managed by Luigi Delneri after José Mourinho had left for Chelsea, won 1-0 thanks to a late Carlos Alberto goal after they had hit the post twice earlier in the game.

One fan who was in Toronto against the advice of a doctor was Andy Hodge from Bootle who was also an Anfield steward. After the Celtic game he had tripped over a kerb, breaking his wrist and two fingers leading to both arms being placed in plaster. The lack of a National Health Service in the United States meant he was not going to have any more treatment than absolutely necessary there but rather than return home as encouraged, he made sure he remained there for the rest of the tour. By the time of the Toronto match the Reds following had significantly increased and many of the banners seen so often around Europe were on display, such as the Bootle Irregulars and Kingfisher Kirkby flags.

The Liverpool players checked out of their Toronto hotel the next morning as next opponents AS Roma checked in, with the Italian side facing Celtic that night before moving on to New Jersey to face the Reds. The Reds now had three days between games so they were allowed a rare rest day on which they were taken on a tour around New York City including a boat trip.

The final game of the tour on 4th August against AS Roma was at the famous Giants Stadium in New Jersey, which had staged seven games in the 1994 World Cup and was home of the New York Giants and New York Jets American football teams. There were plenty of spaces in the 80,000 seat stadium though, just 25,028 turning out to see Liverpool win 2-1, with Michael Owen scoring the winning goal five minutes from time.

The Reds left straight after the game, returning to Liverpool on Miami Heat's plane. They had left a lasting impression, with Academy coaches having run a number of training camps for local schoolchildren. As they left event organiser Chris Unger told the club website:

'In terms of building the Liverpool brand and taking the team to the fans in the United States I'd say it was a good idea and that it's been well received. When you first approach a new market it is a learning experience and you don't know how the fans will react but I think from Liverpool's perspective it has been a very successful tour. When you look at the guys Liverpool have on their team there are so many stars and they've performed so well. They've brought their team with them and played to win every match. Not only do we the event organisers appreciate this, the fans do as well. They want to see the best players and Liverpool have provided this. It probably makes more business sense from the club's point of view to go back to Asia next summer and explore other markets but we don't want it to be 10 years before Liverpool come back here. Hopefully they'll consider coming back the year after next. We'd welcome them back with open arms.'

When the new season began there were some parallels to 1964-65, with a disappointing league campaign being offset by cup glory, this time in the Champions League when the Reds came back from 3-0 down to beat AC Milan on penalties in Istanbul. They would do that without Michael Owen though, who despite having given so much indication that he would sign a new contract ended up joining Real Madrid a week before the start of the season.

NORTH AMERICA 2012

The only surprise about Liverpool's visit to America in 2012 was that it was not until six years after the club had been purchased by American owners that they had gone there. There were no trips there during the four summers that Tom Hicks and George Gillett co-owned the club, but after they sold to John W. Henry's Fenway Sports Group in October 2010, it was made clear that developing the Reds brand in the United States was on the agenda. 2011 saw the Reds go to the Far East, but rumours circulated for some time that they would be going to America in 2012.

The tour was not officially confirmed until March, when it was announced that Liverpool would play AS Roma at Fenway Park, home of the Boston Red Sox baseball team that Henry also owned, in a game that formed part of the venue's centenary celebrations. The Reds confirmed that two other games would be played during the 12-day visit, although arrangements were still to be finalised. Reds boss Kenny Dalglish said that he was looking forward to the tour, saying:

> 'We had a great time playing in front of our supporters in Asia last year and it will be good to give our fans in North America the chance to watch us live this summer. My son Paul worked and played in America and he's told me about just how much interest there is in Liverpool, and English football, right now. We've had some amazing matches against Roma in the past, particularly the 1984 European Cup final, so it should be fantastic.'[66]

By the time the tour came around however Dalglish was no longer the manager, having been sacked by Henry following a disappointing league campaign that saw the Reds finish eighth. Winning the League Cup and also reaching the FA Cup final had failed to save him and he was replaced by Brendan Rodgers, who had guided Swansea to the Premiership and seen the club make a lot of friends with a stylish passing game. His appointment brought a mixed reaction from fans, given Dalglish's iconic status at the club, although on the whole the feeling was that any dissatisfaction should be towards the owners and that the new manager had to be backed. In many ways though Rodgers was taking the job on with one hand tied behind his back as it was made clear to him he would not have the funds available to him that Dalglish had. As such this American trip gave him an opportunity at close hand to see what areas needed strengthening the most in time for the start of the season as well as give players a chance to get used to his methods.

It wasn't just about the playing side though, there was a commercial element as chief executive Ian Ayre explained to the club's online television subscriptions service, LFC Online before departure:

> 'Obviously sponsorship is a very important part of our revenue generation at the club and this is an opportunity for our sponsors to showcase with their customers or their staff, and to bring people to those types of games in markets where they have other business. Warrior is probably the best example as our new kit supplier; they have a head office in Boston. New Balance are based in Boston, so it will be very exciting for them as a new partner to be able to showcase their relationship with Liverpool in their home town.'

Rodgers named a 34-man party for the tour but was forced to make some notable exceptions. Keeper Pepe Reina was still on holiday after Spain's European Championship win and Uruguayan Luis Suárez was away with his country's Olympic squad, as was Craig Bellamy who was part of Team GB. The charter flight that departed Liverpool John Lennon Airport bound for Boston on Monday 16th July contained 27 of the players, with the six England internationals due to join the tour for the second week. Also arriving then would be the one summer signing so far, Italian striker Fabio Borini who insisted on cutting short a planned holiday to be on the tour, despite not having to be back until August as he was part of the Italian squad that had reached the European Championship final.

Two club legends, Robbie Fowler and Ian Rush were also present, with Ayre explaining that this was to help ease the burden on the current players in terms of personal appearances and community coaching sessions. Although the number of players still on breaks after the European Championships meant several youngsters were included, Rodgers didn't see this as a bad thing, saying before departure:

> 'It's a great pre-season for me because I get to look at the younger players and the senior players. So they all feel there's hope right through the club. I've also got some of the staff from the Academy coming with me. I feel it's important that they understand how I work, on and off the field, because when we come back, it all becomes really, really busy and you're getting into your focus for the games. So it's a great integration for the players and the staff and we will enjoy it and work hard which is important.'[67]

This was almost certainly Liverpool's most comprehensively covered tour ever, with all major national newspapers having journalists there in addition to the local press and club media channels. It wasn't just the matches that were being covered, with cameras accompanying the players and officials at their training complexes, hotels and dressing rooms as part of a fly-on-the-wall documentary, *Being Liverpool*, which would later be broadcast as six one-hour episodes on Fox Sports and Channel Five. In addition, the phenomenal rise of Twitter meant that more of the players were now communicating directly with fans, as well as through journalists. Some of the tweets would be interesting, but many more were mundane, with Brad Jones and José Enrique feeling the need to let their followers know that they had boarded the plane.

After touching down in Boston the party transferred to a hotel where Rodgers held a press conference for the U.S. media. He told them that if a player was good enough they would get a chance no matter how young they were. The timing of the tour and Liverpool's entry into the Europa League as League Cup holders rather than via the FA Cup or league route, meant that they would be playing their first qualifying tie on 2nd August, just four days after they were due to arrive home. Rodgers admitted it wasn't the best preparation but that 'we'll be up to speed' come the time of the first game.

The following morning the players were put through their first training session at the prestigious Harvard University's sports complex. A small number of fans attended and the players were happy to pose for pictures and sign autographs. Also present was Reds chairman Tom Werner, who said of the visit: 'It's a great opportunity for the fans in North America to see this squad and I'm excited to see the training here today because we're so pleased that Brendan Rodgers is our coach and that he's implementing the philosophy that he discussed with us. It's also great to see all these young faces.'[68] The session was held in soaring temperatures of over 100 degrees but Jamie Carragher believed this would be beneficial to the players, telling the official club website that the heat would make the players work harder and help build fitness for the season ahead.

On 18th July Fowler and Rush helped out with training at a children's summer camp, which was run in conjunction with the Red Sox Foundation. They were joined there by John W. Henry's wife Linda Pizzuti, who told the website:

'The Liverpool coaches are doing an amazing job over here. They are so talented they can – and do – go all over the world and coach kids regardless of where they come from or what language they speak. Football is such a global sport and Liverpool are such a global club – to have them here today is a real thrill for not just the young people but also me.'

After training on 18th July, Rodgers and defender Daniel Agger went to the Old Yard outside University Hall to visit the statue of John Harvard, unveiled in 1886, six years before the Reds were formed, and carried out the tradition of touching his left foot for luck. As he looked to the season ahead, Rodgers said he hoped a change of formation would help the Reds overcome the problem of lack of goals, which blighted them in 2011-12, telling the website:

> 'People talk about the goalscoring last year. They talk about playing two strikers or one striker, but it's about your players. For a lot of last season the team played 4-4-2. People cry out about playing two strikers up front, yet everyone at the end of the season said we didn't score enough. With 4-3-3 you play with three strikers, depending on the types they are – whether it's one up and two wide or one up and two more narrow. That means the draws can turn into wins and the losses turn into draws. If we can get goals into the team and keep our stability from behind then hopefully we can fly.'

That night an example occurred of just how different the players communicated with fans compared to those earliest tours when letters were printed a week after games took place, as defender José Enrique conducted a live question and answer session on Twitter. Most of the questions were in relation to his career to date and hopes for the coming season, but he did say that the players were not sharing rooms on the tour and Northern Irish winger Ryan McLaughlin had impressed him so far.

Owner John W. Henry attended training on 19th July, telling the website that Liverpool were a local club and that it was important that they get out and meet the fans. In the evening the squad attended a baseball match at Fenway Park between the Boston Red Sox and Chicago White Sox. Some of the players went to the home side's dressing room before the game and exchanged shirts, but a plan for Carragher to carry out the ceremonial first pitch was dropped as there were concerns amongst Red Sox fans that their owners were paying too much attention to the Reds, something that has also been felt vice versa by Liverpool fans.

The following day the Reds party flew to Toronto in readiness for the first game of the tour, against Toronto FC at the ironically named Rogers Center (formerly the Skydome where the Reds played in 2004) on 22nd July. Some 4,000 fans attended a training session held at the stadium and afterwards Rodgers instructed the whole squad to go and pose for photographs and sign autographs. After 15 minutes the players left to get changed and go back to the hotel but Rodgers remained longer, telling reporters that he felt it was his duty to do so. He also chatted for a while to a disabled fan, Khalid Magram, who had waited patiently by the exit tunnel in his wheelchair as he had been unable to go in the stand. He told lfctour.com later that he thought Rodgers would be special for Liverpool and that 'there's something good about him.' The morning of the game was spent relaxing and there was also some opportunity for sightseeing, with the 553-metre CN Tower being situated next to the Rogers Center, from where Brad Jones posted a picture on Twitter.

Rodgers made it known that the game against Toronto was essentially about fitness and that all 11 players would be changed at half-time. The Major League Soccer side, who were halfway through their season, took the lead on 58 minutes but 18-year-old Academy graduate Adam Morgan levelled for the Reds in the 69th minute and neither side could find a winner. Morgan was delighted at the goal afterwards and dedicated it to his grandmother who had recently died. He was also pleased that his father had managed to make it out to Toronto to see him score it. The Reds side contained a mixture of youth and experience, balanced across the two halves of a game played in intense heat, having kicked off at 3pm. A total of 23 players were used in all, with a major boost coming 16 minutes from time when Lucas Leiva, who had missed most of 2011-12 through injury, came on to the pitch to warm applause from the large number of Liverpool supporters in the 33,087 crowd. The game was shown live in England on ESPN and followers of Enrique on Twitter were even treated to a pitchside view from the bench which he posted during the second half.

Joe Cole was one of the players that was desperate to impress Rodgers and convince him that he had a future at Anfield. After his high profile arrival in 2010 he had failed to make an impression and spent 2011-12 on loan at Lille. Cole was keeping a video diary of the tour which was posted on YouTube and he said of the first game: 'The first game is always the toughest one, you're finding your feet, the main thing is to get fitness in. It was nice to get a result and not lose the game, everyone came through unscathed and we're happy.'[69] He also revealed that after flying back to Boston the players were allowed to unwind a little and went out for a meal and watched a Manchester United friendly in a sports bar, with some of them being given a lift back to the hotel late in the night by a police van.

Sunday 22nd July was a day off for the players but not the community coaches, who ran clinics for children from the Boston Supporters' Club as well as local schools. The following day it was back to training at Harvard, with some cruel temptation being thrown the way of two of the players. Dunkin Donuts, one of the sponsors of the tour arranged a question and answer session prior to the morning practice where keeper Brad Jones and midfielder Charlie Adam answered questions from local fans. Even though some special Liverpool donuts were made both players resisted the urge to try any and had a simple fruit breakfast instead. That evening the seven players who had been given extra time off following the European Championships arrived. They were Fabio Borini, Andy Carroll, Stewart Downing, Steven Gerrard, Jordan Henderson, Glen Johnson and Martin Kelly. On arrival Borini explained his decision not to take until the beginning of August off as he could have done due to Italy reaching the final: 'I chose to come early because I think it's important to be with the team, especially because I'm a new player. I could have had a month off but I didn't play at the Euros. I chose to come early to get used to the team and adapt more quickly. I am desperate to get started.'[70]

The new arrivals trained for the first time on Tuesday 24th July, with the 90 minute evening session being held at Fenway Park with John W. Henry in attendance. Rodgers admitted that they definitely would not be playing against Roma the following night and it was too early to say if they could feature in the last game of the tour, against Tottenham in Baltimore on Saturday 28th July.

Liverpool supporters had come from Merseyside, across North America and even as far as Japan and Australia to see this game. Captain Steven Gerrard said he was honoured to have such a following when he was asked about it at the press conference, saying: 'It's no surprise to me. We've got the best support in the world. I'm not being biased, it's fact. The fans travel from all over the world to get to games, they spend a lot of money and they're fanatical.'

Liverpool weren't just concentrating on playing and coaching whilst in Boston though, as commercial links were strengthened. They announced on 24th July that car manufacturer Chevrolet would be the club's new automotive partner, with a four-year agreement being signed. Ian Ayre said of the deal, which gave Chevrolet advertising opportunities at Anfield and in the club's media:

> 'Much like our club, Chevrolet has a long, rich history with a growing, global brand and this landmark partnership once again demonstrates the value of Liverpool's international appeal. Partnerships with blue chip brands like Chevy will help ensure the long-term growth and success of our club, both on-and-off the pitch. We look forward to working closely with Chevy to help reach and engage our supporters, who are among the most passionate and educated fans in the world.'[71]

For the game the Red Sox went out of their way to make the Liverpool fans feel at home, with Yawkey Way, on which the stadium's main entrance is situated, having replica Shankly Gates erected and a huge 'This is Fenway' sign with Liver Bird. Around 400 metres away in Kenmore Square over 600 Liverpool fans gathered outside bars in the hours leading up to the game, draping flags and singing 'Shankly' and 'When The Reds Go Marching In.' The owner of the An Tua Nua bar, where Fowler and Rush had held a meet and greet session with fans the previous day said of the scene: 'I've never seen anything like this, not even around the World Series'[72]

The Reds had a celebrity supporter at Fenway Park with James Bond actor Daniel Craig meeting the players before the game, having earlier signed autographs for fans. But he was unable to inspire them to victory as Roma, who had a reasonable number of supporters in the stadium themselves in the capacity 37,169 crowd, won 2-1 with their American international Michael Bradley scoring the opening goal in the 63rd minute. Alessandro Florenzi doubled their lead in the 69th minute but there was something for the Reds supporters to cheer when Charlie Adam scored from outside the box with 10 minutes left.

Rodgers again utilised the squad to the full, making seven substitutions at half-time and another four after an hour. Despite the result he still took plenty of positives from the game, telling the press afterwards: There were lots of real positives from the game. Roma are ahead of us in terms of games – they've played four or five more than ourselves. We actually created a lot of chances, and once we get that wee bit fitter and introduce our top players, I'll be very hopeful for the future.

Rodgers told his players that playing at Fenway Park was something they could tell their grandchildren about in years to come and had kind words about the way they had been received in Boston, saying: 'It was incredible. I'd like to go on record to say a big thank-you to the people of Boston. We've got one more day here before we fly away on Friday, and it's been absolutely magnificent. The hospitality we've received here, and to climax it by playing at an incredible stadium.' Although Borini hadn't played against his former club, another ex Roma player Alberto Aquilani did feature for the Reds in the game. The midfielder, signed for £17 million in the summer of 2009 had struggled to adapt to the English game and spent the last two seasons on loan back in Serie A, but Rodgers refused to rule him out, telling the assembled media: 'I need to have a close look at Alberto. It's been difficult for him during his time in England, and this is probably the first period where he's felt happy, according to him, and he's working. I need to assess, and that's what I'm doing at the moment.'

On the last day in Boston, 26th July, a Reds backroom staff side that also included Fowler and Rush, played against a Harvard XI. Watched by the current crop of professionals, Rodgers set up head of fitness Darren Burgess for the Reds first goal, then Fowler scored a penalty after being brought down in the box to secure a 2-2 draw. The following morning the Reds party took the short flight to Baltimore where they held their final training session at the 71,000 capacity M & T Bank Stadium, home to the Baltimore Ravens American football team. Some 300 fans were in attendance, including one who had flown in from Kildare in Ireland, as well as members of the New York Supporters' Club with one shouting to Glen Johnson that he needed to teach José Enrique how to dress.

The heat in Baltimore, where the party stayed in a hotel overlooking the Patapsco River, was even more intense than Boston with the LFC Tour blog describing it as 'ridiculous.' There was also a funny moment in the lift, where one of the hotel workers showed that despite the massive increase in interest and awareness of football there in the last few years there were still plenty in blissful ignorance. An American Leeds fan told the employee that the mighty Liverpool were staying there and after taking a look at the tall cameraman from LFC TV replied: 'That's great but I don't really follow basketball.'

Prior to the game, Carragher took time to meet Stuart Hamilton and his four-year-old son Liam. Stuart is originally from Waterloo but emigrated to America in 1992, having been at Hillsborough in 1989 where his father Roy died. Stuart said of meeting the club's vice captain: 'Today means a lot to me but it›s more about Liam. Jamie was great with him though – asking him about his cap and what he thought the score was going to be. He's a great ambassador for the club.'[73]

With a Europa League qualifying tie against Gomel in Belarus coming up the following Thursday Rodgers felt it was important to give those players who had only arrived for the second week of the tour some game time against Spurs. One of those was captain Steven Gerrard, who said of his new manager in an interview with the official website before the game: 'He's an impressive man. He speaks very well, he's come in with a vision and a plan for the club.' Another, defender Martin Kelly who had been a surprise late inclusion to the England squad after Gary Cahill pulled out through injury, said of the training so far: 'The training sessions have been enjoyable and it's total football. It's hard on the fitness but after the session you really feel as though you have benefited from it and in the long term I think everyone will benefit from this style of play.'

Despite the first appearance of some of the squad's strongest members in this game the Reds couldn't find a goal against Spurs with the match ending 0-0 in front of 42,723 fans. Fabio Borini made his Reds debut, making a good impression and Andy Carroll had a 20 minute runout, but couldn't convert any of the half chances created for him. Given the game was played in temperatures of over 90 degrees it still had a competitive edge with plenty of opportunities being created. There was also a backlash from Spurs over a tackle by Charlie Adam on Gareth Bale, which led to him leaving the stadium on crutches.

Liverpool's fans had been far more prominent in the stadium than those of Spurs and afterwards Brendan Rodgers admitted he had been surprised by the volume of support that the club had attracted during the tour, telling the official club website: 'I'd like to put on record a massive thank-you to everyone. The three games have been like home games for us.' With respect to the game itself he said: 'I was very pleased first and foremost with today's game as the concentration and condition of the players was fantastic. In that heat, to keep that level of organisation and concentration at 35 degrees plus was fantastic.' Rodgers was satisfied with the way the tour had gone, highlighting the progress made by some of the younger players:

> 'I'm really satisfied with how the players have coped with the work. It was a big demand for players to think and then pass and then think and each day that has been proved. I have been really, really pleased with them. That was one of the key things today – the development of the youngsters and how they've taken on the concept. If you look at Raheem Sterling over the last two weeks, he came as a young boy, 17-years-old, and he only knew how to beat a defender – but if you look at today's game, he understood when to press and when to be inside. He was playing against an experienced player in Sébastien Bassong and he actually gave him a hard time. That's brilliant for me because it shows he's taken it on board. He's thinking about the game. If he does that, and you add that to his talent, he's going to be a very, very good player for the future.'

The Reds party flew overnight from Baltimore back to Liverpool arriving in the early hours of 29th July. They would not be home for very long though as just three days later they were on their travels again for the Europa League game against Gomel, which they won 1-0. In the coming season the style of play Rodgers tried to introduce on the training camp became a feature not just of the first team but also the reserve side, while Sterling was given a first team opportunity and seized it. Carroll though, was instead sent on loan to West Ham.

18

Down Under

In July 2013 Liverpool FC played in Australia for the first time, where the pulling power of the club was shown as they sold out the huge Melbourne Cricket Ground.

Rumours began to surface early in the year that the Reds were planning a trip to Australia and they gathered pace when Manchester United announced they would be playing in Sydney. In April 2013 it was confirmed that a match against A-League Melbourne Victory would take place on 24th July and tickets sold out within hours of them going on sale.

The Liverpool party arrived in Melbourne on their chartered Garuda Airlines jet at 8.20pm local time on 21st July, with a large crowd being at the airport to greet them. They were taken straight to the Grand Hyatt hotel, where dozens of fans were waiting for them. Striker Luis Suarez, who had arrived on an earlier flight after being given an extended break following the Confederations Cup, was there to meet them. The Uruguayan was the subject of intense speculation over his future following a series of interviews back home in which he indicated a desire to leave the club and there was even speculation that he would not join the tour to force a move.

The following day Brendan Rodgers held a press conference in the hotel, where he described the reception the team had had at the airport as 'incredible.' He then said it was an honour to be playing at 'such an iconic sporting venue' before confirming that he hoped Australian keeper Brad Jones would be fit to play after missing out on the game in Indonesia. He then signed a shirt with Melbourne 2013 on the back for a competition prize. The squad then headed to their first training session at AAMI Park, the 30,050 capacity stadium where Victory are tenants along with rivals Melbourne Heart and two rugby teams. They were watched by the Premier of Victoria, Dr. Denis Napthine, who told the official website that he was 'absolutely thrilled' to have 'one of the most well known and well respected clubs in the world' in Melbourne.

Once training was over, some community work was done with Suarez and Lucas helping promote the club's partnership with the local Reagan Milstein Foundation, which helps disadvantaged youngsters play sport. Andre Wisdom, Iago Aspas, Simon Mignolet, Jay Spearing and Luis Alberto also helped out with a coaching clinic run by the Liverpool FC Foundation.

Wisdom told how this was something he enjoyed and that he had been blown away by the reception they had received:

'It's great to come down to events like these and meet the kids. I'm still only a kid myself so I know how much it means to meet players from another country who you look up to. I grew up in Leeds and I always wanted to meet a professional footballer as a youngster but I never got the chance with any of the teams I played for. It's something I dreamed about – meeting one of my idols in the flesh; so now I'm a player, I jump at the chance to attend events like this. We've been in Australia less than a day but the reaction from the fans to our visit is unbelievable. It's freezing here compared to Jakarta but it hasn't stopped the fans waiting for hours to see us everywhere we go.'

On Tuesday 23rd July hundreds of fans turned up at Federation Square to meet Sebastian Coates and Martin Skrtel at a pop-up store selling Reds souvenirs. The work of the Liverpool FC Foundation was also continuing with some staff meeting with officials from the Aussie Rules Western Bulldogs team to give advice over their men's health programme and others coaching. At the team hotel Dave Cunningham, a Hillsborough survivor now living in Australia met with the players after writing to the club asking if his wife could meet one player, but they were so moved by his email he was invited to meet the whole squad. In the evening the players trained at the MCG for the first time in an open session attended by 10,000 fans. Rodgers told reporters that the milder conditions, it being winter in the Southern Hemisphere, meant that he was looking for the players to step up a gear. Afterwards children from the Reagan Milstein Foundation were given the opportunity to meet Steven Gerrard.

The following morning the players were allowed to rest ahead of the game, but club legend Ian Rush helped with a coaching clinic at a grammar school for the visually impaired and gave out gifts to the children. The players rested ahead of the match, which will go down as one of the most unforgettable non-competitive games the club has ever played. A crowd of 95,446, the largest ever for a football match in Melbourne and second highest for one in Australia packed the MCG where there was a huge rendition of *You'll Never Walk Alone* before the game. The words were flashed up on the big screens but the crowd didn't need them as the whole stadium was a sea of red and white.

The game itself started slowly with little action in the first fifteen minutes, but after both keepers had made good saves Gerrard gave the Reds the lead in the 32nd minute, scoring after being set up by Joe Allen. The crowd were ecstatic and Gerrard responded accordingly, celebrating far more than wold be expected for a game of this nature. In the second half Fabio Borini twice went close to scoring before Rodgers made wholesale changes in the

72nd minute. This included sending Suarez on and he was warmly received by the crowd, before engaging in some trickery that led to him setting up Aspas for a simple tap-in during stoppage time.

Afterwards Rodgers paid tribute to the fans, telling reporters: 'It'd be disrespectful to start with anything other than the crowd. It was a huge honour. I want to put on record a huge thank-you to the people of Melbourne and Australia. They can be very proud of what they put on here tonight. The "You'll Never Walk Alone" at the beginning was a real tear-jerker.' Slovakian defender Martin Skrtel said that the occasion was 'something special' and as the party headed to Thailand for the final leg of their tour managing director Ian Ayre made it clear that they would be back in the near future when asked about it: 'Yes, absolutely. We've said in various different events this week that it's taken us 120 years or so to get here, but it certainly won't take us that long to come back. This has proved just how big Liverpool are in this part of the world and the fans here deserve a reasonably regular visit. It's just about fitting it in with all of those other places people want us to go.'

19

The Future

Over the last decade a clear pattern has now started to emerge when it comes to Liverpool's foreign tours and prestige friendlies. With the exception of 2005 when early entry into the Champions League qualifiers forced the cancellation of a tour of Japan, the Reds have been to the Far East every year when there hasn't been a major international tournament since 2001. Those years where there has been a tournament have seen one off games at various venues around Europe, then in 2012 the squad visited North America for the first time since 2004.

Whether or not there was an international tournament Gérard Houllier, Rafael Benitez and Roy Hodgson were all proponents of training camps in Switzerland, where some low key friendlies were also played. Brendan Rodgers though did not take up this option in 2012, there being little point given the same could be achieved during the ten days that were spent in the one place that they stayed in North America.

Lucrative mid-season friendlies, that were so often a feature of Bob Paisley, Joe Fagan and Kenny Dalglish's time in charge are now a thing of the past. It now seems inconceivable that the team would take a two or three day trip to the Middle East in between weekend games, but the reality of the situation at that time was the fee received was equivalent to the gate receipts from two or three home games.

Pre-season now is all about maximising commercial opportunities and securing new markets. In 2013 the Reds visited Indonesia for the first time, a country with a population of nearly a quarter of a billion people. There remains much work to do to secure more support in China, the world's most populous country with 1.3 billion people. Another country where more than a billion live, India, has yet to be visited and if football begins to become anywhere near as popular as cricket is there, then there are huge opportunities that can be exploited.

In 1964, as Liverpool went on their fourth tour of North America, Everton were in Australia, becoming the first team to play on all six permanently inhabited continents. The Reds only made it there in 2013, distance having been an obvious factor in why they haven't been before but also the huge country has a population barely a third that of the United Kingdom and they are more interested in rugby, cricket and Aussie rules football. However when they did finally make it, they were overwhelmed by the sheer level of support and fanaticism but it remains debatable as to how much revenue trips there can generate compared to other places. Lack of interest in football could be used as an argument not to go to North America, but over there the game has grown in popularity since the staging of the 1994 World Cup and there is a population of over 300 million. In addition the fact that the club has American owners means inroads via commercial partnerships are also quicker to establish, the Warrior kit deal being a prime example.

Liverpool are yet to visit South America, despite the numbers of players from that continent who have played for the club in recent years. The conundrum there though is that fans there are fanatical to their own clubs and although it may be an interesting exercise to visit it is debatable whether any long term fan base could be established there beyond the time players from that particular country were with the club.

One big question of the tours nowadays is, are they the right preparation for the season ahead? Brendan Rodgers' first competitive game in charge was in Belarus on a Thursday after the squad had only returned home from North America jetlagged on the Sunday morning. Commercial gain seems to be the main driving force, with games being played in temperatures of 100 degrees hardly seeming ideal preparation. When the league season began, Liverpool started slowly failing to win any of their first five games and it wasn't until the last third of the season that there was any consistency.

When Bob Paisley was manager tours of the 1970s were not made for profit, more to make sure the team was primed for the season ahead. Success in that season would then bring subsequent profits. It was only in the early 1980s when economic conditions on Merseyside severely reduced income through the turnstiles that the club started accepting invitations to play in strange yet lucrative environments, such as in Marbella in 1982. Today though the profits to be made from being a global brand are so great it is hard to see Liverpool FC ever returning to that way of thinking, especially when every other team is doing the same thing anyway so everyone is at the same disadvantage as each other.

Endnotes

1 Evening Express 6th May 1910

2 Evening Express 19th May 1910

3 Evening Express 31st May 1932

4 Kevin Keegan: My Autobiography; Warner Books 1998.

5 John Williams: Red Men, Liverpool Football Club The Biography; Mainstream Publishing 2010

6 Letter from Tom Bromilow published in Evening Express 5th June 1922

7 Letter from Tom Bromilow, published Evening Express 7th June 1922

8 Stork's Column, *Liverpool Echo* 20th May 1952

9 Letter from Ernie Blenkinsop, published *Liverpool Echo* 20th May 1936

10 Letter from George Kay, published *Liverpool Echo* 23rd May 1946

11 Letter from George Kay, published *Liverpool Echo* 27th May 1946

12 Letter from George Kay, published *Liverpool Echo* 30th May 1946

13 *Liverpool Echo* 1st June 1946

14 Bee's Sportfolk, *Liverpool Echo* 7th June 1946.

15 *Liverpool Echo*, 20th June 1946.

16 Letter from Billy Liddell, published *Liverpool Echo*, 20th May 1953

17 Letter from Billy Liddell, published *Liverpool Echo* 15th June 1953

18 Letter from Ian St John, *Daily Post* 12th May 1964.

19 John Keith: Bob Paisley *Manager of the Millennium*, Robson Books 1999

20 Letter from Ian St John, *Daily Post* 30th May 1964

21 Ian St John: *The Saint* Hodder & Stoughton 2005. Page 140

22 Tommy Smith: Over The Top, Breedon Books 1998

23 Tommy Smith: Over The Top, Breedon Books 1998

24 Liverpool Echo 4th August 1967

25 Liverpool Echo 5th August 1967

26 Daily Post 11th August 1967

27 Liverpool Echo 7th August 1972

28 Email to author 5th December 2012

29 mail to author 5th December 2012

30 Liverpool Echo 5th August 1976

31 Liverpool Echo 6th August 1976

32 Liverpool Echo 6th August 1980

33 Liverpool Echo 10th August 1981

34 Liverpool Echo 12th August 1981

35 Email to author 22nd February 2013.

36 Email to author 22nd February 2013.

37 Graeme Souness: No Half Measures p133;Willow Books 1985

38 John Aldridge: John Aldridge My Story, Hodder & Stoughton 1999

39 Kenny Dalglish: Dalglish, Hoddder & Stoughton 1996

40 *Liverpool Echo*, 27th July 1992

41 *Liverpool Echo*, 3rd August 2002

42 Alan Hansen: A Matter of Opinion p114; Transworld Publishers 1999

43 Liverpool Echo, 15th July 1987

44 Jan Mølby: Jan the Man; Orion Books 1999

45 Liverpool Echo, 28th July 1987

46 Interview with author 10th January 2013

47 Liverpool Echo, 27th July 1991

48 Liverpool Echo 29th July 1991

49 Daily Post 31st July 1991

50 Email to author 11th December 2012

51 Email to author 11th December 2012

52 Interview with author 19th January 2013

53 Email to author 11th December 2012

54 Bruce Grobbelaar: More Than Somewhat p112; Willow Books 1986

55 Graeme Souness: No Half Measures p201; Willow Books 1985

56 Mark Platt & Andrew Fagan: Joe Fagan Reluctant Champion p223; Aurum Press 2011

57 John Aldridge: My Story p 68; Hodder & Stoughton 1999

58 Daily Post 2nd June 1984

59 Phil Thompson: Stand Up Pinocchio p166; Trinity Mirror Sport Media 2005

60 Liverpool Echo 25th May 1994

61 Liverpool Echo 3rd June 1983

62 Phil Thompson: Stand up Pinocchio p 162; Trinity Mirror Sport Media 2005

63 Match Programme Liverpool v Bradford 1st November 1999

64 Sky Sports 18th July 2007

65 Welcome notes, Champions World 2004 official souvenir programme

66 EPLtalk.com 28th March 2012

67 www.lfctour.com 16th July 2012

68 www.lfctour.com 18th July 2012

69 Joe Cole's Video Diary, LFC Tour 23rd July 2012

70 www.lfctour.com 24th July 2012

71 www.lfctour.com 24th July 2012

72 www.boston.com 26th July 2012

73 www.lfctour.com 28th July 1992

About the Author

Born in 1971, Steven Horton has been a Liverpool FC season ticket holder since 1986. He has been writing about the club since the early 1990s, contributing to fanzines, the official website, *Liverpool Echo* and *The Times*.

This is his second book about Liverpool FC, following on from *Ending the Seven Year Itch*, which was published by Vertical Editions in 2012 and recalled the 1972-73 Football League Championship and UEFA Cup winning season. A similarly styled book, *Liverpool – We Love You Yea Yea Yea*, commemorating the 50th anniversary of Bill Shankly's first title, will also be published by Vertical in the spring of 2014.

Steven lives in Childwall, is married with one son and has seen Liverpool FC play in 15 European countries. He is determined to watch them on a different continent, having been disappointed to learn that the Ataturk Stadium is in the European side of Istanbul.